The Emotionally Intelligent Online Tutor

The Emotionally Intelligent Online Tutor foregrounds the tutor within online and blended learning environments, and focusses on desirable skills, qualities and attributes for effective tutoring. It analyses these qualities in relation to prominent psychological constructs, such as emotional intelligence, and the exploration of their value in practice.

This book is focussed on the tutoring of adult learners undertaking study within higher education, commonly on a part-time basis whilst studying vocationally relevant degree programmes. However, the contents are applicable and generalisable to those tutoring within informal environments, such as Massive Open Online Courses. Prominent social constructivist models of e-learning are critiqued with alternative actions provided for tutors now practicing in a digital age. The book provides a conceptual model that represents an interpretation of effective practice in a blended learning context.

This book will be of great interest for academics, scholars and postgraduate students in the field of education and for e-tutors delivering online and blended courses. Furthermore, it will be useful for those undertaking teacher training, psychology and counselling courses.

Andrew Youde is Acting Head of Department of Education and Community Studies at the University of Huddersfield, UK.

The Emotionally Intelligent Online Tutor

Effective Tutoring in Blended and Distance Learning Environments

Andrew Youde

LONDON AND NEW YORK

First published 2020 by Routledge

2 Park Square, Milton Park, Abingdon, Oxon OX14 4RN
605 Third Avenue, New York, NY 10017

Routledge is an imprint of the Taylor & Francis Group, an informa business

First issued in paperback 2021

Copyright © 2020 Andrew Youde

The right of Andrew Youde to be identified as author of this work has
been asserted by him in accordance with sections 77 and 78 of the
Copyright, Designs and Patents Act 1988.

All rights reserved. No part of this book may be reprinted or reproduced or
utilised in any form or by any electronic, mechanical, or other means, now
known or hereafter invented, including photocopying and recording, or in any
information storage or retrieval system, without permission in writing from
the publishers.

Notice:
Product or corporate names may be trademarks or registered trademarks, and
are used only for identification and explanation without intent to infringe.

Publisher's Note

The publisher has gone to great lengths to ensure the quality of this reprint but
points out that some imperfections in the original copies may be apparent.

British Library Cataloguing-in-Publication Data
A catalogue record for this book is available from the British Library

Library of Congress Cataloging-in-Publication Data
A catalog record has been requested for this book

ISBN: 978-0-367-33853-4 (hbk)
ISBN: 978-1-03-217289-7 (pbk)
DOI: 10.4324/9780429322389

Typeset in Bembo
by Cenveo® Publisher Services

This book is dedicated to 'my girls' Philippa, Abigail and Lola

Contents

List of illustrations		ix
Acknowledgements		x
1	E-tutoring: Introduction and context	1
2	Emotional intelligence and its value for tutors in higher education	11
3	The utility of the Mayer–Salovey–Caruso Emotional Intelligence Test (MSCEIT) for identifying effective tutors in online and blended learning contexts	20
4	Emotional intelligence: Trait-based models and their utility for tutors in online and blended learning contexts	38
5	Motivation and the adult learner in online and blended learning environments	58
6	Analysis of prominent distance education theorisations to explore developing relations in online and blended learning	80
7	Effective teaching in online and blended learning environments	95
8	E-tutor competences, skills and beliefs	116
9	Developing effective e-tutors	134

viii Contents

10 Emotionally intelligent tutoring 143

11 Emotionally intelligent tutors and tutoring:
   A summary and concluding thoughts 160

*Appendix 1 An andragogical model for adult learners
        studying in blended learning contexts* 171
Appendix 2 Course Experience Questionnaire 173
Appendix 3 Revised Study Process Questionnaire (R-SPQ) 176
Index 179

List of illustrations

Figures

5.1	Kolb's experiential learning cycle	63
7.1	Laurillard's conversational framework	103
7.2	Community of inquiry framework	104
11.1	Conceptual model of effective tutors and tutoring in a blended learning context	161

Tables

3.1	Structure of the MSCEIT	25
3.2	Tutor's CEQ results – mean and (standard deviation)	29
3.3	Tutor MSCEIT scores	29
3.4	Guidelines for interpreting MSCEIT scores	30
4.1	Goleman's framework of emotional competences	41
4.2	Bar-On's (1997) Model of emotional-social intelligence	42
4.3	A group of competences contributing to the effectiveness of tutors within the context under investigation	52
10.1	Implications of punctuation within asynchronous, text-based online environments	144
11.1	Constructivism Dimension's lower level factors	163
11.2	Care/Nurture Dimension's lower level factors	164
11.3	Instrumentality Dimension's lower level factors	164

Acknowledgements

I would like to thank Professor Roy Fisher for his detailed review and critique of an earlier draft of this book, your time and diligence is very much appreciated. I wish to thank Professor Kevin Orr for his continued advice, guidance and encouragement on all research matters. I would like to thank my EdD supervisors, Dr. Ron Thompson and Heather Dale. Through discussions with Ron, the Model outlined in Chapter 11 was developed, which was a significant outcome from my doctoral research. My discussions with Heather helped progress my understanding of emotional intelligence and other key psychological constructs discussed in this book. I would also like to thank Dr. Wayne Bailey for his help, advice and support along the way.

I would like to thank Lola (our dog) as our walks have provided clear thinking time for the ideas contained within the book. Finally, and above all, I would like to thank my family for their support and encouragement throughout – my wife Philippa, my beautiful daughter, Abigail, Mum, Dad, Joanne, Andrew, Cate, Georgie, Clive, Rae (RIP) and George. I would also like to thank my friends for their support and encouragement – Linz, Matt, Michelle, Jim, Andy, Dick, Sarah and Craig.

Chapter 1

E-tutoring
Introduction and context

Starting points and purpose

The twenty-first century has witnessed an explosion of information technologies, which have presented unprecedented opportunities and challenges in all spheres of economic and social life. This has been particularly the case in the field of education where both formal and informal teaching and learning have been transformed through the introduction and exponential growth of online and blended learning environments. New modes of knowledge production and access to knowledge are changing the roles of teachers and learners in ways which can be seen as both exciting and daunting, as full of potential, but at the same time laden with important questions, which can lead to tensions associated with the need to development new skills and, indeed, new ways of thinking and working. This book seeks to foreground the tutor in these teaching and learning contexts, and focusses on desirable skills, qualities and attributes for effective e-tutoring. It applies a unique analysis of these factors in relation to prominent psychological constructs, particularly emotional intelligence (EI), and offers an exploration of their value in practice. EI and its role in teaching and learning has been rarely discussed in appropriate depth, particularly when considering academics and their interactions with learners. In essence, this book considers effective 'e-tutoring', broadly defined as teaching, supporting, managing and assessing those students engaged in online or blended programmes of study.

Notions of effective tutors and tutoring within this context have a range of extant understandings within educational discourses. For example, a managerialistic ideologically driven perspective may view effectiveness by analysing key educational metrics, such as student achievement, retention and employability, whereas an economistic perspective may consider profitability. When exploring effective tutoring in a distance education context, Jelfs, Richardson, and Price (2009) considered tutor and student perspectives, and this book draws on a range of empirical sources and theorisations rooted in such similar empirical research to discuss notions of effectiveness in online and blended learning. However, the boundaries between ideological views

2 E-tutoring: Introduction and context

are blurred regarding 'effectiveness' as, for example, managerialistic perspectives commonly draw on measures of student satisfaction to judge quality.

Although the focus of this book is on EI in the context of e-tutoring and learning within UK higher education (HE), the implications of the results are potentially much wider. Good teaching practices are generally context specific (Stronge, 2002), and what follows is a critical discussion of effective practice and related influences within online and blended learning environments. Conclusions are drawn with the aim of enhancing the recruitment, selection, training and development of those tutors with a role which involves e-tutoring (see Chapter 9), as well as to encourage further thought and debate on its nature and related issues. As Wheeler (2007, p. 116) notes, "the future success of blended learning will rely heavily on technology-mediated communication, but even more on the skills and knowledge of responsive tutors". More recently, the fields of 'big data', 'data science' and, especially, 'data analytics' have grown substantially, and together with artificial intelligence (AI) and the increasing use of digital algorithms, these hold massive implications for the practice of e-tutoring. At the heart of these developments are people, (tutors, learners and associated professionals), who are faced with unprecedented opportunities to access knowledge. At the same time, there are previously unknown challenges which arise mainly from forms of '24/7' workload intensification with the potential to impact negatively on mental health and welfare. Added to these are ethical dangers arising from digital 'footprints' and the emergence of surveillance cultures that rest at levels below the formal progress monitoring normally associated with academic accreditation systems.

This book focusses on the tutoring of adult learners engaged in part-time (PT) study for undergraduate and postgraduate degrees related to their employment. They generally choose PT study as they require flexibility with many seeking higher-level vocational awards for career enhancement (Holley & Oliver, 2010). In my experience, these learners tend to be well motivated but have often not studied in a formal educational environment for some time and they can lack academic confidence. There are often specific difficulties that are faced by such learners, particularly regarding the influence of events within their daily lives, together with the pressures of demanding employment regimes (Creanor, 2002; Holley & Oliver, 2010). However, they tend to understand clearly what they want to achieve from their studies (Biesta, 2005; Knowles, Holton, & Swanson, 2015). Increasingly, universities are developing delivery models to meet their needs (Beetham, 2012, p. 8) with a greater use of online learning and e-tutoring, together with an increasing number of blended learning delivery patterns. University tutors' roles have been changing to meet these challenges (Dykman & Davis, 2008, p. 159), but the adaption of their pedagogy to this context can be difficult as related training is often unavailable or difficult to access (Guasch, Alvarez, & Espasa, 2010), which can result in negative teaching and learning experiences.

When tutoring in online contexts, teaching, learning and communication media are commonly asynchronous. A range of theories, models are available to advise tutors and associated professionals how to approach teaching within this context (see Chapter 7), but there is little written about who can deliver effective practice in both online and blended learning environments, and the skills, competences and attributes that they should either acquire or possess. This book takes steps to address this gap in understanding of this area.

The e-tutors' competences and skills outlined throughout this study are generalisable to informal online learning contexts outside educational institutions. Within formal HE contexts, learners tend to be motivated by a need to be successful in assessments and to gain accredited qualifications: this is different from e-tutoring on informal courses, such as Massive Open Online Courses (MOOCs), where a general interest in a topic area normally drives study. However, on such courses, non-completion rates can be high (see The Current E-tutoring Context section for a further discussion of MOOCs). The conclusions and guidance within this book regarding tutor competences and skills are rooted in practices on formal courses leading to recognised awards, but they will have salience for e-tutors teaching and supporting learners in informal environments.

E-tutoring is of particular interest to me as a former blended learning student, as leader of a blended learning course and as manager of a university department that offers a range of such programmes. Each of these roles provided insight into practices within online and blended learning contexts and how tutors' behaviours influenced student learning and motivation. Electronic communications do not have the benefit of body language, facial expression or tone of voice to aid the receiver's understanding, with messages often taken literally. Attempts at humour can be misinterpreted as sarcasm or derision. Tutor competence in this area is important and needs to go beyond technical proficiency to include empathy to enable a successful learner experience (Barker, 2002; Youde, 2016).

Once I began teaching adult learners in blended contexts, the importance of appropriately responding to these students as they managed the challenges of study, work and their personal life became increasingly apparent. One particular incident remains significant. On the course in question, students were encouraged to get in contact if they were unsure about aspects of their study or university life more generally. One student e-mailed a tutor to ask a question about their studies, with the tutor's response being – "I don't have time for this, do you know how much work I have to do at the minute?" The student was devastated by this and contacted me immediately in a distressed state. What was apparent to me was not only the loss of trust that the learner had experienced but also the power of the written word. Such negative expression towards the student in written form had a damaging effect on their confidence. In contrast, I have frequently had the pleasure of hearing about a number of complimentary e-mails written to learners by tutors, which they have re-read and taken inspiration from when they were struggling. It is the understanding of this phenomenon; the motivational and demotivational actions an online tutor can take, which this study seeks to explore. Learning at a distance from tutors and peers is challenging, and this book aims to analyse theory and practice that can help to address the issues which can arise.

Salmon (2011, p. 104) expressed the view that EI and the ability to influence others are necessary attributes when tutoring online. She particularly emphasised the importance of tutor self-awareness and interpersonal sensitivity. However, her opinion was not based on empirical evidence. Both Mortiboys (2005) and Corcoran and Tormey (2012) argue that teacher training courses should focus on pedagogy with a brief discussion of subject expertise, and that EI should be considered when developing trainees. Mortiboys (2005) outlines two goals for tutors in relation to the development of EI in educational contexts:

- to be able to recognise and respond to the feelings of both yourself and your learners in the classroom, in order to make you both more effective in your respective roles
- to encourage an emotional state in your learners that is conducive to learning (Mortiboys, 2005, p. 8).

Whilst these goals refer to classroom-based teaching, they are pertinent to online and blended learning environments but are difficult to achieve given the limited face-to-face interaction these contexts afford. Mortiboys (2005) outlined numerous activities to develop teachers' emotional competence (EC) in face-to-face settings, which he felt would improve performance; however, they had limited relevance for online contexts. Lopes, Salovey, and Straus (2003), in their study of emotion regulation and the quality of social interactions, found those with higher EI reported more positive interactions and relations with other people. On the face of it, these are valuable outcomes for teaching contexts. In her earlier work, Salmon (2002, p. 150) gave practical examples of how tutor emotional competences might be developed, such as through the use of capital letters and emoticons, but, again, there was no evidence provided for the link between EC and tutor quality.

To explore effective e-tutors and e-tutoring, particularly through an EI lens, the book is structured as follows. Chapter 2 presents compelling evidence to explore EI for tutors operating within online and blended learning environments. This, further justifies the book's overall purpose and, in particular, the choice of theories and competences unpinning the analyses throughout. Chapters 3 and 4 critically examine prominent theorisations of EI and suggest competences that appear valuable for online and blended tutors. Chapter 5 considers the needs of adult learners and, in particular, their learning preferences in the digital age, while Chapter 6 examines prominent theorisations in distance education discourses to argue that tutor EC underpins their effective implementation in practice. Chapter 7 considers effective teaching and learning within online and blended contexts with Chapter 8 developing this discussion by presenting a range of empirical sources regarding tutor competences, skills and beliefs that appear to enhance practice. Throughout Chapters 4 to 8, the book suggests aspects of theoretical triangulation (Denzin, 1970) within distance education and the EI-related academic literature, and the growing body of empirical work around online e-tutor competences. In light of the discussion of effective e-tutors and e-tutoring already presented, Chapter 9 considers potential training and development within HE contexts. This is further developed in Chapter 10, which suggests practical actions that tutors can take to both enhance practice and appear 'emotionally intelligent' in their learners' eyes. Finally, Chapter 11 summarises the key arguments in the book and presents a conceptual model of effective e-tutors and e-tutoring within a specific HE context, which may be generalisable to other blended learning environments.

Definitions of key concepts

Two key terms used throughout this study are now defined. 'Online learning' is conceived as that which occurs purely through computer-mediated communications with no face-to-face contact between a tutor and their learners, or between learners and their peers. Whereas 'blended learning' is seen as that which typically involves significant online teaching, learning and support, but which includes some face-to-face contact (De George-Walker & Keeffe, 2010; Halverson, Graham, Spring, & Drysdale, 2012). Throughout this book, when online learning is discussed, this refers either to purely online contexts or to the online elements of blended learning.

The current e-tutoring context

Before considering effective tutors and tutoring within online and blended courses, it is helpful to briefly discuss the current e-tutoring context more broadly, and the skills and qualities learners are bringing to their study. This discussion will be developed further in Chapter 5 where tutoring adult learners in HE is specifically considered.

MOOCs, or scaled open courses, have seen a steady expansion in student numbers over recent years with recent estimates suggesting the total figure is beyond millions (Poquet et al., 2018). Such courses are commonly open access, free of charge, with universities generally providing them to enhance their marketing and branding. Educational resources are freely available providing open learning opportunities for all. Due to the large numbers of students attached to such courses, tutor-peer interaction is normally unavailable. The absence of interpersonal interaction within these environments has often

6 E-tutoring: Introduction and context

negatively influenced the educational experience, and course completion rates have tended to be poor.

The current e-tutoring context was expertly summarised by Wheeler (2012, 2015) who accounted for the affordances of the recent technological developments. Mobile technologies are now pervasive in many societies with learners accessing content and communicating with peers via such devices. Social media is becoming increasingly integral to student learning as a mechanism for communicating with both peers and extended networks. This is facilitated by both technology convergence, where devices and software are getting better at sharing user-generated content, and by ubiquitous connections, either via wifi or mobile networks. Finally, there is increased 'gamification' in HE learning contexts, where learning activities are turned into games with rewards for success. For example, a university library might reward students for accessing electronic journals and books, with prizes given when a certain threshold is achieved.

Building on the context described above, Wheeler (2012, 2015) provided an overview of the type of learners emerging within HE contexts. He described them as 'new' learners, and compared to previous generations, they were seen as:

- more self-directed
- better equipped to capture information
- more reliant on feedback from peers
- more inclined to collaborate
- more orientated to being their own 'nodes of production'.

Open access resources and a proliferation of user-generated information and resources have helped facilitate greater self-direction in learning. This has been enhanced with access to social media channels, for example, by following the work of scholars within a student's disciplinary area. Mobile devices have enhanced learners' ability to capture information, such as videoing examples of their practice whilst on placement and photographing summaries of a discussion on a classroom board. This increased ability to capture information also supports learners in developing content, or being a node of production. Examples could be videos, blogs and screencasts, which can be developed in collaboration with others, either with peers on their course or those in external networks.

Effective peer-to-peer interaction in online and blended learning environments

The challenge of peer-to-peer interaction and learning within online environments is a theme throughout this study. Smith and Hill's (2019) review of 97 journal articles relating to blended learning identified flexibility, increased tutor-learner interaction, personalisation, enhanced learner outcomes, and the development of autonomy and self-directed learning as key benefits. However, little empirical support was provided espousing the educational value of peer-to-peer interaction in the online elements of these programmes. Boelens, De Wever, and Voet (2017), in their systematic literature review of blended learning environment design, regarded the stimulation of peer-to-peer interaction as a key challenge. However, little justification was provided regarding why this was the case. The 20 studies reviewed as part of their research generally highlight the benefits of face-to-face elements, with some also recognising the value of tutor-peer interaction within online elements of blended learning. None of these studies reported effective peer-to-peer interaction within the online elements of blended learning environments. Social constructivist models of e-learning have commonly promoted opportunities for peer interaction within online, formal, university learning environments (Garrison & Kanuka, 2004; Goodyear, Banks, Hodgson, & McConnell, 2004; Salmon, 2011); however, it would appear that, in practice, such interaction is both challenging for tutors and of little benefit for learners (see Chapter 7 for a further discussion effective teaching in online contexts).

Today's HE learners have the affordances of a wealth of university resources to support their study. These include virtual learning environments (VLEs), lecture capture, library resources and databases and online access to support services, such as finance and wellbeing. However, these resources encompass a fraction of the learning resources now available to learners online, outside their university, particularly in a social media–rich external environment (Dabbagh & Kitsantas, 2012).

It is useful here to draw upon Wheeler's (2015) Personal (or Professional) Learning Network (PLN) conception. This refers to an informal network of people a student interacts with to support aspects of learning for their degree studies. This could include, but is not restricted to, colleagues at work, fellow students, family, friends or relative strangers connected to online forums. These networks of people are accessed through an individual's Personal Learning Environment, which includes both the PLN and the tools used by learners to support their lifelong learning (Wheeler, 2015, p. 124). These tools can include traditional print media, learning through TV or radio, or social media software, such as, content management systems (blogs), relationship management systems (for example, Facebook) and file sharing systems (for example, Dropbox). A relevant example comes from a PT student on a BA (Hons) Educational Management and Administration course who asked a question about her research for a particular assignment to a group of school business managers on Twitter. This group commonly discussed issues relevant to their roles by using an appropriate hashtag. She was quickly able to acquire relevant data for her assignment, ask follow up questions and discuss the issue in some depth by drawing on this professional learning network. These interactions appeared far more valuable than discussing the issue with her course

8 E-tutoring: Introduction and context

peers, particularly given the increased knowledge base available from a group drawn exclusively from the same specific job role. Siemens (2005) states that "formal education no longer comprises the majority of our learning. Learning now occurs in a variety of ways – through communities of practice, personal networks, and through completion of work-related tasks". This appears relevant for adult learners studying in online and blended contexts.

There is a growing research base into the influence of PLNs on student learning (e.g., see Casquero, Ovelar, Romo, Benito, & Alberdi, 2016; Dabbagh & Kitsantas, 2012); however, such work has yet to be undertaken in relation to adult learners on PT vocational courses. This book considers what universities can do to both accommodate and enhance new approaches to learning. This is at a time when many universities are investing significant sums to improve their digital estates by, for example, improving VLEs and introducing lecture capture technology.

Digital literacies

When setting the e-tutoring context for adult learners in online and blended learning environments, it is important to discuss the skills and qualities they will need to be successful. These skills and qualities are commonly referred to as digital literacies, which JISC (2013) define as:

> … those capabilities which fit an individual for living, learning and working in a digital society. For example, the use of digital tools to undertake academic research, writing and critical thinking; digital professionalism; the use of specialist digital tools and data sets; communicating ideas effectively in a range of media; producing, sharing and critically evaluating information; collaborating in virtual networks; using digital technologies to support reflection and PDP; managing digital reputation and showcasing achievements.

For all those undertaking vocationally relevant qualifications, identity management is significant as prospective clients, customers and employers will often search for an individual's online profile and presence. This can be enhanced by the effective use of social and business networking sites, privacy maintenance, creating accessible and engaging content and strategic self-presentation.

In summary

This introductory chapter has provided important background and contextual information regarding the purpose of this study, and the context in which online and blended tutors' competences and skills are developed. What follows in subsequent chapters is an exploration and critical analysis of the value of tutor EI and EC.

References

Barker, P. (2002). On being an online tutor. *Innovations in Education and Teaching International, 39*(1), 3–13.

Beetham, H. (2012). *Institutional approaches to curriculum design: Full synthesis report*. Retrieved from http://repository.jisc.ac.uk/5081/1/JISC_Curriculum_Design_Final_Synthesis_i1.pdf

Biesta, G. (2005). Against learning: Reclaiming a language for education in an age of learning. *Nordisk Pedagogik, 25*, 54–66.

Boelens, R., De Wever, B., & Voet, M. (2017). Four key challenges to the design of blended learning: A systematic literature review. *Educational Research Review, 22*, 1–18. doi: 10.1016/j.edurev.2017.06.001.

Casquero, O., Ovelar, R., Romo, J., Benito, M., & Alberdi, M. (2016). Students' personal networks in virtual and personal learning environments: A case study in higher education using learning analytics approach. *Interactive Learning Environments, 24*(1), 49–67. doi: 10.1080/10494820.2013.817441.

Corcoran, R., & Tormey, R. (2012). *Developing emotionally competent teachers: Emotional intelligence and pre-service teacher education*. Bern, Switzerland: Peter Lang.

Creanor, L. (2002). A tale of two courses: A comparative study of tutoring online. *Open Learning: The Journal of Open, Distance and e-Learning, 17*(1), 57–68.

Dabbagh, N., & Kitsantas, A. (2012). Personal learning environments, social media, and self-regulated learning: A natural formula for connecting formal and informal learning. *Internet and Higher Education, 15*(1), 3–8. doi: 10.1016/j.iheduc.2011.06.002.

De George-Walker, L., & Keeffe, M. (2010). Self-determined blended learning: A case study of blended learning design. *Higher Education Research & Development, 29*(1), 1–13. doi: 10.1080/07294360903277380.

Denzin, N. K. (1970). *The research act: A theoretical introduction to sociological methods*. Chicago: Aldine.

Dykman, C. A., & Davis, C. K. (2008). Online education forum: Part two - teaching online versus teaching conventionally. *Journal of Information Systems Education, 19*(2), 157–164.

Garrison, D. R., & Kanuka, H. (2004). Blended learning: Uncovering its transformative potential in higher education. *The Internet and Higher Education, 7*(2), 95–105.

Goodyear, P., Banks, S., Hodgson, V., & McConnell, D. (2004). Research on network learning: An overview. In P. Goodyear, S. Banks, V. Hodgson, & D. McConnell (Eds.). *Advances in research on networked learning* (pp. 1–10). Dordrecht: Kluwer Academic Publishers.

Guasch, T., Alvarez, I., & Espasa, A. (2010). University teacher competencies in a virtual teaching/learning environment: Analysis of a teacher training experience. *Teaching and Teacher Education, 26*(2), 199–206.

Halverson, L. R., Graham, C. R., Spring, K. J., & Drysdale, J. S. (2012). An analysis of high impact scholarship and publication trends in blended learning. *Distance Education, 33*(3), 381–413. doi: 10.1080/01587919.2012.723166.

Holley, D., & Oliver, M. (2010). Student engagement and blended learning: Portraits of risk. *Computers & Education, 54*, 693–700. doi: 10.1016/j.compedu.2009.08.035.

Jelfs, A., Richardson, J. T., & Price, L. (2009). Student and tutor perceptions of effective tutoring in distance education. *Distance Education, 30*(3), 419–441.

JISC. (2013). *The design studio*. Retrieved from http://jiscdesignstudio.pbworks.com/w/page/46421608/Developing%20digital%20literacies

Knowles, M. S., Holton, E. F., & Swanson, R. A. (2015). *The adult learner: The definitive classic in adult education and human resource development* (8th ed.). Abingdon: Routledge.

10 E-tutoring: Introduction and context

Lopes, P. N., Salovey, P., & Straus, R. (2003). Emotional intelligence, personality, and the perceived quality of social relationships. *Personality and Individual Differences*, *35*, 641–658.

Mortiboys, A. (2005). *Teaching with emotional intelligence*. Abingdon, Oxfordshire: Routledge.

Poquet, O., Kovanović, V., de Vries, P., Hennis, T., Joksimović, S., Gašević, D., & Dawson, S. (2018). Social presence in massive open online courses. *The International Review of Research in Open and Distributed Learning*, *19*(3), 43–68. doi: 10.19173/irrodl.v19i3.3370.

Salmon, G. (2002). *E-tivities: The key to teaching & learning online*. London: RoutledgeFalmer.

Salmon, G. (2011). *E-moderating: The key to teaching & learning online* (3rd ed.). London: RoutledgeFalmer.

Siemens, G. (2005). *Connectivism: A learning theory for the digital age*. Retrieved from http://www.itdl.org/journal/jan_05/article01.htm

Smith, K., & Hill. J. (2019). Defining the nature of blended learning through its depiction in current research. *Higher Education Research & Development*, *38*(2), 383–397. doi: 10.1080/07294360.2018.1517732.

Stronge, J. H. (2002). *Qualities of effective teachers*. Alexandria, VA: Association for Supervision and Curriculum Development.

Wheeler, S. (2007). The influence of communication technologies and approaches to study on transactional distance in blended learning. *ALT-J*, *15*(2), 103–117.

Wheeler, S. (2012). Digital learning futures. Retrieved from http://www.steve-wheeler.co.uk/2015/03/social-mobile-and-personal-learning.html#!/2015/03/social-mobile-and-personal-learning.html

Wheeler, S. (2015). *Learning with 'e's*. Carmarthen: Crown House Publishing.

Youde, A. (2016). Tutor emotional competences valued by learners in a blended learning context. *European Journal of Open, Distance and E-Learning (EURODL)*, *19*(2), 81–97. doi: 10.1515/eurodl-2016-0008.

Chapter 2

Emotional intelligence and its value for tutors in higher education

Introduction

This chapter outlines the conceptual background to the book with a particular focus on emotional intelligence (EI) including key definitions, the associated constructs and issues related to measurement. The link between EI and emotional competence (EC) is established and key empirical studies are reviewed that discuss the value of EI in non-educational contexts where interpersonal relationships are considered important. This discussion is developed to outline similar research within educational contexts with the Chapter arguing that there is compelling evidence to explore the value of EI and EC for tutors practicing within online and blended learning environments.

Emotional intelligence: Background and relevant definitions

Daus and Ashkanasy (2005, p. 455) outlined 'three streams' of EI constructs and the respective ways in which they could be measured:

- stream 1 is based on the Mayer-Salovey-Caruso (2002) 'ability' model of EI (outlined below) and uses the Mayer-Salovey-Caruso Emotional Intelligence Test (MSCEIT) as its measure
- stream 2 is also based on the Mayer-Salovey-Caruso (2002) ability model of EI; however, this uses either a peer or self-report strategy as its measure
- stream 3 comprises a group of broader 'mixed' models that include dimensions or components not included in Salovey and Mayer's (1990, p. 189) original definition of EI. These are commonly termed trait-based measures and include Goleman's (2001) Framework of ECs and Bar-On's (1997) Five-Dimensional Model.

Although other models have been developed, such as Trait EI (Perez, Petrides, & Furnham, 2005), the Daus and Ashkanasy (2005) streams are still highly influential, although later conceptions of EI incorporated a greater focus on

12 Emotional intelligence and its value for tutors

'ability' models and 'mixed' models as overall descriptive categories (e.g., see Corcoran & Tormey, 2012; Zeidner, Matthews, & Roberts, 2009).

The 'ability' model of EI, as measured by the MSCEIT, is a "valid model of emotional intelligence" (Daus & Ashkanasy, 2005, p. 463), with a supported factor structure (Corcoran & Tormey, 2012; Day & Carroll, 2004; Palmer, Gignac, Manocha, & Stough, 2005), and acceptable levels of reliability (Brackett & Mayer, 2003; Lopes, Salovey, & Straus, 2003; Mayer, Salovey, & Caruso, 2012). Although Maul has been critical of the MSCEIT regarding, for example, factor structure (Maul, 2011) and validity (Maul, 2012), he still regards it as the "flagship test of EI" (Maul, 2012, p. 394). In response to Maul's criticisms, Mayer et al. (2012, p. 407) stated:

> the argument for the MSCEIT's overall validity is growing and arguably quite strong, notwithstanding the technical imperfections that are a part of any real-life form of measurement, and acknowledging that improvements in the MSCEIT and measurement in the area are desirable (Mayer et al., 2012, p. 407).

Although the term 'emotional intelligence' was popularised by Goleman (1996) in his book *Emotional Intelligence: Why it can matter more than IQ,* the construct EI[1] was first proposed by Salovey and Mayer (1990). By 1997, Mayer and Salovey defined EI as follows:

> Emotional intelligence involves the ability to perceive accurately, appraise, and express emotion; the ability to access and/or generate feelings when they facilitate thought; the ability to understand emotion and emotional knowledge; the ability to regulate emotions to promote emotional and intellectual growth (Mayer & Salovey, 1997, p. 10).

Throughout this book, the Mayer and Salovey's (1997) definition will be used when considering the construct and measurement of EI.

When referring to EI and EC I consider them to be close constructs. Wakeman (2006, p. 72) argues that Mayer and Salovey's definition of EI embodies "the distinction between EI and EC", with EI factors allowing the development of ECs. For example, the ability to perceive emotions in others would aid the development of EC in conflict management or empathy (Wakeman, 2006, p. 72). It is common for intelligence to be measured by tests of competence, Intelligence Quotient (IQ) being a relevant example. When discussing the relationship between EI and EC, Vaida and Opre state:

> The relation between these two concepts is a symbiotic one. Emotional intelligence is a prerequisite that forms the building bricks for developing emotional competence which, in turn, leads to performance. And in

order to achieve the results that many training programs claim to bring (improved academic and job performance, personal development) emotional intelligence is a must yet not enough on its own. For long lasting results, emotional competence must be developed, based on improved emotional intelligence (Vaida & Opre, 2014, p. 26).

Goleman (2001, p. 1) similarly considers there to be a relationship between the two constructs when stating an EC is "a learned capability based on emotional intelligence that results in outstanding performance at work". Although Zeidner et al. (2009, p. 11) are critical of Goleman's link between EI and learning, they do acknowledge that higher EI increases "the capacity to acquire mental skills through learning". Thus, the definition of EC within this book is a learned capability based on EI that leads to effective performance in online and blended learning environments.

To aid understanding when considering EI, clear definitions of emotions are needed, and also for related areas such as feelings, behaviours and traits. Emotions are organised responses typically in reaction to an event, whereas traits (see stream 3 measures of EI) are characteristic or preferred ways of behaving, such as, extroversion or shyness (Mayer & Salovey, 1997, p. 8). The use of the word 'organised' is surprising as emotions would generally be considered more disorganised or random as implied in McLeod's (2007, p. 171) definition, "an immediate, bodily response to a situation". Mayer and Salovey's definition of emotion refers to cognitive activities in response to an event and the adaptive nature of subsequent action, and this led to the cognitive underpinning of the definition of EI. Feelings are similar to emotions in that they are internal, embodied responses to events, however, a "feeling can be regarded as an ever-present inner sensing that can be referred to at any moment" (McLeod, 2007, p. 173) and is typically multifaceted, whereas emotions can be identified individually. Behaviours are typical ways in which a person acts or conducts themselves, especially towards others (McLeod, 2007, p. 189) and are closely related to individual traits. For example, a trait, such as being trusting, drives the typical behaviour when interacting with others. The consideration and understanding of emotions, feelings, behaviours and traits are instructive for an online or blended tutor and can support their practices, particularly when responding to learners (see Chapter 9 for a discussion of effective responses to student questions).

An introduction to some of the key literature relating to emotional intelligence

EI is an area which has generated substantial scholarly interest and by the close of the twentieth century a very considerable academic literature had already developed with key foundational texts including Goleman's (1996)

14 Emotional intelligence and its value for tutors

and Mayer and Salovey's (1997). To begin to understand the value of EI for those tutoring in online and blended contexts, an initial literature review was undertaken. The literature incorporated into this study was chosen on the basis of the following criteria:

- that which focussed on the measurement of EI/EC
- studies exploring EI/EC in work-contexts, particularly those which involve extensive interpersonal interaction
- contributions which considered key definitions relevant to this area of study, such as emotions, traits, feelings and behaviours.

Empirical studies formed the majority of sources reviewed.

As stated in Chapter 1, the stimulus for this book came from Salmon's (2011, p. 104) view that EI and the ability to influence others are important attributes which are necessary when tutoring online (as they are in conventional teaching). It follows from this that being emotionally competent would be a valuable quality for tutors operating in blended learning environments (see the previous Section for a discussion of the link between EC and EI).

A range of ECs have been found to enhance performance in work environments. Individuals with high EI are more pleasant to be around generally (Mayer, Roberts, & Barsade, 2008), and this is particularly the case in relation to teachers (Brackett & Katulak, 2006). A study by Lopes, Grewal, Kadis, Gall, and Salovey (2006) found that the EI of clerical workers was positively related to supervisor ratings of interpersonal skills, stress tolerance and leadership potential. EI has been found to positively relate to leadership effectiveness (Edelman & van Knippenberg, 2018; Rosete & Ciarrochi, 2005). Caruso (1999) claims that managers with high EI can plan flexibly and adapt, motivate others and themselves, and have improved decision making skills (such as not reacting out of anger). Further, higher EI enables more creative thinking, such as the ability to see issues from multiple perspectives, and being effective in social environments. He identified the following characteristics of emotionally intelligent managers:

- they are enjoyable to be with
- they are good at influencing people
- they can build consensus
- they are believable and trusting
- they are empathic (Caruso, 1999, p. 6).

The above qualities appear important when exploring contexts where inter-personal relationships are important. Next, research considering ECs within educational contexts is outlined and discussed.

Emotional intelligence and educational research

The majority of the education-focussed empirical literature exploring EI has been in relation to learners, not tutors [e.g., see Han and Johnson (2012), who explored the relationship between students' EI, social bond and interactions in online learning; Kingston (2008), who researched EI and reasons for student drop-out; and Vega-Hernández, Patino-Alonso, Cabello, Galindo-Villardón, and Fernández-Berrocal (2017), who explored EI and learning strategies]. There is, however, a growing literature, largely quantitative in nature, exploring teacher EI and its impact on teachers themselves and their practice (e.g., see Mérida-López & Extremera, 2017, who explored EI and its relationship with teacher 'burnout'). In teaching, success, to some extent, depends on the quality of relationships with managers, colleagues and learners, and research suggests that being emotionally intelligent would be beneficial. Ignat and Clipa (2012) conducted research to determine if teachers' EI is correlated with a positive attitude towards work and a general job satisfaction. They found it did and, more broadly, with life generally. Similarly to Ignat and Clipa, Anari (2012) found a significant positive relationship between teachers' EI and both job satisfaction and organisational commitment. This discussion, together with Salmon's view outlined in Chapter 1, strengthens the need for emotionally competent tutors when operating in online and blended learning environments. Further, it establishes the value of EI in work contexts, and teaching in particular, where inter-personal relationships are important.

Further research is emerging around the impact of teacher EI on student outcomes. Ghanizadeh and Moafian (2010) found a significant positive relationship between English foreign language teachers' EI and their pedagogical success in language institutes. Whereas, Corcoran and Tormey (2013) explored whether or not student teachers' levels of EI are associated with their teaching performance and found no relationships, stating that their findings raised serious questions about understandings of emotions in this context. The contradictory nature of these studies points to the multifaceted and complex issues underpinning teachers' EI and its influence on their learners' outcomes. However, Dolev and Leshem (2016, p. 87) found that as Israeli secondary school teachers' EI developed through related training they directly and indirectly improved the social and emotional learning of their pupils.

Research exploring EI and its impact on higher education (HE) lecturers and their practices is scant within Western contexts, however, there is an emerging literature conducted within Asian universities. Similar to the findings regarding teachers outlined above, EI has been found to have a significant impact on the job effectiveness of HE lecturers (Shah, Saad, Mohan, & Poniran, 2018), with self-regulation found to be a key factor. Shah et al. (2018) suggested that EI should be used to predict organisational effectiveness as they found that employees can appropriately apply their personal emotional experience to their work. Also, it helped them to develop a strong emotional bond with those people associated with their work, which could include students. Building on this, Asrar-ul-Haq, Anwar, and Hassan (2017) undertook a quantitative study to explore the impact of EI on lecturers' performance within Pakistani HE. Through an analysis of 166 staff, a significant correlation was found between EI and their job performance. Further, they found that emotional self-awareness, self-confidence, achievement, developing others and conflict management have a positive and significant relationship with job performance. Again, these studies are both suggesting the value of EI generally, and identifying potentially valuable competences for tutors in online and blended learning contexts.

So far, the studies outlined in this chapter have generally fallen within, broadly, the quantitative paradigm, which is currently dominant in EI educational research. However, qualitative approaches have made a significant contribution to this area. Fineman (2004) argued for a greater use of qualitative research when exploring EI and stated that emotion could be researched without being subject to measurement. He outlines a number of studies exploring emotions qualitatively and states "the understandings so produced are inherently less precise than the simplifications of measurement, but they are likely to be abundant in insight, plausibility and texture" (Fineman, 2004, p. 736). Analysis of data in Youde's (2014) doctoral study identifies the same kind of imprecision and insight that qualitative data can give rise to. When analysing interview data from an HE blended learning tutor, the main difficulty found was that of identifying and classifying emotionally intelligent competences, for example, consider the following statement:

> I meet all my deadlines and if I say I'm going to do something I do it. I find out answers [to students' questions] that I don't know and I always get back to them [students].

On first reading it appears as just the statement of a conscientious tutor, however, when considered in the context of the interview, and the passion in the tutor's voice at the time, it revealed ECs such as self-awareness (including self-confidence), self-management (including trustworthiness and conscientiousness) and social awareness (including service orientation; Goleman, 2001). Undertaking qualitative research around ECs involves complex interpretation of data, often going beyond both the spoken word and written text.

Within educational contexts there has been limited, but valuable, qualitative research regarding EI and leadership. Parrish (2015) undertook case study research to explore EI for effective HE academic leadership. The construct was found to be an important requirement in this leadership context with the study ascertaining that EI traits related to empathy, inspiring and guiding others, and responsibly managing oneself, were the most applicable for academic leadership. Further, Cliffe (2011) explored the relationship between

EI and educational leadership amongst female secondary school headteachers and found that, both knowingly and unknowingly, they made positive use of their emotions in practice. However, to date, there is limited qualitative research into value of EI or EC for HE lecturers and, in particular, for HE online and blended tutors. This provided an impetus for qualitative research in this area, which is detailed in Chapter 4.

In summary

This chapter has presented evidence to suggest that EI has value for tutors operating within online and blended learning contexts. It has argued that there has been a dominance of the quantitative paradigm in EI research and identified a need for further qualitative research in this area. Further, there has been a paucity of literature regarding ECs and tutors within HE online and blended learning environments, a deficit that this book seeks to remedy. The sources discussed in this Section have suggested a number of potential benefits that flow from emotionally intelligent tutoring, including enhanced achievement of work outcomes, improved interpersonal skills, stress tolerance, leadership potential, a general positive attitude towards work, job satisfaction and improved communication. Stakeholder views are important when researching and understanding EI, with this Chapter outlining a range of studies considering their perceptions, including students. Although limited in number, the studies discussed that were undertaken in educational contexts point to the multifaceted and complex issues underpinning teachers' EI and its influence on their learners' outcomes. This background literature review has identified a need for further exploration of EC for HE tutors, with a fuller review integrated into the following two Chapters. The following Chapter explores the utility of the MSCEIT, and its underpinning theory, within the context of HE.

Note

1. The term emotional intelligence was first used in 1985 by Wayne Payne (1985) in his doctoral dissertation – "A study of emotion: developing emotional intelligence; self-integration; relating to fear, pain and desire".

References

Anari, N. N. (2012). Teachers: Emotional intelligence, job satisfaction, and organizational commitment. *Journal of Workplace Learning, 24*(4), 256–269.

Asrar-ul-Haq, M., Anwar, S., & Hassan, M. (2017). Impact of emotional intelligence on teacher's performance in higher education institutions of Pakistan. *Future Business Journal, 3*(2), 87–97.

Bar-On, R. (1997). *Bar-On emotional quotient inventory: Technical Manual.* Toronto: Multi-Health Systems.

18 Emotional intelligence and its value for tutors

Brackett, M. A., & Katulak, N. A. (2006). Emotional intelligence in the classroom: Skill-based training for teachers and students. In J. Ciarrochi & J. D. Mayer (Eds.) *Applying emotional intelligence: A practitioner's guide* (pp. 53–88). New York, NY: Psychology Press.

Brackett, M. A., & Mayer, J. D. (2003). Convergent, discriminant, and incremental validity of competing measures of emotional intelligence. *Personality and Social Psychology Bulletin, 29*, 1147–1158.

Caruso, D. R. (1999). *Applying the ability model of emotional intelligence to the world of work.* Retrieved from http://www.leadershipcoachacademy.com/handouts/EQ_articleEQ_at_Work.pdf

Cliffe, J. (2011). Emotional intelligence: A study of female secondary headteachers. *Educational Management, Administration & Leadership, 39*(2), 205–216.

Corcoran, R. P., & Tormey, R. (2012). How emotionally intelligent are pre-service teachers? *Teaching and Teacher Education, 28*(5), 750–759.

Corcoran, R. P., & Tormey, R. (2013). Does emotional intelligence predict student teachers' performance? *Teaching and Teacher Education, 35*, 34–42.

Daus, C. S., & Ashkanasy, N. M. (2005). The case for the ability-based model of emotional intelligence in organisational behaviour. *Journal of Organizational Behaviour, 26*, 453–466.

Day, A. L., & Carroll, S. A. (2004). Using an ability-based measure of emotional intelligence to predict individual performance, group performance, and group citizenship behaviours. *Personality and Individual Differences, 36*, 1443–1458.

Dolev, N., & Leshem, S. (2016). Teachers' emotional intelligence: The impact of training. *International Journal of Emotional Education, 8*(1), 75–94.

Edelman, P., & van Knippenberg, D. (2018). Emotional intelligence, management of subordinate's emotions, and leadership effectiveness. *Leadership & Organisational Development Journal, 39*(5), 592–607.

Fineman, S. (2004). Getting the measure of emotion - and the cautionary tale of emotional intelligence. *Human Relations, 57*(6), 719–740.

Ghanizadeh, A., & Moafian, F. (2010). The role of EFL teachers' emotional intelligence in their success. *ELT Journal, 64*(4), 424–435.

Goleman, D. (1996). *Emotional intelligence: Why it can matter more than IQ.* London: Bloomsbury.

Goleman, D. (2001). An EI-based theory of performance. In C. Cherniss & D. Goleman (Eds.) *The emotionally intelligent workplace: How to select for, measure, and improve emotional intelligence in individuals, groups, and organization* (pp. 27–44). San Francisco: Jossy-Bass.

Han, H., & Johnson, S. D. (2012). Relationship between students' emotional intelligence, social bond, and interactions in online learning. *Educational Technology & Society, 15*(1), 78–89.

Ignat, A. A., & Clipa, O. (2012). Teachers' satisfaction with life, job satisfaction and their emotional intelligence. *Procedia – Social and Behavioral Sciences, 33*, 498–502.

Kingston, E. (2008). Emotional competence and drop-out rates in higher education. *Education & Training, 50*(2), 128–139.

Lopes, P. N., Grewal, D., Kadis, J., Gall, M., & Salovey, P. (2006). Evidence that emotional intelligence is related to job performance and affect and attitudes at work. *Psicothema, 18*, 132–138.

Lopes, P. N., Salovey, P., & Straus, R. (2003). Emotional intelligence, personality, and the perceived quality of social relationships. *Personality and Individual Differences, 35*, 641–658.

Maul, A. (2011). The factor structure and cross-test convergence of the Mayer-Salovey-Caruso model of emotional intelligence. *Personality and Individual Differences, 50*(4), 457–463.

Maul, A. (2012). The validity of the Mayer-Salovey-Caruso emotional intelligence test (MSCEIT) as a measure of emotional intelligence. *Emotion Review, 4*, 394–402.

Mayer, J. D., & Salovey, P. (1997). What is emotional intelligence? In P. Salovey & D. Sluyter (Eds.) *Emotional development and emotional intelligence: Implications for educators* (pp. 3–31). New York: Basic Books.

Mayer, J. D., Roberts, R. D., & Barsade, S. G. (2008). Human abilities: Emotional intelligence. *Annual Review of Psychology*, *59*, 507–536.

Mayer, J. D., Salovey, P., & Caruso, D. (2002). *Mayer-Salovey-Caruso emotional intelligence test manual*. Toronto, Canada: Multi-Health Systems.

Mayer, J. D., Salovey, P., & Caruso, D. (2012). The validity of the MSCEIT: Additional analyses and evidence. *Emotion Review*, *4*(2) 403–408.

McLeod, J. (2007). *Counselling skill*. Maidenhead: Open University Press.

Mérida-López, S., & Extremera, N. (2017). Emotional intelligence and teacher burnout: A systematic review. *International Journal of Educational Research*, *85*, 121–130. doi: 10.1016/j. ijer.2017.07.006.

Palmer, B. R., Gignac, G., Manocha, R., & Stough, C. (2005). A psychometric evaluation of the Meyer-Salovey-Caruso emotional intelligence test version 2.0. *Intelligence*, *33*, 285–305.

Parrish, D. R. (2015). The relevance of emotional intelligence for leadership in a higher education context. *Studies in Higher Education*, *40*(5), 821–837. doi:10.1080/03075079.2 013.842225.

Payne, W. L. (1985). *A study of emotion: Developing emotional intelligence; self-integration; relating to fear, pain and desire.* (Unpublished PhD Thesis, The Union for Experimenting Colleges and Universities). Retrieved from http://eqi.org/payne.htm

Perez, J. C., Petrides, K. V., & Furnham, A. (2005). Measuring trait emotional intelligence. In R. Schulze & R. D. Roberts (Eds.) *Emotional intelligence: An international handbook* (pp. 181–201). Cambridge, MA: Hogrefe & Huber.

Rosete, D., & Ciarrochi, J. (2005). Emotional intelligence and its relationship to workplace performance outcomes of leadership effectiveness. *Leadership & Organization Development Journal*, *26*(5), 388–399.

Salmon, G. (2011). *E-moderating: The key to teaching & learning online* (3rd ed.). London: RoutledgeFalmer.

Salovey, P., & Mayer, J. D. (1990). Emotional intelligence. *Imagination, Cognition and Personality*, *9*(3), 185–211.

Shah, N. A., Saad, M., Mohan, N. M. M., & Poniran, H. (2018). Working in private universities: Does emotional intelligence matter for job effectiveness? *International Journal of Accounting, Finance and Business (IJAFB)*, *3*(10), 87–96.

Vaida, S., & Opre, A. (2014). Emotional intelligence versus emotional competence. *Journal of Psychological and Educational Research*, *22*(1), 26–33.

Vega-Hernández, M. C., Patino-Alonso, M. C., Cabello, R., Galindo-Villardón, M. P., & Fernández-Berrocal, P. (2017). Perceived emotional intelligence and learning strategies in Spanish university students: A new perspective from a canonical non-symmetrical correspondence analysis. *Frontiers in Psychology*, *8*, 1888. doi: 10.3389/fpsyg.2017.01888.

Wakeman, C. (2006). Emotional intelligence: Testing, measurement and analysis. *Research in Education*, *75*, 71–93.

Youde, A. (2014). *A mixed methods exploration of effective tutors and tutoring in blended learning contexts* (Unpublished EdD Thesis, The University of Huddersfield, Huddersfield). Retrieved from http://eprints.hud.ac.uk/id/eprint/20351/

Zeidner, M., Matthews, G., & Roberts, R. D. (2009). *What we know about emotional intelligence: How it affects learning, work, relationships, and our mental health.* Cambridge, MA: MIT Press.

Chapter 3

The utility of the Mayer-Salovey-Caruso Emotional Intelligence Test (MSCEIT) for identifying effective tutors in online and blended learning contexts

Introduction

Chapter 2 referred to the MSCEIT (Mayer, Salovey, & Caruso, 2002) as the "flagship test of emotional intelligence" (Maul, 2012, p. 394) and this Chapter analyses its underpinning definition and model (the Four-Branch Model of Emotional Intelligence) in relation to its value within online and blended tutoring. It provides an in-depth critique of the Model and Test regarding their value in exploring the EI of tutors in this context. The Chapter firstly presents evidence to argue the benefits of 'ability' measures of emotional intelligence (EI) before providing an analysis of the Four-Branch Model to suggest a set of abilities, such as perceiving learners' emotions, which could support effective tutoring. Further, the MSCEIT and Four-Branch Model are refined with relevant definitions amended to suit the context. As stated in Chapter 2, there is limited empirical research to link EI and teaching effectiveness in higher education (HE) online and blended learning environments and this Chapter presents empirical evidence regarding use of the MSCEIT in educational contexts and suggests strengths and limitations of the instrument for identifying effective tutors. The analysis of the Four-Branch Model in relation to this context offered here provides a new perspective, which develops current understandings of EI.

Ability measures of emotional intelligence

This Section justifies the use of an 'ability' measure of EI when considering effective tutoring in online and blended learning contexts. Chapter 2 noted that the MSCEIT was a prominent ability measure of EI, which tests the construct directly, with this being a potentially important factor when considering tutors in HE. Self-report measures require self-judgement and, therefore, limit the intelligent reasoning about emotion or the enhancement of intelligence through the use of emotions and emotional knowledge (Mayer, Roberts, & Barsade, 2008, p. 519). Therefore, the validity of using such approaches to measure intelligence is questionable. There is evidence

The utility of the MSCEIT 21

to suggest self-reported measures of EI correlate with measures of personality (Day & Carroll, 2004; Rosete & Ciarrochi, 2005) and, therefore, are unlikely to measure a distinct construct. Further, self-reporting tests can be subject to 'reporting bias' where respondents in work contexts may want to be seen in a favourable light (Rosete & Ciarrochi, 2005), with this being particularly pertinent for academics and any measure of 'intelligence'. Corcoran and Tormey (2012, p. 751) used the MSCEIT in their study to explore the EI of pre-service teachers as, they argued, it strengthened the validity in relation to self-report and 360 degree evaluation mechanisms. Ability measures only slightly correlate with measures of personality, correlate modestly with intelligence, and are harder for respondents to determine 'correct' answers (Rosete & Ciarrochi, 2005). From my experience, academics tend to deconstruct self-report tests rather than approach them at face value, and this is a factor which strengthens the validity of ability measures for research in HE contexts.

The term 'ability' implies something that can be improved, which is generally not the case in relation to personality traits (Groves, McEnrue, & Shen, 2006, p. 19). Further, an individual's 'intelligence' can be improved overtime (Matthews, Zeidner, & Roberts, 2002). If EI, as measured by the MSCEIT, was classified as an intelligence, training could be provided for its improvement, thus, of potential value to online and blended tutors. Matthews et al. (2002, p. 228) state that the MSCEIT is the only measure of EI to satisfy the following criteria and, therefore, is a measure of intelligence:

- it reflects performance (through the use of an ability-based measure) rather than perceived ways of behaving
- it correlates, but not too highly, with existing Intelligence Quotient (IQ) measures
- it has been found to improve from childhood to middle adulthood
- it is predictive of emotion-related outcomes and general life satisfaction (Matthews et al., 2002, p. 228).

More recent research has continued to confirm that EI, as measured by the MSCEIT, is related to other IQ measures, although not so closely as to make the test redundant (MacCann, 2010, p. 490; Zeidner, Matthews, & Roberts, 2009, p. 101). With the MSCEIT satisfying Matthews et al. (2002, p. 228) criteria, this strengthens its value when considering its analysis in relation to tutors and suggests face validity. However, there has been limited empirical research within online and blended learning environments to verify this view (Youde, 2014). Teaching and learning in any context is certainly an emotion-related process whether an individual lesson or tutorial, or something longer such as a unit of study or course. Youde (2016) suggested that being emotionally competent was a valuable quality for tutors operating in online and blended learning environments, and it is potentially beneficial to practice, as the above literature suggests, that it could improve with age and be developed. Dolev and Leshem (2016) found that emotional competences can be developed through training within educational contexts, however, their research did not adopt the MSCEIT as its measure of EI.

The Four-Branch Model of emotional intelligence

The MSCEIT measures an individual's perceptions, use of, understanding of and management of emotion (Mayer et al., 2002). It is based on the Mayer and Salovey Four-Branch Model of Emotional Intelligence (1997) and measures the following four abilities:

- Perceiving emotions (Branch 1)
- Using emotions to facilitate thought (Branch 2)
- Understanding emotions (Branch 3)
- Managing emotions (Branch 4).

Abilities associated with each branch are developed below and contextualised in relation to online and blended learning. Mayer and Salovey (1997) describe four 'boxes' for each branch, with higher numbered boxes indicating higher EI. Throughout this Section, the MSCEIT and Four-Branch Model have been refined with relevant definitions amended to suit the context.

Perceiving emotions (Branch 1)

This Branch indicates a person's ability "to perceive emotions in oneself and others, as well as in objects, art, music, and other stimuli" (Mayer et al., 2002, p. 7). The four 'boxes' are:

- box 1 – the tutor can accurately express own feelings
- box 2 – the tutor can evaluate emotion in others or artwork etcetera
- box 3 – the tutor can express feelings and express needs around these feelings
- box 4 – the tutor is sensitive to false or manipulative expression.

Corcoran and Tormey (2012, p. 751) argue that "the ability to perceive emotion in self and others has repeatedly been identified as important for teachers". Tutors in online and blended learning use various media beyond face-to-face interactions through which they have to evaluate emotions in others whilst expressing their own. Many of these media are text-based such as e-mail, discussion forums and wikis, however, some are speech-based including the telephone and online conferencing. Therefore, the ability of a tutor to appropriately express their own feelings and accurately perceive emotions in others appears important in both face-to-face and online contexts.

The utility of the MSCEIT   23

Using emotions to facilitate thought (Branch 2)

This Branch indicates a person's ability "to generate, use and feel emotion as necessary to communicate feelings" (Mayer et al., 2002, p. 7). The four 'boxes' are:

- box 1 – the tutor will complete a necessary job as they know it will affect their enjoyment of another activity if left
- box 2 – the tutor can anticipate feelings which help their decision making, for example, should they criticise a learner?
- box 3 – the tutor allows shifting moods to give more possibilities when making decisions and affords more creative thinking
- box 4 – recognition that "different forms of work and different forms of reasoning (e.g., deductive/inductive) may be facilitated by different kinds of moods" (Mayer & Salovey, 1997, p. 13).

Emotionally intelligent blended learning tutors should recognise the influence of differing emotional states on learners' cognitive processes (Corcoran & Tormey, 2012, p. 751). On the face of it, it would be expected that tutors exhibiting these ECs would be perceived as more effective by learners. This could be achieved by tutors generating their own emotional state to be conducive to teaching whilst also encouraging the emotional states of learners, such as trust and anticipation, which are beneficial to the tasks in hand, most commonly learning. Further, it would be expected that tutors recognise the creative ideas that can come from differing moods, both within themselves and their learners. For example, avoiding focussed discussions with an overjoyed student as very positive emotions frequently result in inductive as opposed to deductive reasoning (Brackett & Katulak, 2006).

Understanding emotions (Branch 3)

This Branch indicates a person's ability "to understand emotional information, how emotions combine and progress through relationship transitions, and to appreciate such emotional meanings" (Mayer et al., 2002, p. 7). The four 'boxes' are:

- box 1 – the tutor can recognise emotions and the differences between them, for example, joy and elation, anxiety and worry
- box 2 – the tutor has an increased understanding of emotional meanings, for example, sadness from loss, fear from threat
- box 3 – the tutor can recognise complex contradictory emotions, for example, awe as a combination of fear and surprise
- box 4 – the tutor can reason about sequences of emotions in interpersonal relationships, for example, anger may lead to rage, and then guilt or satisfaction.

24 The utility of the MSCEIT

For tutors to understand emotion in themselves and their students it may be expected that they know what causes emotion, and be able to describe a full range of emotions when considering their own and other's feelings (Brackett & Katulak, 2006). A confident student may not mind a tutor saying their answer was not correct, but others may find this embarrassing and become anxious, both in face-to-face and online contexts. Further, it is expected that learners would value tutors' understanding of students' emotions to motivate them, that they would respond to varying points of view, and that they would handle various group reactions (Caruso, 1999).

This Branch considers tutors' ability to identify emotions that combine into other emotions, for example, malice might arise from a combination of envy and aggression (Mayer, Salovey, Caruso, & Sitarenios, 2003, p. 99), and variations in emotions over time, such as when anger changes to sadness (Kerr, Garvin, Heaton, & Boyle, 2006, p. 269). This is relevant for tutors as they seek to understand how a learner's emotions are interlinked and how they change. For example, it appears beneficial for tutors to understand a learner's anger from receiving a poor mark and this may result in sadness in the near future. A tutor can then action support around this understanding as the learner works on the next piece of work. This emotional competence proves significant as the analysis develops throughout this book with Chapter 11 synthesising this discussion when arguing the importance of tutor/learner relationships in this context.

Managing emotions (Branch 4)

This Branch indicates a person's ability "to be open to feelings, and to modulate them in oneself and others so as to promote personal understanding and growth" (Mayer et al., 2002, p. 7). The four 'boxes' are:

- box 1 – the tutor stays open to feelings, both agreeable and disagreeable
- box 2 – the tutor can separate emotion and behaviour, for example, a tutor who is angry can take a step back and be calm with learners, and then discuss the issue later with more calm confidents
- box 3 – the tutor becomes "consistently reflective or meta–experience of mood and emotion" (Mayer & Salovey, 1997, p. 14), for example, this feeling of anger is influencing the approach to teaching
- box 4 – emotions are understood without exaggerating or minimising their importance.

The ability to manage and regulate emotions in oneself and others appears important for tutors (Corcoran & Tormey, 2012, p. 751). This Branch considers Emotional Management, where respondents judge the actions required for effective emotional outcomes for individuals in certain scenarios, and Emotional Relations, which is similar to Emotional Management, but considers a respondent's ability to judge actions that constitute effective management of another person's feelings. This

The utility of the MSCEIT 25

Branch appears particularly important for tutors and is at the heart of generating a correct emotional state, in themselves and their learners, for effective learning to take place in both face-to-face and online environments.

Tutors who manage their own and learners' emotions in a classroom can create a more open and effective learning environment with fewer distractions (Brackett & Katulak, 2006; Mortiboys, 2005), and it is reasonable to assume the same would be true in online environments. It is anticipated that online and blended learning tutors, who can control their emotional reactions, are more accomplished at dealing with difficult conversations, such as might arise when a learner feels they deserve a higher mark for their coursework.

Summary

The analysis of the Four-Branch model revealed a number of abilities that appear relevant to online and blended tutoring and which are considered further in this book. Each of the abilities would be apparent in face-to-face and a variety of online media, the latter being particularly difficult given the lack of para-lingual and emotional cues in predominantly text-based environments (Gilmore & Warren, 2007, p. 581; Murphy, Shelley, White, & Baumann, 2011, p. 410). The analysis moves on now from the Four-Branch Model to further explore the MSCEIT's utility in measuring the EC of tutors.

Analysis of the MSCEIT's constituent tasks to evaluate their utility in measuring the emotional intelligence of tutors in online and blended learning environments

To further explore the face validity of the MSCEIT for tutors in online and blended learning contexts, its constituent tasks were reviewed (see Table 3.1 for an overview of the MSCEIT's structure). This provides an in-depth critique of the Test to explore its value in evaluating online and blended tutors EI.

The MSCEIT measures an individual's overall EI and also scores their performance on the four branches of the model, with each having two sets of underpinning tasks. The Perceiving Branch consists of a 'Faces task' and a 'Pictures task'

Table 3.1 Structure of the MSCEIT (Adapted from Mayer et al., 2002, p. 8)

Overall Score	Two Areas of the MSCEIT	Four Branches of the MSCEIT	Task Level
Emotional Intelligence (EI)	Experiential Emotional Intelligence (EEI)	Perceiving Emotions	Faces Pictures
		Using Emotions	Facilitation Sensations
	Strategic Emotional Intelligence (SEI)	Understanding Emotions	Changes Blends
		Managing Emotions	Emotional Management Emotional Relations

with respondents identifying emotions in each. There is relevance here for tutors as they will need to perceive emotions in faces, but it would also be valuable to get information on their ability with other media, in this case pictures, as this may be important when teaching in online environments.

The Using Branch consists of a 'Facilitation task', which involves identifying emotions that are beneficial in five differing activities, and a 'Sensations task' which requires emotions to be linked to differing sensations, for example, considering the emotion guilt and deciding its coldness (Mayer et al., 2003, p. 99). The Facilitation task appears particularly relevant for tutors given the range of activities learners undertake across a range of media. The Sensations task's face validity is less apparent as tutors are unlikely to be required to link emotions to differing sensations, however, it does give a picture of the cognitive ability to generate emotions and, therefore, is relevant when considering EI as an intelligence.

The Understanding Emotions Branch consists of a 'Blends task', where respondents identify emotions that combine into other emotions (Mayer et al., 2003, p. 99), and a 'Changes task' where respondents identify variations in emotions over time (Kerr et al., 2006, p. 269). Both of these tasks are relevant for tutors as they seek to understand how a learner's emotions are interlinked and how they change over time.

The Managing Emotions Branch consists of an 'Emotional Management task' where respondents judge the actions required for effective emotional outcomes for individuals in certain scenarios, and the 'Emotional Relations task', which is similar to the Emotional Management task, but asks respondents to judge actions that are most effective management of another person's feelings. This Branch appears particularly important for tutors and is at the heart of generating a correct emotional state, in themselves and their learners, for effective learning to take place in both face-to-face and online environments. This Branch, however, raises an interesting contradiction as it more closely resembles a self-report rather than an ability measure of EI. This brings into question its face validity for assessing a tutor's EI, as stated earlier, academics tend to deconstruct self-report tests rather than approach them at face value. In the Emotional Management task an example question considers what an individual may do to reduce their anger, however, the respondent is not angry at the time of completing the test and therefore may provide a preferred response. Similarly, the Emotional Relations task asks respondents how they would manage another person's feelings in certain circumstances, but again, they have to imagine themselves in such a situation.

The MSCEIT also generates two 'area' scores and a Positive-negative Bias score. Firstly, Experiential Emotional Intelligence (EEI), which combines the Perceiving and Understanding Branches and is a measure of an individual's ability to "perceive emotional information, to relate it to other sensations such as colour and taste, and to use it to facilitate thought" (Mayer et al., 2002, p. 17). Secondly, Strategic Emotional Intelligence (SEI), which combines the Using and Managing Branches and measures an individual's ability to "understand emotional information and use it strategically for planning and self-management" (Mayer et al., 2002, p. 17). The Positive-negative Bias score provides a "metric of an individual's tendency to respond to the pictorial stimuli in the MSCEIT with positive or negative emotions" (Mayer et al., 2002, p. 15) and higher scores indicate relatively positive responses.

The MSCEIT provides scores for total EI, two areas and four branches. An actual score is provided for each aspect of the MSCEIT and these are further categorised from Consider Development to Significant Strength to guide the interpretation of the ability level (Mayer et al., 2002). These scores allow quantitative analysis with other studies comparing the MSCEIT's scores with a range of other variables, such as, learners' perceptions of their tutors in online and blended learning environments as measured by an attitude survey (see Chapter 10 for an example survey developed for blended learning contexts).

Although the MSCEIT and the Four-Branch Model have some limitations for measuring tutors' EI, they still have utility and are a valid and reliable measure in this context. The Sensations task may have limited face validity for tutors and the Managing Emotions Branch may be difficult to accurately complete due to its 'self-report' nature, but the remaining tasks are relevant for analysis of EI in online and blended learning contexts.

Empirical research utilising the MSCEIT in educational contexts

This Section outlines a small number of empirical studies and discusses their findings regarding the utility of the MSCEIT in exploring the EI of teachers and lecturers. In particular, the Section outlines the quantitative findings from Youde's (2014) mixed-methods exploration of effective tutors and tutoring in an educational blended learning context.

Brackett (2008) cites a number of studies that use the MSCEIT to predict academic performance, but each is focussed on students' EI and not that of their teachers. As detailed in Chapter 2, Corcoran and Tormey (2013) used the MSCEIT to analyse student teachers' levels of EI in relation to their teaching performance, and found no relationships. They stated that their findings raised serious questions about current understandings of emotions in this context. Curci, Lanciano, and Soleti (2014) utilised the MSCEIT to investigate the effects of teachers' EI ability, self-efficacy, and emotional states and students' self-esteem, perceptions of ability, and metacognitive beliefs in predicting school achievement. Their findings showed that teachers' EI has a positive role in promoting students' achievement by enhancing the effects of students' self-perceptions of ability and self-esteem. Again, these studies point to the contradictory findings regarding EI and teacher performance. Further, these studies did not provide a detailed analysis of the MSCEIT at branch and task level, something that Youde's (2014) research provided within an educational disciplinary area.

28 The utility of the MSCEIT

Youde (2014) explored the practices of experienced HE tutors in blended learning contexts. Their skills, qualities and competences, particularly emotional competences, were investigated using a mixed methods approach (Creswell, 2014) to conduct a detailed exploration of eight tutors' practice in relation to blended learning with data gathered from four principal sources. The study used the MSCEIT to assess tutors' EI scores and results were compared to their learners' perceptions of quality, assessed using an attitude survey (n = 72). Interviews with tutors explored their approaches to delivery and considered factors that impacted on quality. Analysis of virtual learning environment (VLE) content and communications provided insight into tutors' online practice.

The learner attitude survey conducted by Youde (2014) included a modified version of the Course Experience Questionnaire (CEQ; Ramsden, 1991) and an Online Tutoring Questionnaire (OTQ; see Chapter 10 for a discussion of the CEQ's development for a blended learning context). The CEQ was designed as an indicator of teacher effectiveness on courses in HE institutions and draws on learners' perceptions of teaching, curriculum and assessment, and was modified for blended learning contexts. The scale items adopted for this research were largely the same as the original CEQ, and were:

- good teaching communication
- good teaching feedback on, and concern for, student learning
- clear goals and standards
- appropriate workload.

The OTQ was similar in focus, but elicited feedback purely on learners' perceptions of tutors in the online elements of their blended modules. The study explored competences, particularly emotional competences, which contributed to the effectiveness of tutors within blended learning environments. The MSCEIT was, in part, used to identify these and this Section argues that it has limited utility in identifying effective tutors. However, two constituent MSCEIT tasks and the Positive–negative Bias measure did suggest interesting abilities that could influence learners' perceptions of quality.

The modules investigated as part of Youde (2014) were successful with students achieving and happy with their progress. Preliminary analysis revealed a CEQ mean total of 3.72 and similar high scores were evident across the constituent scales, indicating that learners considered their tutors were effective (see Table 3.2 for overall CEQ scores with standard deviations). Standard deviation scores were relatively small for a five-point scale, which suggested a common perception from the groups of learners. Overall module pass-rates, whilst a crude measure of educational success, were greater than 95% with some of the remaining 5% expected to complete in the near future. Learners were asked to rate their module achievement on a five-point scale (very disappointed to very good) and the resultant mean score was 3.83 indicating broad satisfaction with their results and academic development. During the

The utility of the MSCEIT 29

Table 3.2 Tutor's CEQ results – mean and (standard deviation)

Tutor (Pseudonym)	N	CEQ Total	Clear Goals and Standards	Good Teaching Communication	Good Teaching Feedback	Appropriate Workload
Ann	6	4.06 (0.36)	4.29 (0.40)	4.50 (0.35)	4.25 (0.45)	3.71 (0.68)
Bill	7	3.86 (0.64)	3.96 (1.09)	4.33 (0.69)	3.93 (0.72)	3.89 (0.66)
Claire	7	4.10 (0.35)	4.29 (0.57)	4.62 (0.36)	3.64 (0.35)	4.25 (0.64)
Daisy	4	3.23 (0.45)	3.69 (0.24)	3.58 (0.74)	2.87 (1.18)	2.94 (0.31)
Emily	15	3.99 (0.26)	4.42 (0.28)	4.15 (0.44)	4.12 (0.44)	3.48 (0.47)
Frank	5	3.43 (0.37)	3.45 (0.62)	4.00 (0.97)	3.30 (0.67)	2.90 (0.88)
George	14	3.55 (0.40)	3.59 (0.74)	4.31 (0.53)	3.68 (0.56)	2.99 (0.55)
Harry	14	3.42 (0.67)	3.42 (1.15)	3.55 (1.06)	3.13 (0.80)	3.46 (0.47)
Mean		3.72 (0.53)	3.89 (0.83)	4.12 (0.79)	3.73 (0.77)	3.38 (0.63)

interviews, when tutors were asked to provide an overall impression of their groups, there was a consensus around motivated learners, students' engagement with their studies, and the production of good quality student work. These indicators, together with the generally high CEQ scores received, suggested successful modules with students learning and achieving, therefore, are worthy of a detailed analysis of effective tutoring in this context.

Discussion of the MSCEIT's utility in identifying effective tutors in an education disciplinary area

A number of issues were apparent that question the MSCEIT's utility in identifying effective tutors in blended learning contexts for mature learners studying vocationally relevant degrees (Youde & Marsden, 2012; Youde, 2014). Below average scores[1] were achieved by tutors at total EI, strategic area and branch levels, the Understanding Emotions Branch being the only exception (see Table 3.3 for tutor MSCEIT scores and Table 3.4 for guidelines to interpret the MSCEIT scores).

Table 3.3 Tutor MSCEIT scores

Tutor Pseudonym	Total EI	Experiential	Strategic	Perceiving	Using	Understanding	Managing
Ann	98	93	103	93	97	102	103
Bill	104	97	110	93	110	115	96
Claire	98	100	94	109	84	108	82
Daisy	84	85	91	81	98	95	89
Emily	107	107	105	109	97	108	98
Frank	80	77	89	73	98	109	74
George	75	75	86	82	74	94	81
Harry	117	118	112	108	133	104	122
Mean	96	94	99	93	99	104	93

30 The utility of the MSCEIT

Table 3.4 Guidelines for interpreting MSCEIT scores (Mayer et al., 2002)

Emotional Intelligent Quotient (EIQ) Range	Qualitative Range
69 or less	Consider Development
70 – 89	Consider Improvement
90 – 99	Low Average Score
100 – 109	High Average Score
110 – 119	Competent
120 – 129	Strength
130 or more	Significant Strength

Earlier, this Chapter established the MSCEIT's potential value as it identified abilities appearing beneficial for online and blended tutors. Higher MSCEIT average scores were anticipated from a group of experienced HE lecturers who had established careers, with this overall finding questioning its validity in identifying successful tutors. In addition, limited correlations were found with learners' perceptions of quality determined through results following their completion of two attitude surveys (the CEQ and OTQ). Whilst tutors were advised to answer questions on instinct, they reported a desire to offer the 'correct' answer. The Test's length was raised as an issue with two tutors noting the frustration this caused at the latter stages when answering questions. Finally, another tutor's responses could have been influenced by her state of mind following two recent bereavements of close family members. She reflected that these events resulted in more negative responses than would have been provided in normal circumstances.

Branch- and task-level analysis of the MSCEIT's utility in identifying effective tutors in an education disciplinary area

The MSCEIT's overall and area scores did not highlight desirable abilities of tutors in relation to learner perceptions of quality, however, some were revealed at branch and task level. Each branch is now analysed to consider its value in identifying effective blended tutors.

The perceiving branch

This Branch, incorporating Faces and Pictures tasks, received varied mean tutor scores and significant positive correlations with the CEQ and some constituent scales. The Branch scores displayed a positive correlation ($r = .243$, $p < .05$) with the CEQ's total mean score which indicates learners' view tutors who are more adept at perceiving emotions as more effective. However, a Low Average (93) mean score was achieved by tutors on this Branch. Further

The utility of the MSCEIT 31

analysis at task level revealed Faces having a significant effect on the Branch. Mean tutors' scores revealed a Competent value (111) on Pictures but a Consider Improvement value on Faces. Only Faces positively correlated with the CEQ. Interviews noted that tutors were experienced and self-efficacious in face-to-face environments, and it was anticipated they would have a greater ability at perceiving emotions in images of peoples' faces. Significant positive correlations between the Perceiving Branch and Faces task, with the CEQ, suggest ability to perceive emotions in faces is associated with learner views of tutor quality. Given the low mean score achieved on this task, it may have utility in ranking tutors but should not be used in isolation when identifying successful tutors in the eyes of learners.

Although Pictures received a Competent mean score by tutors it did not correlate with the CEQ and OTQ. Seven tutors achieved above average scores on this task that tests ability at perceiving emotions in certain images or landscapes (Mayer et al., 2002, p. 20). This ability could be supporting the apparent module success as tutors were perceiving emotions through other media, predominantly text-based in this instance. Further, ability to perceive emotions aids the development of empathic competences (Wakeman, 2006, p. 72), which interview data suggested was noticeable in tutors receiving higher CEQ scores. However, although the Pictures task indicates a potentially important ability for tutors, its lack of correlation with the CEQ and OTQ indicates that other factors are influencing learner perceptions of quality.

The using branch

This Branch, incorporating Facilitation and Sensations tasks, received average mean tutor scores, but some significant negative correlations with constituent scales of the CEQ and OTQ. Significant correlations were:

- the Using Branch had a significant negative relationship with the OTQ ($r = -.365$, $p < .01$)
- the Sensations task had a significant negative relationship with the CEQ ($r = -.257$, $p < .05$)
- the Sensations task had a significant negative relationship with the OTQ ($r = -.477$, $p < .01$)
- further significant negative correlations were found with Clear Goals and Good Teaching Feedback CEQ scale items.

Earlier within this Chapter, the Facilitation task's relevance for this research was highlighted as the identification and use of appropriate and beneficial emotions could facilitate the creation of effective learning environments, however, no significant correlations were found. Further, the earlier discussion outlined limited face validity of the Sensations task as tutors are unlikely to be required to link emotions to differing sensations. The task was included to provide a picture of the cognitive ability to generate emotions and, therefore, relevant when considering EI as an intelligence. Examining the descriptive data for Sensations revealed the two tutors receiving the lowest CEQ and OTQ scores getting high results on this task, with the opposite occurring for the tutor achieving the highest score. The remaining five tutors received largely similar task scores and it was clear that further qualitative analysis was needed to interrogate these correlations.

Qualitative analysis following the interviews revealed relevant examples of tutors' effectively 'using' emotions that diminish the Sensations task's value in identifying effective blended tutors. A flavour of tutors' effective use of emotions was described in face-to-face contexts as tutors generated emotions to "set the tone" for the module, get learners interested and engaged, and try to "win them over" with the aim of these approaches to keep them motivated on to the submission of summative assessments. Two tutors felt their enthusiasm for the subject was an important motivational factor for learners on their modules. Emotions evident in tutors' teaching were generally positive, however, some were negative around online elements of practice and workload. One tutor, though, outlined effective use of negative emotions when stating:

> that's why you worry when you're frustrated and tired and you have to manage your workload – sometimes you have to walk away so you're in the right mind to give the right feedback.

Following the qualitative analysis, it was difficult to rationalise strong negative correlations between the Sensations task and the CEQ and OTQ, and it has limited utility in identifying effective blended tutors. Qualitative evidence indicated tutors are using emotions to generate sessions intended to interest and motivate students in face-to-face environments.

The understanding branch

This Branch, incorporating Changes and Blends tasks, received the highest branch mean score with Blends having significant positive correlations with constituent scales of the CEQ and OTQ. Ability in these areas allows a better understanding of learners' emotions, their cause, and how these may change over time. This Branch score was the highest, and only, in the High Average range with both task scores also located at this level. The Understanding Branch had a significant positive relationship with the CEQ ($r = .255$, $p < .05$) and, when analysed at task level, Blends had a significant positive relationship with the CEQ ($r = .333$, $p < .01$) and OTQ ($r = .305$, $p < .01$). Further, significant positive correlations were found with Clear Goals and Good Teaching Feedback scales of the CEQ. It is clear that Blends is significant in identifying effective blended tutors and further analysis was needed to interrogate these results.

Qualitative analysis revealed a number of tutor strategies to motivate learners, particularly in face-to-face contexts, which could indicate competence at understanding emotions in others. The Understanding Branch indicates a person's ability "to understand emotional information, how emotions combine and progress through relationship transitions" (Mayer et al., 2002, p. 7), and highlights the importance of tutors developing relationships with learners (see Chapter 11 for a discussion regarding the importance of tutor/learner relationships). As tutors develop relationships with learners, a better understanding of their emotions can be achieved and, in particular, an appreciation of how these will change over time. A confident student may not mind a tutor saying their answer was not correct, but others may find this embarrassing and become anxious; and, over time, a tutor's ability in this area will develop with regard to understanding individual learners. Ability to understand emotions, and therefore respond appropriately to learners, can help build productive relationships and potentially impact on the quality of support provided. Tutors' previous relationships with the learner groups was found to influence CEQ scores, in that, those who had either taught students before, or had some involvement in courses inductions, received higher ratings. Therefore, this could be a factor in tutors' increased ability in understanding their students' emotions.

The managing branch

Earlier, this Chapter argued the potential utility of abilities outlined in the Managing Emotions Branch for effective blended tutors, but was critical of its face validity as this section was self-reported rather than based on a measure of their ability. Tutors' achieved Low Average scores at both branch and task levels. This Branch is particularly important for blended tutors and is at the heart of generating a conducive emotional state, in themselves and their learners, for effective learning to take place (Brackett & Katulak, 2006; Mortiboys, 2005). However, given Low Average scores, few significant CEQ correlations, a negative OTQ correlation, and concern about face validity for academics with tendencies for deconstructing tests, the Branch's utility in identifying effective blended tutors appears limited.

Positive-negative bias scores

The MSCEIT's Positive-negative Bias scores identified seven tutors whose tendency was to respond to pictorial stimuli with positive emotions (Mayer et al., 2002, p. 15). This could have been a contributory factor in the module success described earlier. Qualitative data analysis revealed that tutors described being enthusiastic and motivational in face-to-face environments, with the most effective (as shown by the CEQ) positive about the affordances of blended learning and seeing opportunities to deliver effective practice.

34 The utility of the MSCEIT

Further, interview data revealed that tutors were self-confident and self-efficacious in face-to-face environments and determined to support learners throughout modules. Chapter 8 discusses the importance of enthusiasm for the subject and teaching as a vital personal quality when working with adults (Biggs & Tang, 2011; Smith, 2004) and the Positive-negative Bias score could be identifying this trait. Bar-On (2006, p. 4) argues that being emotionally intelligent requires individuals to be optimistic, positive and self-motivated. The link between a tutor being generally positive in identifying emotions and these broader traits is questionable, however, qualitative analysis of data in Youde's (2014) research did suggest association. Further, caution must be taken when reading positive-negative values as overly positive values may indicate tutors are misreading situations, which could have been occurring with one tutor. The tutor in question described confidence in his blended tutoring abilities, but he did not proactively support learners or contribute to online elements of modules, and received a low CEQ score.

The Positive-negative Bias score potentially identified an important trait for effective blended tutoring, however, other factors need to be considered to provide a broader picture of emotional competences associated with learner perceptions of quality.

In summary

Within this Chapter, the MSCEIT and Four-Branch Model have been refined with relevant definitions amended to suit the context of blended learning. The Chapter firstly argued that the MSCEIT potentially provides a robust measure of tutors' EC and the use of qualitative data might bridge its potential limitations.

Through an analysis of empirical studies, the Chapter has noted a number of limitations of the MSCEIT in identifying effective blended tutors, although Blends, Faces and Positive-negative Bias scores have potential utility (Youde, 2014). An ability measure of EI was chosen to alleviate academics' tendency to deconstruct tests of intelligence, however, although advised to answer questions on instinct, tutors reported a desire to determine 'correct' answers. The Chapter noted that one tutor's responses could have been influenced by her state of mind following two recent bereavements of close family members, making answers more negative than in normal circumstances. Further, two tutors reported the questionnaire's length as an issue, and feelings of frustration caused by this affected later stages of completion. Mayer et al. (2002, p. 15) advised interpreting task scores with "great caution" and, whilst there is potential utility in Blends and Faces in the identification of effective blended tutors, further evidence is required from the findings from broader EI constructs and identified good practice in blended tutoring, which is outlined in Chapter 4 and Chapter 7 respectively. Blends potentially provided a stronger indication of effective blended tutoring in learner's eyes, whereas Faces' value may lie in ranking tutors. Whilst small scale in nature, Youde's (2014) research provides a rigorous analysis of the most prominent model and measure of EI in relation to tutors operating in online and blended learning environments.

Empirical studies (Corcoran & Tormey, 2013; Curci, Lanciano, & Soleti, 2014) have pointed to the multifaceted and complex issues underpinning teachers' EI and its influence on their learners' perceptions. The detailed analysis of the MSCEIT and its underpinning model provided within this Chapter suggests agreement with those findings. In support of this view, Corcoran and Tormey (2013, p. 41) stated:

> The emotional intelligence framework and the MSCEIT provide a nuanced roadmap to investigate teachers' abstract ability in this domain, but there is also an urgent need for the development of a more contextually specific tool for assessing the ability and disposition to draw upon emotional skills in teaching/learning situations.

This argues that further research is needed to explore and measure EI within broad educational contexts. The following Chapter utilises Goleman's (2001) Framework of Emotional Competences to broaden the analysis to propose potential traits that are valuable for effective online and blended tutors.

Note

1. Scores are calculated as empirical percentiles, positioned on a normal curve with 100 being the average MSCEIT score (Mayer, Salovey, & Caruso, 2002, p. 18).

References

Bar-On, R. (2006). The Bar-On model of emotional-social intelligence (ESI). *Psicothema*, *18*, 13–25.

Biggs, J., & Tang, C. (2011). *Teaching for quality learning at university* (4th ed.). Maidenhead: Open University Press.

Brackett, M. A. (2008). Emotional intelligence as a basic competency in pre-service teacher training: Some evidence. *Electronic Journal of Research in Educational Psychology*, *15*(6), 437–454.

Brackett, M. A., & Katulak, N. A. (2006). Emotional intelligence in the classroom: Skill-based training for teachers and students. In J. Ciarrochi & J. D. Mayer (Eds.) *Applying emotional intelligence: A practitioner's guide* (pp. 53–88). New York, NY: Psychology Press.

Caruso, D. R. (1999). *Applying the ability model of emotional intelligence to the world of work*. Retrieved from http://www.leadershipcoachacademy.com/handouts/EQ_articleEQ_at_Work.pdf

Corcoran, R. P., & Tormey, R. (2012). How emotionally intelligent are pre-service teachers? *Teaching and Teacher Education*, *28*(5), 750–759.

Corcoran, R. P., & Tormey, R. (2013). Does emotional intelligence predict student teachers' performance? *Teaching and Teacher Education*, *35*, 34–42.

36 The utility of the MSCEIT

Creswell, J. W. (2014). *Research design: Qualitative, quantitative and mixed approaches* (4th ed.). London: Sage Publications.

Curci, A., Lanciano, T., & Soleti, E. (2014). Emotions in the classroom: The role of teachers' emotional intelligence ability in predicting students' achievement. *The American Journal of Psychology*, *127*(4), 431–445.

Day, A. L., & Carroll, S. A. (2004). Using an ability-based measure of emotional intelligence to predict individual performance, group performance, and group citizenship behaviours. *Personality and Individual Differences*, *36*, 1443–1458.

Dolev, N., & Leshem, S. (2016). Teachers' emotional intelligence: The impact of training. *International Journal of Emotional Education*, *8*(1), 75–94.

Gilmore, S., & Warren, S. (2007). Emotion online: Experiences of teaching in a virtual learning environment. *Human Relations*, *60*(4), 581–608.

Goleman, D. (2001). An EI-based theory of performance. In C. Cherniss & D. Goleman (Eds.) *The emotionally intelligent workplace: How to select for, measure, and improve emotional intelligence in individuals, groups, and organization* (pp. 27–44). San Francisco: Jossy-Bass.

Groves, K. S., McEnrue, M. P., & Shen, W. (2006). Developing and measuring the emotional intelligence of leaders. *Journal of Management Development*, *27*(2), 225–250.

Kerr, R., Garvin, J., Heaton, N., & Boyle, E. (2006). Emotional intelligence and leadership effectiveness. *Learning & Organisational Development Journal*, *27*(4), 265–279.

MacCann, C. (2010). Further examination of emotional intelligence as a standard intelligence: A latent variable analysis of fluid intelligence, crystallized intelligence, and emotional intelligence. *Personality and Individual Differences*, *49*(5), 490–496.

Matthews, G., Zeidner, M., & Roberts, R. D. (2002). *Emotional intelligence: Science and myth.* London: The MIT Press.

Maul, A. (2012). The validity of the Mayer-Salovey-Caruso emotional intelligence test (MSCEIT) as a measure of emotional intelligence. *Emotion Review*, *4*, 394–402.

Mayer, J. D., & Salovey, P. (1997). What is emotional intelligence? In P. Salovey & D. Sluyter (Eds.) *Emotional development and emotional intelligence: Implications for educators* (pp. 3–31). New York: Basic Books.

Mayer, J. D., Roberts, R. D., & Barsade, S. G. (2008). Human abilities: Emotional intelligence. *Annual Review of Psychology*, *59*, 507–536.

Mayer, J. D., Salovey, P., & Caruso, D. (2002). *Mayer-Salovey-Caruso emotional intelligence test manual.* Toronto, Canada: Multi-Health Systems.

Mayer, J. D., Salovey, P., Caruso, D., & Sitarenios, G. (2003). Measuring emotional intelligence with the MSCEIT V2.0. *Emotion*, *3*(1), 97–105.

Mortiboys, A. (2005). *Teaching with emotional intelligence.* Abingdon, Oxfordshire: Routledge.

Murphy, L. M., Shelley, M. A., White, C. J., & Baumann, U. (2011). Tutor and student perceptions of what makes an effective distance language teacher. *Distance Education*, *32*(3), 397–419.

Ramsden, P. (1991). A performance indicator of teaching quality in higher education: The course experience questionnaire. *Studies in Higher Education*, *16*, 129–150.

Rosete, D., & Ciarrochi, J. (2005). Emotional intelligence and its relationship to workplace performance outcomes of leadership effectiveness. *Leadership & Organization Development Journal*, *26*(5), 388–399.

Smith, A. (2004). "Off-campus support" in distance learning - how do our students define quality? *Quality Assurance in Education*, *12*(1), 28–38.

Wakeman, C. (2006). Emotional intelligence: Testing, measurement and analysis. *Research in Education*, *75*, 71–93.

Youde, A. (2014). *A mixed methods exploration of effective tutors and tutoring in blended learning contexts* (Unpublished EdD Thesis, The University of Huddersfield, Huddersfield). Retrieved from http://eprints.hud.ac.uk/id/eprint/20351/

Youde, A. (2016). Tutor emotional competences valued by learners in a blended learning context. *European Journal of Open, Distance and E-Learning (EURODL)*, *19*(2), 81–97.

Youde, A., & Marsden, F. (2012). Developing a transactional presence amongst adult learners in blended learning contexts: An exploration of the skills, qualities and traits required of the tutor. In *EDULEARN12 Proceedings of International Conference on Education and New Learning Technologies, Barcelona, Spain* (pp. 6334–6342). ISBN 978-84-695-3491-5

Zeidner, M., Matthews, G., & Roberts, R. D. (2009). *What we know about emotional intelligence: How it affects learning, work, relationships, and our mental health*. Cambridge, MA: Mit Press.

Chapter 4

Emotional intelligence

Trait-based models and their utility for tutors in online and blended learning contexts

Introduction

This Chapter outlines common trait-based models of emotional intelligence (EI) and explores their value when identifying effective online and blended learning tutors. It establishes Goleman's (2001) Framework of Emotional Competences (ECs) and the Bar-On (1997) Model of Emotional-Social Intelligence[1] (ESI) as useful templates to evaluate tutor competences. This analysis was instructive when considering ECs that underpin the practices of effective blended learning tutors. Research is presented that utilised Goleman's (2001) Framework to provide a lens through which to analyse blended tutors' practices in relation to learner perceptions. Of significance, in this Chapter are examples of tutor actions that contextualise these competences in online and blended learning environments, with these of potential value for other studies in this area. The Chapter proposes a framework of ECs that, in the views of adult learners, appeared to contribute to tutor effectiveness within an Education disciplinary area (Youde, 2016). Conclusions are drawn that continue to build a picture of the emotionally intelligent tutor within online and blended learning contexts.

Trait-based models of emotional intelligence

Chapter 2 identified a number of traits, such as leadership and being empathic, that are associated with higher EI. This Section outlines prominent trait-based models of EI to consider their value in identifying attributes that may be beneficial when tutoring in online and blended learning environments. Two predominant trait-based models of EI, Goleman's (2001) and Bar-On's (1997), were considered and their constituent clusters analysed for utility in this context. Chapter 2 noted the importance of qualitative research when exploring emotional intelligence. A challenge when tutoring online is that emotional cues are difficult to identify in text-based environments, which still account for a significant proportion of communications in this learning context. Therefore, it can be difficult for tutors to express their emotions

Emotional intelligence 39

as well as interpret the emotions their learners are experiencing. Further, when analysing qualitative data in this area, such as interview transcripts with tutors or content analysis within online, text-based environments, emotional states can be difficult to identify. However, traits such as being empathic, are more easily identified through qualitative analysis (Youde, 2014). This, again, adds weight to the adoption of broader trait-based models of EI when considering effective tutors and tutoring.

Trait-based models of EI such as Bar-On's (1997) and Goleman's (2001) have proved more popular in the literature despite the research supporting Mayer and Salovey's Four-Branch Model and its resultant measure (Day & Carroll, 2004). These models consist of a list of traits that are related to emotions and are different constructs of EI than those represented by ability models (Mayer, Roberts, & Barsade, 2008; Petrides & Furnham, 2003; Zeidner, Matthews, & Roberts, 2009). During the 1990s, three lines of research were established, Salovey and Mayer (1990), Goleman (1996) and Bar-On (1997), with Matthews, Zeidner, and Roberts (2002, p. 175) highlighting these as "the major conceptualisations of EI appearing in the literature". Further, Zeidner et al. (2009) note Goleman's and Bar-On's Models as prominent 'mixed' EI constructs.

When comparing the definitions of prominent ability and trait-based constructs of EI there is clear commonality. As stated in Chapter 3, the most prominent ability-based model, the Mayer-Salovey-Caruso model of emotional intelligence (Mayer, Salovey, & Caruso, 2002), adopted the following definition:

> Emotional intelligence involves the ability to perceive accurately, appraise, and express emotion; the ability to access and/or generate feelings when they facilitate thought; the ability to understand emotion and emotional knowledge; the ability to regulate emotions to promote emotional and intellectual growth. (Mayer & Salovey, 1997, p. 10).

Bar-On (2006, p. 15) stated that most descriptions, definitions, conceptualisations of ESI include one or more of the following components:

- the ability to recognise, understand and express emotions and feelings
- the ability to understand how others feel and relate with them
- the ability to manage and control emotions
- the ability to manage change, adapt and solve problems of a personal and interpersonal nature
- the ability to generate positive affect and be self-motivated.

There is clear similarity between the first three bullet points and Mayer and Salovey's (1997) definition. However, the latter two bullet points suggest a broader understanding of EI, in that new competences are included, such as

40 Emotional intelligence

solving problems of a personal and interpersonal nature, and being self-motivated. This moves trait-based models away from a definition of EI that could be considered an 'intelligence' [see Chapter 3 for a discussion of the Mayer-Salovey-Caruso Emotional Intelligence Test (MSCEIT) as the only measure of EI to be considered a true intelligence]. Goleman outlined EI as non-cognitive in nature with both himself and Bar-On raising a number of non-cognitive traits, such as self-confidence and optimism, which could be valuable in online and blended tutoring environments. Bar-On (1997, p. 14) characterises EI as "an array of non-cognitive capabilities, competencies, and skills that influence one's ability to succeed in coping with environmental demands and pressures". Whilst 'ability' and 'trait-based' models are potentially measuring different constructs there is certainly commonality between them and a broader measure of EC may be more appropriate for the diverse array of skills and qualities required to tutor in online and blended learning environments.

Goleman's (2001) Framework of ECs and Bar-On's (1997) Five-Dimensional Model consist of a similar cluster of personality traits (Matthews et al., 2002, p. 15). While Goleman's model is directed at organisational and workplace success, Bar-On's (1997) conceptualisation of EI has a greater focus on general life success. Both Goleman and Bar-On's later work has largely continued with this general divergence in focus. Goleman, building on his EI research, has explored social intelligence and its impact on leadership (Goleman & Boyatzis, 2008, p. 52) to suggest managers develop "a genuine interest in and talent for fostering positive feelings in the people whose cooperation and support you need". Whereas, Bar-On (2010, p. 54) suggests that EI is an integral part of positive psychology. He argues:

> emotional intelligence has a significant impact on successful performance, happiness, well-being and the quest for a more meaningful life, which are important topics of study in the area of positive psychology. (Bar-On, 2010, p. 55).

Goleman's framework of emotional competences

Goleman's (2001, p. 1) Framework (see Table 4.1) was derived from "internal research at hundreds of corporations and organisations as distinguishing outstanding performers". This four-domain version was refined from the previous five-domain framework (Goleman, 1998), but still with the vision of EI as a theory of organisational effectiveness, therefore, being pertinent for tutors in higher education (HE). The Framework outlines 20 competences[2] in four clusters of general EI traits, but under two main headings – Self (personal competence) and Other (social competence), with two clusters recognising and regulating competence. Goleman's Framework and subsequent development into the Emotional Competence Inventory (ECI) (Sala, 2002), with a revision into

Emotional intelligence   41

Table 4.1 Goleman's framework of emotional competences (Adapted from Goleman, 2001, p. 2)

	Self *Personal Competence*	*Other* *Social Competence*
Recognition	Self-awareness • Emotional self-awareness • Accurate self-assessment • Self-confidence	Social Awareness • Empathy • Service orientation • Organisational awareness
Regulation	Self-management • Self-control • Trustworthiness • Conscientiousness • Adaptability • Achievement drive • Initiative	Relationship Management • Developing others • Influence • Communication • Conflict management • Leadership • Change catalyst • Building bonds • Teamwork & Collaboration

the ECI 2 in 2006 (Sharma, 2012), continues to be extensively used to research links between EI and a variety of dependent variables within business and leadership contexts (e.g., see Araujo & Taylor, 2012; Grimm & Cherniss, 2010).

It is not the intention of this book to critique Goleman's Framework, rather to use it as a template to evaluate competences for tutors in online and blended learning contexts. The definitions of Goleman's competences are broad, which provides a useful complement to the Four Branch Model (see Chapter 3), when exploring effective practice in this context.

Bar-On's Model of emotional-social intelligence

The theoretical foundation of Bar-On's Model is based on Darwin's work (1872/1965) regarding the emotional expression for survival and adaption (Bar-On, 2006, p. 15). Further, the works of Thorndike (1920) (social intelligence), Wechsler (1943) (intelligent behaviour), Sifneos (1967) (alexithymia) and Appelbaum (1973) (psychological mindedness) also impacted on the Model's ongoing development.

The Model has five key components, or EQ-i scales, with each comprising of closely related competences, skills and facilitators (Bar-On, 2006, p. 15). These are outlined in Table 4.2. When describing his Model, Bar-On (2006, p. 15) states:

emotional-social intelligence is a cross-section of interrelated emotional and social competencies, skills and facilitators that determine how effectively we understand and express ourselves, understand others and relate with them, and cope with daily demands.

42 Emotional intelligence

Table 4.2 Bar-On's (1997) Model of emotional-social intelligence

EQ-i SCALES	The EI Competencies and Skills Assessed by Each Scale
Intrapersonal	Self-awareness and self-expression:
• Self-regard	• To accurately perceive, understand and accept oneself
• Emotional Self-awareness	• To be aware of and understand one's emotions
• Assertiveness	• To effectively and constructively express one's emotions and oneself
• Independence	• To be self-reliant and free of emotional dependency on others
• Self-actualization	• To strive to achieve personal goals and actualize one's potential.
Interpersonal	Social awareness and interpersonal relationship:
• Empathy	• To be aware of and understand how others feel
• Social Responsibility	• To identify with one's social group and cooperate with others
• Interpersonal Relationship	• To establish mutually satisfying relationships and relate well with others
Stress Management	Emotional management and regulation:
• Stress Tolerance	• To effectively and constructively manage emotions
• Impulse Control	• To effectively and constructively control emotions.
Adaptability	Change management:
• Reality-testing	• To objectively validate one's feelings and thinking with external reality
• Flexibility	• To adapt and adjust one's feelings and thinking to new situations
• Problem-solving	• To effectively solve problems of a personal and interpersonal nature.
General Mood	Self-motivation:
• Optimism	• To be positive and look at the brighter side of life
• Happiness	• To feel content with oneself, others and life in general.

The final component, General Mood Scale, is an example of a facilitator to the other components, as Optimism and Happiness can facilitate, for example, Interpersonal Relationships and Stress Tolerance.

Whilst Bar-On's (2006) conception of ESI was not rooted in organisational effectiveness in the same way that Goleman's (1998) study targeted, there are affordances contained within the theory to suggest value for those in work environments, and in particular for this book, tutoring within HE, online and blended learning environments. Bar-On (2006, p. 16) states "being emotionally and socially intelligent means to effectively manage personal, social and environmental change by realistically and flexibly coping with the immediate situation, solving problems and making decisions". Such intelligence and resulting competence appear valuable for any social situation either within face-to-face or online environments. For example,

Emotional intelligence   43

should an educational technology fail, such as a synchronous conference in a virtual learning environment (VLE), could a tutor cope with this situation and solve this problem of having learners waiting for a session, and make a solution finding decision that appeases those who have taken the time to participate? In order to be emotionally intelligent in the manner described in this example Bar-On (2006, p. 16) adds that "we need to manage emotions so that they work for us and not against us, and we need to be sufficiently optimistic, positive and self-motivated". This emphasises the importance of the tutor both managing their own emotions and those of their learners, as well as providing a reminding that 'facilitators' can enhance this process.

The Emotional Quotient Inventory (EQ-i), as stated earlier, is a self-report measure of an individual's emotional and social intelligence (Bar-On, 2006). Bar-On states that this inventory played an instrumental role in the development of the ESI model. Further, the ESI model is operationalised by the EQ-I (Bar-On, 2006). Dawda and Hart's (2000) research, with a sample of 243 university students, indicated that the EQ-i had good item homogeneity and internal consistency at domain and scale level. It also had meaningful convergent validities in relation to measures of normal personality, with Dawda and Hart (2000) arguing that, overall, the EQ-i was a promising measure of emotional intelligence. The inventory continues to be extensively used to research the relationship between EI and a variety of dependent variables within a range of contexts (e.g., see Başoğul & Özgür, 2016; Megreya, 2015).

Like Goleman's Framework outlined above, it is not the intention of this book to critique Bar-On's Model, but rather to use it as a template to evaluate competences for tutors in online and blended learning contexts. These competences are considered further in this Chapter, and then in Chapter 8, where tutor competences and skills supporting effecting teaching in online and blended learning contexts are discussed.

Summary

Within this Section, Goleman's (2001) Framework of ECs and Bar-On's (1997) Five-Dimensional Model were presented as valid constructs of EI that have undertaken extensive scrutiny in academic research and literature. A range of pertinent EI traits have been discussed that have potential utility for tutors in online and blended learning contexts. The two theories consist of a similar cluster of personality traits (Matthews et al., 2002, p. 15), thus providing some construct validity to their consideration within this book. Both include intrapersonal, interpersonal, emotional regulation, relationship management and self-confidence traits. They provide a set of traits to support the analysis of effective tutors and tutoring in online and blended learning environments.

Emotional competences associated with effective blended tutoring

This Section presents a group of ECs that support the effective blended tutoring of mature learners, studying part-time (PT), vocationally relevant degrees, within an education disciplinary area (Youde, 2014, 2016). The discussion draws heavily on Youde (2016) who adopted a mixed methods approach to conduct a detailed exploration of the practice of eight tutors. Youde assessed the perceptions of learners' experiences using a questionnaire [a modified version of Ramsden's (1991) Course Experience Questionnaire (CEQ) was used, see Chapter 10 for further discussion of its development]; interviews with tutors explored their approaches to delivery and considered factors that impacted on quality; and an analysis of the content and communications in the VLE provided insight into tutors' online practices. As detailed in Chapter 3, the modules investigated by Youde (2014, 2016) were successful in terms of student achievement and satisfaction indicators. Therefore, the analysis of tutor ECs had merit as, in learners' eyes, these modules were effective. Competences associated with these effective blended learning experiences were identified from factors described in all modules taught, such as timely feedback on formative assessments. In addition, competences were identified from those tutors receiving higher CEQ scores, which appeared to have influenced learner perceptions of quality.

The competences identified by Youde (2016) were analysed in relation to Goleman's (2001) Framework of ECs. This provided a lens through which to consider blended tutors' practices in relation to learner perceptions. This decision was particularly pertinent given the Framework's focus on organisational and workplace success, as this aligned with the HE context of the research. Goleman's Framework includes a range of ECs categorised into four clusters: Self-awareness, Self-management, Social Awareness and Relationship Management. Although there is theoretical significance in examining each cluster for emotional competence in that area (Goleman, 2001, p. 10), to be considered emotionally intelligent, individuals must exhibit proficiency across all areas (Goleman, 2001, p. 1). As Goleman summarises:

> people exhibit these competencies in groupings, often across clusters, that allow competencies to support one another. Emotional competencies seem to operate most powerfully in synergistic groupings (Goleman, 2001, p. 10).

In light of this, tutor ECs were considered in relation to each cluster in the first instance, followed by analysis for potential groupings (Youde, 2016). In this Chapter, examples of tutor actions that appeared to contextualise these competences in online and blended learning environments are provided, with these of potential value for other studies in this area. Further ECs evident are highlighted, which do not form part of Goleman's Framework. Some of Goleman's competences are rejected and, with the addition of further competences, the Section suggests a new group required for effective tutoring in this context (Youde, 2014, 2016). In addition, Goleman's definitions have been adapted to suit the context under investigation.

Self-awareness cluster

This cluster comprises three competences:

- Emotional Self-awareness – tutors recognise own feelings and how they impact on performance
- Accurate Self-assessment – tutors are aware of their abilities and limitations, seek feedback and learn from mistakes, are aware of areas of improvement, and work with others who can support improvement
- Self-confidence – a belief and self-assurance about the tutor's own abilities.

Examples are provided below of tutor actions that appeared to contextualise these competences within this Education disciplinary area. Common to all tutors was the competence Accurate Self-assessment, however, varying levels of Self-confidence were apparent (Youde, 2014, 2016). The examples of competence in Emotional Self-awareness provided an interesting comparison with results of tutors' Positive-negative Bias scores achieved on the MSCEIT (see Chapter 3 for a discussion of tutors' MSCEIT Positive-negative Bias scores).

Tutors featured in Youde (2016) described examples that indicated competence at identifying their strengths and weaknesses with regard to their practice within modules, which could be understood as Accurate Self-assessment. Further, they were aware of areas to improve, particularly around online delivery. They would seek out and act on feedback and work with others to improve practice. Tutors appeared aware of their strengths in face-to-face contexts outlining a number of positive aspects to practice, however, they were equally aware of their limitations regarding online pedagogy. All tutors either collaborated with colleagues about educational technology and pedagogy, or had informal mentors available if needed and worked with others to improve their practice. Therefore, they worked with others to support improvement, providing some evidence of Accurate Self-assessment as defined by Goleman (2001).

Building on this discussion of Self-awareness by Youde (2016), tutors generally exhibited Self-confidence, with the evidence justifying this statement mirroring that of self-efficacy, which Goleman (2001, p. 6) argued, was "a form of self-confidence". Whilst Goleman's comparison appears a little imprecise, analysis of tutors suggested similarities (see Chapter 8 for a discussion of tutor self-efficacy in online and blended learning contexts). All tutors

46 Emotional intelligence

described Self-confidence in face-to-face environments with this appearing to be a factor in the generally high CEQ scores achieved. Three tutors showed similar confidence whilst arguing online elements were focussed around student support. Two were more experimental in their pedagogy beyond face-to-face elements but, despite limited success, were confident in their approaches. Two tutors exhibited a lack of Self-confidence at times around differing areas, both receiving lower CEQ scores. One outlined problems with his module including the online resources developed and with elements of assessment, but had not changed practice. The second displayed a lack of confidence in delivering the module on a blended basis and also about their online pedagogy.

Analysis of Youde's (2016) interview data for Emotional Self-awareness provided an interesting similarity with results of tutor's Positive-negative Bias MSCEIT scores (see Chapter 3). Commonly, emotions outlined were positive and were often related to enthusiasm for face-to-face teaching and the motivational effects this had on learners. This resonates with Bar-On's (2006, p. 23) facilitator 'Optimism' which states that such individuals are "positive and look on the brighter side of life". Only one tutor in Youde's (2016) study received feedback that indicated they responded to pictorial stimuli with more negative emotions (Mayer et al., 2002, p. 15). Further, she described a number of negative emotions when referring to practice both generally and within the module under investigation. However, she showed emotionally intelligent competences by using these emotions to advise and inform practice (see Chapter 3 for further evidence supporting this claim). With regard to Emotional Self-awareness, it appeared unimportant whether positive or negative emotions are exhibited as long as they were used to inform and improve practice. The importance of tutors' enthusiasm in face-to-face contexts was outlined in Chapter 3, where it was suggested as influential in motivating learners and the generally high CEQ scores achieved on the modules, and is considered further in Chapter 8. Therefore, the trait enthusiasm, and the emotions leading to that trait, are likely to be beneficial when interacting with learners.

Self-management cluster

This cluster comprises six competences:

- Self-control – tutors' absence of distress and disruptive feelings
- Trustworthiness – tutors letting others know own values and principles, intentions and feelings, and acting in ways consistent with them
- Conscientiousness – tutors being careful, self-disciplined and attending to responsibilities
- Adaptability – tutors are open to new information, let go of old assumptions and adapt practice

Emotional intelligence   47

- Achievement Drive – tutors having an optimistic striving to continually improve performance
- Initiative – tutors act before being forced to by external events.

Examples are provided below of tutor actions that appeared to contextualise these competences within this Education disciplinary area. Competences common to all tutors were Conscientiousness and elements of Achievement Drive, with those achieving the higher CEQ scores exhibiting greater Trustworthiness, Adaptability and Initiative (Youde, 2014, 2016). Self-control was difficult to evaluate as, after the event, tutors outlined difficulties and resultant actions rationally, which may not have been a true reflection of events. Further self-management competences were evident beyond those included in Goleman's Framework (Youde, 2014, 2016).

Youde's (2016) study identified aspects of Achievement Drive, indicated by past experiences and commitment to supporting learners, however, the tutors did not describe actions that could be considered "optimistically striving to continually improve performance" (Goleman, 2001, p. 7). Tutors were selected as they were experienced teachers/lecturers and, in life generally, could be considered successful individuals in a range of contexts, including holding management positions and having studied PT qualifications. These factors indicated a certain level of Achievement Drive. However, throughout the research, tutors were also managing competing objectives in their work as lecturers and some were aware of weak practice but felt that, overall, their modules were successful. One tutor's comment was illustrative:

> So, I suppose, I could do with standing back and looking it afresh – I need another day in the week. But, it works, it's quite good so it stays as it is. It's not a problem.

Another outlined improvement that would strengthen the module assessment strategy, but had not made the desired changes after three iterations of the assignment. Whilst these examples illustrate that tutors were not continually striving to improve performance, the levels of support given by all tutors indicated Achievement Drive (see Chapters 7 and 10 for a more detailed discussion of effective learner support). The high levels of support described may also be understood as conscientiousness.

Tutors' Conscientiousness in Youde (2014, 2016) was most apparent around formative and summative assessment, and their commitment to student support, however, there were further competences evident beyond Goleman's definition. Each tutor highlighted quick turnaround of feedback and determination to achieve this even with competing pressures (see Chapter 5 for a more detailed discussion of the assessment support provided by the tutors). Further, this determination was apparent when supporting learners and meeting individual needs, which was particularly evident from the two tutors

48   Emotional intelligence

receiving the highest CEQ scores. Goleman's definition of Conscientiousness includes 'being careful' and 'self-disciplined' and this competence was found to be insufficient with Youde's (2014, 2016) research adding the competences Coping Potential and Organised with these underpinned by a strong ability to prioritise. In this context, coping potential refers to competence in focusing on key tasks and not being influenced by less important demands of the role. This competence is supported by organisation, the ability to plan work activities efficiently, and the ability to prioritise. The two tutors with the highest CEQ scores did not spend a great deal of time learning differing educational technologies and focussed on their strengths of learner support. Another tutor receiving a higher CEQ score also displayed elements of Coping Potential when managing extensive support they provided for other colleagues. However, they were mindful of supporting learners and other key demands of the role. The motives behind tutor Conscientiousness are unclear and could be influenced by intrinsic and extrinsic factors. For example, it could be due to a lack of tutor support they described when they were students themselves, or possibly their previous experiences in pastoral care roles. Alternatively, it could be influenced by the culture of performativity (Ball, 2003) and target setting within which the University academic staff operated, with staff potentially fearful of weak quality indicators. Whatever the source, tutor Conscientiousness could have fostered trust from learners and be a factor in the high CEQ scores generally received.

All tutors in Youde's (2014, 2016) study described practices indicating Trustworthiness, however, there were a greater number of significant examples demonstrated by those achieving the higher CEQ scores. As outlined above, Trustworthiness could have developed from tutor Conscientiousness around assessment and learner support. Further, adherence to standards, as demonstrated by the high score on the CEQ scale Clear Goals and Standards (see Chapter 3, Table 3.2), is evidence of Trustworthiness. This was exemplified by two tutors who spoke passionately about developing autonomous learners and the actions taken to achieve this, whilst maintaining a dialogue to support the process. The following two quotes are illustrative of this:

> So there are students that if they want the constant attention, they can get it. If they don't want it, they don't get it. I think, and hope, they are all mature enough to respond to that in the way that suits their learning needs best.

> I won't mither you. If I don't hear from you I'll ask how you are and might follow up with a phone call rather than an email sometimes. Because I know myself about the volume of email people receive.

Further, Chapter 3 (when discussing the Understanding Branch of the MSCEIT) highlighted the importance of tutors' previous relationships with learners. Tutors receiving the three highest CEQ scores had each had course management responsibilities on learners' courses and two had taught earlier modules. It is reasonable to assume that learners knew these tutors were available, and that trust had emerged through positive exchanges.

Youde's (2014, 2016) research explored tutors who had previously taught in traditional HE contexts, before moving into roles with a greater focus on online and blended teaching and learning. The shift of practice allowed analysis and evaluation of tutor adaptability. Tutors receiving higher CEQ scores appeared open to a new delivery model, they let go of old assumptions, and they amended their practice, demonstrating competence in Adaptability. These tutors outlined opportunities afforded by the delivery model with these including learner support, synchronous web conferencing to replicate face-to-face contact, and increased space for reflection and learning. Whereas, others who received lower CEQ scores adopted a greater 'blame' response to changes primarily around time affordances. For example, one tutor stated:

> So, for example, 10 years ago the delivery pattern was weekly, in class sessions over an academic year. 24 weeks of 2 hour classes in the evening. That got knocked back … and now it's just two Saturdays.

Some tutors demonstrated a number of short-term adaptations to practice, which, again, suggests Adaptability. For example, two used an alternative VLE, which was perceived to be better than the University offer, and there was close overlap evident here with the competence, Initiative.

A number of short-term examples of initiative were evident both from tutors' past experiences and from analysis of the modules themselves, however, a longer term picture was hard to accurately determine (Youde, 2014, 2016). Two tutors showed initiative in their studies when experiencing a lack of support. Initiative was evident in the description of one tutor whose face-to-face teaching was disrupted by snow. Learners were e-mailed all the materials, further resources were uploaded to the VLE, and tutorials were arranged. The quality of student work was not affected and feedback received through module surveys indicated the tutor's initiative had a positive impact. As the research focused on short-term cases rather than being a longitudinal study, it was difficult to get a longer-term view of tutors taking initiative, however, initiative appeared to be a valuable competence when unforeseen problems arose.

Social awareness cluster

This cluster comprises three competences:

- Empathy – tutors have an astute awareness of others' emotions, concerns and needs

50 Emotional intelligence

- Service Orientation – tutors' ability to identify learners' often unstated needs and concerns, and match them to HE provision
- Organisational Awareness – tutors' ability to read currents of emotions and political realities in groups.

Examples are provided below of tutor actions that appeared to contextualise these competences within this Education disciplinary area (Youde, 2014, 2016). Empathy and Service Orientation were described, however, Organisational Awareness was not a competence apparent from the data and therefore of less value for tutors in online and blended learning contexts as it refers to "behind-the-scenes networking and coalition building that allows individuals to wield influence" (Goleman, 2001, p. 8). This competence would appear more valuable for management issues and potentially important in lecturers' broader roles.

Whilst the analysis of tutors' awareness of other's emotions was difficult to interpret, largely due to a lack of interaction in module VLEs, there was awareness of learners' concerns and needs, particularly as adults with competing pressures (see Chapter 5). Holmberg (1989, p. 162) stated that empathy was central to effective distance education and this was integral to learner feelings of belonging, with this being a key EC demonstrated by tutors. The tutors who participated in Youde's study (2014, 2016) were empathic, with the most effective describing awareness of learners' concerns and needs. These were met with timely management of formative and summative assessments with tutors aware of the external pressures learners face (see Chapter 5 for a more detailed discussion of learner assessment). The most effective tutors created space for adult learning, focussed on assignment work outside of face-to-face teaching, and were mindful of individual needs. Aligned with empathic tutoring were numerous examples of actions to meet needs whilst developing high achieving, autonomous learners. Two illustrative quotes were:

> They have got to find their own way through the piece of work they have chosen to do and if I am saying I need you to be online for a synchronous group discussion on a particular day; I wonder what impact that has on their other progress?

> …they shouldn't assume they can go to Blackboard [the University VLE] and everything they need will be there, … because one of the key things about this is that the students need to be developed as autonomous learners.

These actions may be understood as Service Orientation as tutors receiving higher CEQ scores described awareness of learners' often unstated needs. This was demonstrated through proactive steps to support learners whilst taking measures to provide space for learning within modules, which appeared appropriate for adult PT learners undertaking vocationally relevant qualifications.

Whilst tutors appeared empathic and exhibited a service orientation, these competences were frequently demonstrated in actions which may be understood as relationship management.

Relationship management cluster

Goleman's (2001) Relationship Management cluster is focussed on leadership roles and, therefore, not all of the competences are relevant when researching a tutor's module delivery. Tutors are, however, leading learners and require a number of relevant competences to do this effectively, therefore, the use of this cluster is appropriate. It comprises eight competences with the following five being most relevant for tutors in online and blended learning contexts (Youde, 2014, 2016):

- Developing Others – tutors sense learners' development needs and bolster their abilities
- Influence – tutors handle and manage emotions effectively and are persuasive
- Communication – tutors effectively give and take emotional information, deal with difficult issues straightforwardly, listen, and foster open communication
- Conflict Management – tutors spot trouble as it is brewing and take steps to calm all involved
- Leadership – tutors inspire others and arouse enthusiasm.

Examples are provided below of tutor actions that appeared to incorporate these competences. The three remaining competences, Change Catalyst, Building Bonds, and Collaboration and Teamwork, were not as evident as those listed above.

Tutors appeared adept at Relationship Management with the competence Communication being significant (Youde, 2014, 2016). Whilst it was difficult to evaluate the tutors' abilities to 'give and take' emotional information, they described fostering open communication and listening to learners. There were a range of measures that tutors used, particularly those achieving higher CEQ scores, to be 'available' and 'visible' to learners, including proactive e-mails to check on progress. These measures were particularly evident in relation to the management of formative and summative assessments, but were also related to strategies for student support, which fostered dialogue. The highest CEQ score was achieved on the Good Teaching Communication scale (mean = 4.12; see Chapter 3, Table 3.2), which includes questions about clear communication, motivational comments to improve work, and the tutor making the subject interesting. Motivational comments were described in face-to-face contexts as tutors aimed to maintain the interest of learners between such sessions and in the periods leading up to summative assessment submission. Further, tutors maintained interest by using learner-centred activities in face-to-face sessions, adopting a facilitative teaching style throughout modules, and using problem-based assessments linked to work contexts (see Chapter 5 for a more detailed discussion of learner assessment). Clear goals and standards were apparent in detailed assessment briefs and, in some cases, in the use of exemplar material. Tutors outlined that assessment strategies were supported through the provision of timely and constructive feedback. These factors again highlight effective communication, but may also be understood as Developing Others, Influence and Leadership.

Examples of tutors developing individual learners were not evident. However, Youde (2014, 2016) argues that an emotionally competent and effective blended tutor should sense learner development needs and bolster abilities. Tutors developing learners would most likely occur during formative and summative assessments as feedback was provided on plans of assignments and draft work. The effectiveness of these processes was not known beyond the high mean score achieved on the Good Teaching Feedback CEQ scale (3.73; see Chapter 3, Table 3.2), as individual examples did not emerge within the study. The research presents a framework of ECs (see Table 4.3) that may help understanding of other instances of online and blended learning and developing learners and bolstering their abilities is integral to this, even without specific examples having become evident from Youde's (2014, 2016) study.

Influence and, to some extent, Leadership were demonstrated through assessment and support strategies, but also through tutor practices to motivate

Table 4.3 A group of competences contributing to the effectiveness of tutors within the context under investigation (Youde, 2014, 2016, adapted from Goleman, 2001, p. 2)

	Self *Personal Competence*	*Other* *Social Competence*
Recognition	Self-awareness • Emotional self-awareness • Accurate self-assessment • Self-confidence	Social Awareness • Empathy • Service orientation
Regulation	Self-management • Trustworthiness • Conscientiousness • Adaptability • Organisation • Coping potential • Initiative	Relationship Management • Developing others • Influence • Communication

Emotional intelligence 53

learners. Tutors generally enthused learners in face-to-face contexts, stated the value of student learning, drew on student experiences, discussed exemplar work, while some prompted those who had not been in touch. Further, tutors receiving the higher CEQ scores appeared committed to student support and developing autonomous learners, actions that may be understood as the competence, Influence.

Competence at Conflict Management appeared to be important, however, there were limited examples from practice in delivery of the modules to justify generalised comments. Quick actions taken by a tutor to deal with disrupted face-to-face teaching potentially evidenced Conflict Management competence whilst building on the abilities of Adaptability and Initiative, but further examples were limited.

Emotional competences contributing to the effectiveness of tutors within blended learning environments

Youde's (2014, 2016) analysis of individual clusters revealed a group of competences contributing to the effectiveness of tutors within the context under investigation (see Table 4.3). It was found that competences across clusters could be supporting one another, for example, Trustworthiness and Conscientiousness require Self-awareness, and this was evident amongst the most effective tutors. Tutors receiving higher CEQ scores appeared to be exhibiting proficiency across all four clusters, indicating emotional intelligence (Goleman, 2001, p. 1). Goleman (2001, p. 10) argues that "emotional competences seem to operate most powerfully in synergistic groupings", and this Section considers possible synergies between competences. However, whilst Youde (2014, 2016) argued that these competences influenced learner perceptions of quality, he found insufficient evidence to conclude that they were operating in synergistic groupings.

Youde's (2014, 2016) study argued that emotionally competent blended learning tutors appeared self-aware with a clear understanding of their abilities and limitations. They sought feedback and learned from mistakes and they worked with others to support improvement. This was strengthened by their Self-confidence regarding pedagogy in blended contexts, and in supporting mature learners studying PT vocational courses. Emotions, both positive and negative, were recognised and there was an understanding of their impact on performance, moreover, the tutors' positive emotions were seen as likely to be beneficial when interacting with learners.

Self-aware tutors studied by Youde (2014, 2016) appeared more likely to be competent at Self-management with Trustworthiness, Conscientiousness, Adaptability, Initiative and elements of Achievement Drive most relevant for blended learning contexts. Self-awareness of abilities and limitations, learning from mistakes, using the support of others, and Self-confidence, could strengthen self-management competences. For example, Self-confidence could

54 Emotional intelligence

assist a tutor's ability to be adaptable to new pedagogy and emerging educational technologies. Conscientiousness appeared important in all aspects of a tutor's role, which can support and foster the competence, Trustworthiness. Effective tutors in Youde's (2014, 2016) study provided support to learners whilst developing their autonomy and they exhibited Initiative when problems arose during module delivery. Further relevant Self-management competences were Coping Potential and being Organised, with these supported by the ability to prioritise. Competence in Self-awareness and Self-management appeared to support tutors' Social Awareness. Empathy and Service Orientation appeared necessary for effective blended tutors building on the competences of accurate Self-awareness, Self-confidence, Trustworthiness, Conscientiousness, Adaptability, Achievement Drive and Initiative. Emotionally competent blended tutors appeared to understand the emotions, concerns and needs of learners, some of which were unstated. These are competences which need to be exhibited in relation to the work of tutoring adult learners studying PT vocational degrees through online and blended learning. However, more than understanding of needs is required and actions are needed that draw on relationship management competences.

Emotionally competent blended tutors appeared to foster open communication, influence and develop learners, whilst inspiring others and arousing enthusiasm. Competence at Conflict Management also seemed to be important, however, it was not evident in the modules under investigation as part of Youde's (2014, 2016) study. These competences are underpinned by the abilities outlined above from the Self-awareness, Self-management and Social Awareness clusters.

This Section has described competences across Goleman's clusters that appear to support one another. Tutors receiving higher CEQ scores seemed to be exhibiting proficiency across all four clusters, indicating emotional intelligence within a blended learning context (Goleman, 2001, p. 1).

In summary

This Chapter has identified a group of competences contributing to the effectiveness of tutors, as measured by learner perceptions of quality, within the context under investigation. These competences were present in Goleman's Framework of ECs and literatures discussing online and blended tutoring (see Chapter 8 for a discussion of these literatures). It was shown that there is a relationship between some tutor ECs and effectiveness in blended learning environments. Examples of tutor actions that appeared to contextualise these competences in online and blended learning environments were provided, with these of potential value for further studies in this area. These competences provide a basis for the development of a conceptual model relating to the data from Youde's (2014) study. This represents an interpretation of effective practice in a blended learning context and is developed in Chapter 11. The competences suggested in this Chapter have been extracted from the analysis of eight modules and for some, a longer-term view may be required before a comprehensive framework of competences can be established.

This Chapter has identified that Goleman's Framework was valuable when considering a group of ECs for a broad range of business organisations and particularly in relation to leadership roles. The Framework was utilised to outline ECs, with associated definitions, for effective tutoring in blended learning contexts. This could inform the recruitment and selection of tutors and form part of further empirical research into this area, particularly across differing subject disciplines. Youde's (2014, 2016) research study questions the value of some of Goleman's competences, primarily those with a focus on leadership. Whilst online and blended learning tutors do lead learners in some respects, it is not as significant in their role with developing learning structures and providing effective support being of greater importance. These require a specific group of competences with Goleman's Model in need of development to add further Self-management competences. This is due, in part, to the greater autonomy over work practices the online and blended contexts afford over traditional teaching approaches.

The next chapter considers the needs of adult learners in relation to emotionally intelligent tutor practices.

Notes

1. Bar-On (2006, p. 13) refers to the construct of EI as emotional and social intelligence (ESI) in his earlier work. Or, later, the abbreviated version - emotional-social intelligence.
2. Literature generally classifies Goleman's model as 'mixed' or 'trait- based'. However, Goleman used the term 'competencies' to outline the components of his model.

References

Appelbaum, S. A. (1973). Psychological mindedness: Word, concept and essence. *International Journal of Psycho-Analysis, 54*, 35–46.

Araujo, S. V. A., & Taylor, S. N. (2012). The influence of emotional and social competencies on the performance of Peruvian refinery staff. *Cross Cultural Management, 19*(1), 19–29.

Ball, S. (2003). The teacher's soul and the terrors of performativity. *Journal of Education Policy, 18*(2), 215–228.

Bar-On, R. (1997). *Bar-On emotional quotient inventory: Technical manual.* Toronto: Multi-Health Systems.

Bar-On, R. (2006). The Bar-On model of emotional-social intelligence (ESI). *Psicothema, 18*, 13–25.

Bar-On, R. (2010) Emotional intelligence: An integral part of positive psychology. *South African Journal of Psychology, 40*(1), 54–62.

56 Emotional intelligence

Başoğul, C., & Özgür, G. (2016). Role of emotional intelligence in conflict management strategies of nurses. *Asian Nursing Research*, *10*(3), 228–233. doi: 10.1016/j.anr.2016.07.002.

Darwin, C. (1872/1965). *The expression of the emotions in man and animals*. Chicago: University of Chicago Press.

Dawda, D., & Hart, S. D. (2000). Assessing emotional intelligence: Reliability and validity of the bar-on emotional quotient inventory (EQ-i) in university students. *Personality and Individual Differences*, *28*(4), 797–812. doi:10.1016/S0191-8869(99)00139-7.

Day, A. L., & Carroll, S. A. (2004). Using an ability-based measure of emotional intelligence to predict individual performance, group performance, and group citizenship behaviours. *Personality and Individual Differences*, *36*, 1443–1458.

Goleman, D. (1996). *Emotional intelligence: Why it can matter more than IQ*. London: Bloomsbury.

Goleman, D. (1998). *Working with emotional intelligence*. London: Bloomsbury.

Goleman, D. (2001). An EI-based theory of performance. In C. Cherniss & D. Goleman (Eds.) *The emotionally intelligent workplace: How to select for, measure, and improve emotional intelligence in individuals, groups, and organization* (pp. 27–44). San Francisco, CA: Jossy-Bass.

Goleman, D., & Boyatzis, R. (2008). Social intelligence and the biology of leadership. *Harvard Business Review*, *86*(9), 74–81.

Grimm, L. G., & Cherniss, C. (2010). Process-designed training: A new approach for helping leaders develop emotional and social competence. *The Journal of Management Development*, *29*(5), 413–431.

Holmberg, B. (1989). *Theory and practice of distance education*. London: Routledge.

Matthews, G., Zeidner, M., & Roberts, R. D. (2002). *Emotional intelligence: Science and myth*. London: The MIT Press.

Mayer, J. D., & Salovey, P. (1997). What is emotional intelligence? In P. Salovey & D. Sluyter (Eds.) *Emotional development and emotional intelligence: Implications for educators* (pp. 3–31). New York, NY: Basic Books.

Mayer, J. D., Roberts, R. D., & Barsade, S. G. (2008). Human abilities: Emotional intelligence. *Annual Review of Psychology*, *59*, 507–536.

Mayer, J. D., Salovey, P., & Caruso, D. (2002). *Mayer-Salovey-Caruso emotional intelligence test manual*. Toronto, Canada: Multi-Health Systems.

Megreya, A. M. (2015). Emotional intelligence and criminal behavior. *Journal of Forensic Sciences*, *60*(1), 84–88. doi: 10.1111/1556-4029.12625.

Petrides, K. V., & Furnham, A. (2003). Trait emotional intelligence: Behavioural validation in two studies of emotion recognition and reactivity to mood induction. *European Journal of Personality*, *17*(1), 39–57.

Ramsden, P. (1991). A performance indicator of teaching quality in higher education: The course experience questionnaire. *Studies in Higher Education*, *16*, 129–150.

Sala, F. (2002). *Emotional competence inventory (ECI) technical manual*. Boston, MA: McClelland Center for Research and Innovation, Hay Group.

Salovey, P., & Mayer, J. D. (1990). Emotional intelligence. *Imagination, Cognition and Personality*, *9*(3), 185–211.

Sharma, R. (2012). Measuring social and emotional intelligence competencies in the Indian context. *Cross Cultural Management*, *19*(1), 30–47.

Sifneos, P. E. (1967). Clinical observations on some patients suffering from a variety of psychosomatic diseases. *Acta Medicina Psychosomatica*, *21*, 133–136.

Thorndike, E. L. (1920). Intelligence and its uses. *Harper's Magazine*, *140*, 227–235.

Wechsler, D. (1943). Nonintellective factors in general intelligence. *Journal of Abnormal Social Psychology*, *38*, 100–104.

Youde, A. (2014). *A mixed methods exploration of effective tutors and tutoring in blended learning contexts* (Unpublished EdD Thesis, The University of Huddersfield, Huddersfield). Retrieved from http://eprints.hud.ac.uk/id/eprint/20351/

Youde, A. (2016). Tutor emotional competences valued by learners in a blended learning context. *European Journal of Open, Distance and E-Learning (EURODL)*, *19*(2), 81–97.

Zeidner, M., Matthews, G., & Roberts, R. D. (2009). *What we know about emotional intelligence: How it affects learning, work, relationships, and our mental health.* Cambridge, MA: MIT Press.

Chapter 5

Motivation and the adult learner in online and blended learning environments

Introduction

This Chapter considers the nature of adult learners and, in particular, their learning preferences in the digital age. It proposes a new way of analysing and understanding online and blended learning and contributes to current debates about these learners' motivations for study (Youde, 2018). It argues that, whilst Knowles, Holton, and Swanson's (2015) Andragogical Model has been criticised, it has provided a useful framework of analysis in the context of online and blended learning to meet the needs of adult learners studying part-time (PT), vocationally relevant degrees, at a distance. The Chapter develops the discussion from Chapter 1 regarding today's learners and considers the implications of a technology rich environment for adults. It discusses learner self-direction, intrinsic and extrinsic motivations for study, experiential learning, and introduces tutor actions to help motivate adult learners. A model is presented for effective tutoring of these learners within higher education (HE) blended learning contexts (Youde, 2018). In addition, factors are provided to operationalise the Model, which could support tutors' delivery within similar teaching and learning contexts.

Twenty-first century adult learners

A key element of this book is to explore tutors' effective teaching and learning approaches, within online and blended contexts, specifically for learners studying vocationally relevant courses on a PT basis. This can include groups of learners returning to study who may not have engaged in formal learning for a number of years. They may not have previously experienced recent digital technologies and the pedagogic affordances of computer mediated communications (CMCs). Prensky (2001) categorises these learners as "digital immigrants" and this label provides a useful reminder of their potential background and inexperience in online learning contexts. PT study in online and blended learning contexts affords learners flexibility and autonomy to plan their own learning, however, this can be challenging with competing pressures such as work and

Effective teaching and learning for adult learners   59

family life (Creanor, 2002; Smyth & Houghton, 2012). Further, Chapter 1 noted the challenges of engaging learners in online communication and collaboration, and this Chapter explores effective practice in teaching adults within online and blended learning contexts and motivating them to be successful.

There is limited research and accompanying literature exploring the experiences and outcomes of PT adult learners on blended learning programmes. Ausburn's (2004) study explored the course design elements most valued by 67 adult learners. The key findings were those containing options, personalization, self-direction, variety and a learning community. McDonald (2014) explored the experiences of ten adult learners in a blended learning context and found they valued adaptable learning and that all learners enjoyed interaction, both in online and face-to-face elements, something unusual in the blended learning literature. These two studies suggest the value that adult learners place on interaction with tutors and peers within online learning environments, which is contrary, in part, to the argument presented in Chapter 1 regarding the challenge of encouraging meaningful peer-to-peer collaboration in this context. Again, this begs the question, who are adult learners communicating with and through what channels?

Although this book's focus is towards HE study, I am aware of the large volume of informal learning that occurs in online contexts, for example, within massive open online courses (MOOCs) (see Chapter 1). The discussion and findings presented in this Chapter are still relevant for online tutors delivering units that are targeting informal learners who are not studying qualifications. This type of study is commonly related to learners' hobbies and interests.

The broad, underpinning theoretical foundation of this book could be described as Humanist in orientation, even though the key theories discussed, such as emotional intelligence, are commonly considered within the field of Psychology. Humanist theories of learning, drawing on the work of Dewey (1938), take a person-centred approach in which true learning comes from within (Mclay et al., 2019, p. 94). These theories are considered in more depth in Chapter 6, however, they have influenced many developments in student-centred learning, including one of the most prominent theories, Malcolm Knowles' andragogy (Mclay et al., 2019, p. 94). Therefore, this Chapter adopts the andragogical model's core principles as a lens to explore teaching and learning in this context. Further, although reporting on a small-scale study, this Chapter tentatively presents an empirical base to Knowles' Model (Youde, 2018).

The andragogical model within online and blended learning contexts

Knowles et al. (2015) claim that the andragogical model and the six core principles on which it is based provide an insight into adult learning. Adult learners bring substantial previous knowledge, viewpoints and life experiences (Knowles et al., 2015) to face-to-face and online learning environments. It is

60 Effective teaching and learning for adult learners

important to apply flexibility when applying the andragogical model and the context of study drives the teaching and learning strategies to be adopted (Knowles, 1984, p. 418). This latter point was included by Knowles, Holton, and Swanson (2011, p. 146) in their 'andragogy in practice' model, which included the six core principles and consideration of the goals and purposes for learning, as well as individual and situational differences, and these are evaluated in the context under exploration within this book. The model recognises "the lack of homogeneity among learners and learning situations, and illustrates that the learning transaction is a multifaceted activity" (Knowles et al., 2011, p. 146). This stresses that the model is not a set of strict criteria, but a set of premises through which to consider adult learning.

Knowles' notion of andragogy has been one of the most widely cited concepts in adult education literatures (Jarvis, 2012; Kember, 2007; Savicevic, 2008). Knowles was part of the learning theory development that brought learners' experiences to the fore, although, he did not explore how adults actually learn, or discuss the nature of their experiences (Jarvis, 2012, p. 135). Andragogy is an ideal position on which adult learning should be based (Hartree, 1984). It offers offer a starting point to create learner-centred approaches within online educational contexts (Blondy, 2007, p. 110), particularly in terms of developing students capable of self-directed learning who are able to manage with limited tutor input (Kember, 2007, p. 89). This is pertinent for online and blended delivery models as they offer less face-to-face tutor/learner contact than traditional teaching approaches. However, for effective learning, tutors should respond to the different experiences of their learners (Jarvis, 2012, p. 142). In the context under discussion here, learners' work experiences, hobbies and interests would be relevant.

The andragogical model's core principles are now analysed to further scrutinise their value in evaluating adult learning within online and blended contexts. The model's core principles are:

- need to know: adults need to know why they are learning a topic before learning commences
- learners' self-concept: adults need to be responsible for their decisions on education
- role of learners' experiences: adults use experiences as the basis for learning activities
- readiness to learn: adults are more interested in learning if there is an immediate relevance to work
- orientation to learning: adult learning is problem-centred rather than content orientated
- motivation to learn: adults' most potent motivators are intrinsic.

The tutor can facilitate andragogical learning, both in face-to-face and online environments, by adopting strategies within their teaching to address

Effective teaching and learning for adult learners 61

the core principles. Adult learners *need to know* the reason for learning a topic is particularly relevant in this area as learners are commonly studying vocationally relevant programmes or courses. This core principle overlaps with *readiness to learn* as this type of self-directed learner, in general, wants to know the relevance of their study to their work context or other interests. Tutors can clearly articulate their teachings' relevance and establish clear goals and purposes for learning, both in relation to the course and general work contexts, either within face-to-face or online environments. Adults often want to be passive in the learning process (Knowles et al., 2011, p. 63), but treating adults in such a manner can cause tensions considering their need to be self-directing, with Knowles et al. (2011, p. 63) referring to this as *the learners' self-concept*. Some HE learners are non-traditional university entrants, who may not have experienced formal education since school and may feel more comfortable in passive learning environments. As Knowles et al. state:

> as adult educators become aware of this problem, they make efforts to create learning experiences in which adults are helped to make the transition from dependent to self-directing learners (Knowles et al., 2011, p. 65).

To address this, tutors can give appropriate consideration to academic skills and robust learner support mechanisms, however, these issues have to be addressed in both face-to-face and online environments. The structuring and learner engagement within this support can be challenging for tutors (Smith, 2004, p. 31), particularly for those learners who are experiencing a number of competing pressures. Both formative and summative assessments provide an opportunity for tutors to consider the core principles, *the role of the learners' experiences* and *orientation to learning,* by allowing students to contextualise their learning to ensure its relevance to their vocational area or interests. Assessment strategies could include case method, problem solving and peer support as a means of integrating learner experiences (Knowles et al., 2011, p. 64), and the use of such methods are discussed further throughout this Chapter.

Knowles' notion of andragogy has been extensively critiqued (Youde, 2018, p. 257) particularly in terms of empirical support, uniqueness to adults and a lack of sociological consideration (see Grace, 1996; Hartree, 1984; Jarvis, 2012). The andragogical model lacks empirical support (Brookfield, 1986; Hartree, 1984) and whilst it provides premises to explore adult learning, it is not a theory of adult learning, nor does it consider how learning occurs (Grace, 1996; Jarvis, 2012). Andragogy is commonly viewed as a framework of practice, rather than a process of adult learning (Taylor & Laros, 2014, p. 136), however, Youde (2018) has taken steps to provide empirical underpinning in relation the model within a blended learning context, which is outlined later in this Chapter. Critics argue the premises on which the

62 Effective teaching and learning for adult learners

andragogical model is based are not unique to adults (Merriam & Caffarella, 1999, p. 20). A further limitation of andragogy is that it lacks consideration of sociological factors (Grace, 1996) and views the adult learner, and the educational process in which they are participating, in relative isolation, ignoring the constraints of social structures (Jarvis, 1985, p. 68). However, this Chapter takes steps to address this concern by exploring teaching approaches suitable for those learners with completing demands and who require flexibility of study, which is commonly those who are undertaking online or blended learning. The flexibility of the model's application is pertinent to the underexplored context of adult learners within this context and is discussed further throughout the Chapter.

Experiential learning

Learning through experiences, whether from work contexts or more generally, is consistently cited as significant within theories of adult learning. Experiential learning is inherent within humanistic theories of learning and is described as a complex integration of theory and practice, which is essentially democratic and inclusive (Mclay et al., 2019, p. 95). Democratic, within online and blended contexts, refers to learning with tutors and peers rather this in isolation, with inclusive meaning a larger number of learning opportunities for a wider spectrum of people, such as the increased accessibility provided by MOOCs. Mclay et al. (2019, p. 95) continue by stating that experiential learning "aims to involve the whole person in an encounter with learning: the experience is of immersion in knowledge, action and practice". This is of significance when considering online and blended environments as the learner commonly drives the area of study, therefore, this is more likely to be relevant to their experiences. Experiential learning is based on educational processes that are created between equals, either as facilitators or peers, and which are not directed or devolved from above – commonly conceptualised as a teacher imparting their knowledge to learners (Gregory, 2002, p. 95). Given the separation of tutors and learners in online and blended learning, coupled with humans' general short attention span for viewing instructional media, experiential approaches to learning are appropriate in this context. Further, Chapter 1 stated that 'new' learners are more self-directed, better equipped to capture information, more reliant on feedback from peers, more inclined to collaborate and more orientated to being their own 'nodes of production' (Wheeler, 2012, 2015), again suggesting an experiential approach to learning would be preferable in this context.

Building on the work of Dewey, Kolb developed the Experiential Learning Cycle (see Figure 5.1; Kolb, 1984), which suggests a process of how experiences are transformed into learning. He considered that learning is defined as "the process whereby knowledge is created through the transformation of experience" (Kolb, 1984, p. 38). The Cycle is based on the

Effective teaching and learning for adult learners 63

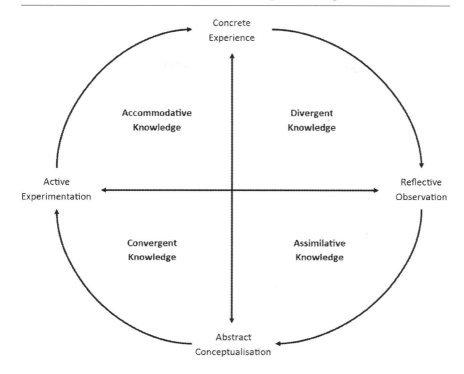

Figure 5.1 Kolb's experiential learning cycle (Kolb, 1984, p. 42).

four stages of the Experiential Learning Model: Concrete Experience (CE), Reflective Observation (RO), Abstract Conceptualisation (AC), and Active Experimentation (AE; Kolb & Fry, 1975). Kolb (1984) considers that in order to learn effectively all four stages in the cycle are needed:

- an ability to involve oneself fully and openly and without bias in new experiences (CE)
- an ability to observe and reflect on these experiences from different angles (RO)
- an ability to create concepts that bring these observations together (AC)
- an ability to use these concepts in making decisions and problem solving (AE).

A 'mature learner' is one who is competent in each mode when it is appropriate, although a totally balanced profile is not necessarily the best. These modes or stages are paired as opposites, AE is "dialectically opposed" to RO and CE to AC (Kolb, 1984, p. 41). The key to effective learning is being competent in each mode when it is appropriate. However, Kolb (1981) discovered that most people develop learning approaches that emphasise some learning abilities over others; each approach has its own strengths and weaknesses. Because of the direction that a person's learning might take as a result of, for example, formal education and subject specialisation, particular approaches may develop at the expense of others. Mclay et al. (2019, p. 95) outline examples of the types of knowledge arising from these nodes. Assimilative knowledge, they state, "results from grasping experience by means of abstract concepts and transforming the experience so grasped by reflective observation" (Mclay et al., 2019, p. 95). Alternatively, they state "Accommodative knowledge derives from apprehending the immediate qualities of experience, which is then transformed into knowledge by the results of AE (2019, pp. 95–96).

Kolb's theory provides a framework for tutors in online and blended environments to incorporate learner experiences within their delivery. This can be achieved by encouraging learners to engage with new learning experiences relevant to the area of study (CE); encouraging them to research and reflect on these experiences from differing perspectives (RO); providing opportunities to create concepts, possibly through an assessment strategy, to pull these observations together (AC), whist using these concepts to solve problems and make decisions (AE). There is clear resonance here with the andragogy model (Knowles et al., 2015) in bringing adult learner experience to the fore, thus providing some theoretical triangulation to the incorporation of such experiences into a unit of study's design.

The adult learner: Intrinsic and extrinsic motivators

An interesting consideration for online and blended tutoring is the andragogical model's core principle, *motivation*, the notion that adults respond better to intrinsic motivators rather than extrinsic. This suggests the role of a tutor regarding motivation is not particularly important, but Youde (2018, p. 258) regards this perspective is too simplistic. He argued that, firstly, this core principle appears a little contradictory to the other five, in that, if learners are intrinsically motivated then there appears limited need for the others. Secondly, both intrinsic and extrinsic motivators have been found to positively influence adult learner achievement in HE contexts (Feinstein, Anderson, Hammond, Jamieson, & Woodley, 2007; Swain & Hammond, 2011). As some adult learners undertake study for instrumental purposes, such as to increase promotional opportunities (Feinstein et al., 2007), tutors would need to incorporate extrinsic motivators when teaching in online and blended contexts.

Building on this discussion, Biggs and Tang (2007, p. 34) support the notion of student intrinsic motivation by highlighting its importance for successful learning experiences, but outline the important role tutors play in building fascination for the area of study. Reference to Biggs and Tang (2007, p. 32) was instructive here. They posit two factors that make

Effective teaching and learning for adult learners   65

students want to learn a topic area, and tutors play a pivotal role in the achievement of both:

- the learner sees value in the area of study
- the learner should expect success when undertaking activities within a unit of study.

Tutors can aid learners in appreciating the value of study through strategies such as linking theory to practice, building on previous learning, and allowing contextualisation of learning to the workplace or area of interest. In addition, tutors can provide an appropriately structured knowledge base, with clear learning goals established, and building on previous learning experiences (Bailey & Card, 2009, p. 154; Biggs & Tang, 2007, p. 25). Further strategies include tutors providing something to stimulate learners' interests and not have them passively receiving information, and questions should be posed to engage the learners, possibly through linking to work contexts (Knowles et al., 2011). In order for learners to 'expect success', formative assessment and tutor feedback can have a powerful effect on a learner's belief that they can achieve (Biggs & Tang, 2007, p. 33; Murphy, Shelley, White, & Baumann, 2011, p. 408).

Whilst it is encouraging that, in general, adult learners would be intrinsically motivated, this Section has highlighted the importance of extrinsic motivators in leading to successful online and blended learning experiences. Extrinsic motivators, such as building self-esteem (Maslow, 1968) by, for example, providing good quality feedback and an appropriately structured teaching approach (Ramsden, 1991), can influence learner perceptions of tutoring quality and adopted approaches to study, which are now discussed in more depth.

Learners' approaches to study

It would be incomplete to discuss effective tutor practices in online and blended environments without also briefly considering the influence of learners and their approaches to study. This Section firstly outlines differing approaches to study and then considers how tutors in online and blended contexts can facilitate learners in adopting the most effective approaches. Other influences on student learning are then discussed which, again, are instructive when considering effective practice in this context.

Marton and Säljö (1976) identified predominant approaches to learning and outlined the notion of Deep and Surface learning, which are influenced by the content, context and requirements of a specific task. Students habitually adopting deeper approaches use the highest level of learning activities (Biggs, Kember, & Leung, 2001, p. 138), such as wide reading and relating concepts to work environments, whereas those deploying surface approaches

66 Effective teaching and learning for adult learners

at any given time complete only the required activities in order to achieve desired outcomes. Biggs and Tang (2007, p. 24) eloquently outline the benefits for tutors when students adopt Deep approaches when they state "they automatically try to focus on underlying meanings, on main ideas, themes, principles, or successful applications". Kember, Leung, and McNaught (2008) develop these ideas by considering influencing factors. They state:

> the relational nature of approaches to learning imply that the curriculum design and the nature of the teaching and learning environment have some bearing on the learning approach the student adopts (Kember et al., 2008, p. 45).

This suggests that identifying learners' approach to study is a factor in understanding their evaluation of a teaching experience, but it may be difficult for tutors to influence within a relatively short time period, such as a unit of study lasting only a few months.

Biggs and Tang (2007, p. 24) state that even with the best teaching some learners will adopt Surface approaches. This is pertinent for two key stakeholder groups who commonly undertake online and blended programmes. Firstly, adult learners studying formal HE programmes have outside influences such as family and work pressures. Secondly, those studying informally, such as on MOOCs, may have enrolled without being deeply committed to the programme of study.

Having established the beneficial factors of students adopting Deep approaches to study, identification of other factors that influence student learning strategies can instruct effective online and blended teaching. The structure of the learning environment, with clear goals and timely, constructive feedback has a significant influence on the student's approach to study (Entwistle & Ramsden, 1983). Biggs and Tang (2007, p. 25) add to these points and associate the following tutor influences with the Deep approach: an appropriate motivational context, assessing for structure and not facts, and aligning teaching and learning methods to the intended outcomes of the unit of study. Further, Gibbs (1992, p. 9) articulates characteristics of teaching and learning environments which tend to encourage a Surface approach:

- a heavy student workload
- an excessive amount of course material
- a lack of opportunity to pursue subjects in depth
- a lack of choice over subjects and the method of study
- an anxiety provoking assessment system.

The nature of assessment and the resultant student workload are important factors in the approaches to study adopted by learners, which coincide with the core principles of the andragogical model (Knowles et al., 2011),

Effective teaching and learning for adult learners   67

particularly with regard to the structuring of teaching units and the choice available within assessment strategies.

Vermetten, Lodewijks, and Vermunt (1999) found that the quality of teaching could impact on learners' approach to studying and it could be assumed this would be similar for online and blended learning environments. However great the tutor impact on approaches to study, it would be incomplete to explore their effectiveness without considering learner motivation and their approach to their study. To do this, a revised version of Biggs et al. (2001) Revised Study Process Questionnaire (R-SPQ) has been developed to evaluate learners' approaches and motivation towards their study within online and blended contexts (Youde, 2014, 2019; see Chapter 10 for a discussion of the questionnaire's development).

An andragogical model for blended learning environments

This Section proposes a new way of analysing and understanding blended learning and contributes to current debates about adult learner motivations for study. Research is reported that adopted a mixed methods approach to conduct a detailed exploration of eight tutors' practice in one of their modules based in an Education disciplinary area (Youde, 2014, 2018). Data were gathered from three principal sources. Interviews with tutors explored their approaches to delivery and considered factors that impacted on quality; students' perceptions of their learning experiences were assessed using an attitude survey [a modified version of Ramsden's (1991) Course Experience Questionnaire (CEQ) was used, see Chapter 10 for further discussion of its development]; an analysis of the content and communications in the virtual learning environment (VLE) provided insight into tutors' online practice. The andragogical model (Knowles et al., 2015) and its six constituent core principles provided a lens through which to evaluate the modules under investigation, but also to consider in greater depth the influence tutors were having in meeting adult learner needs. Further, other factors present within modules that are suitable for these learners and their particular circumstances were considered. Youde's (2014, 2018) research found that the predominant approaches to teaching and assessment adopted by tutors were mainly congruent with the andragogical model's core principles, which was in part due to the structured, assessment driven learning environment, but particularly the type of problem and case-based assessments undertaken by learners on the courses investigated. The andragogical model offered an analytical lens that was valuable as it provided a number of actions appearing to influence learner perceptions of quality, which can support practice for tutors and HE institutions in similar contexts. Further, this analysis highlighted the importance to tutors of providing extrinsic motivators and an addition to the andragogical model to accommodate this is suggested (Youde, 2014, 2018).

68 Effective teaching and learning for adult learners

The learners under investigation were classed as 'mature', as a significant number were aged between 25 and 54 and brought previous knowledge, viewpoints and life experiences to the blended learning context (Knowles et al., 2011). They were studying PT vocationally relevant degrees at a distance (Youde, 2014, 2018).

The core principles are now addressed in turn to consider their strengths and limitations for the blended learning context under investigation. In the next Section, factors are presented to demonstrate how online and blended learning tutors could operationalise each core principle in practice. These factors are provided to potentially guide online and blended learning practitioners, within similar contexts to Youde's (2014, 2018), in meeting the adult learner needs. Tutors' skills, qualities and competences are considered where appropriate to evaluate their influence in addressing the andragogical model's core principles.

Need to know: Adults need to know why they are learning a topic before learning commences

Knowles et al. (2015, p. 44) state that adult learners should know why they are learning and be engaged in the collaborative planning of their studies. Further, that a tutor's first task is to help learners become aware of the 'need to know', that is to make the intellectual case for the learning in improving the effectiveness of the learners' performance or the quality of their lives.

Youde (2014, 2018) found that this core principle was addressed by tutors, but was facilitated by the vocational nature of learners' courses. The immediate relevance of some topics would have been apparent to learners as they were linked to work roles, however, tutors facilitated this process by, for example, connecting theory to practice. Throughout study related to the modules, learners appeared to know what was expected, which was enhanced with the predominant facilitative teaching style and support when required. The CEQ scale item Clear Goals and Standards received a high mean score (3.89; see Chapter 3, Table 3.2) indicating learners knew what was expected of them. Qualitative analysis revealed some instruction of key module information within face-to-face sessions, such as submission dates, assessment requirements, and key subject knowledge in the area of study. All face-to-face sessions included a range of learner-centred activities to develop understanding of key concepts and apply theory to practice, with tutors encouraging learners to see the value of their study by contextualising their learning. One tutor was illustrative of all tutors here when outlining "what's in it for you" to learners, as activities and assignments were introduced, thus supporting learners' need to know. To summarise, tutors related theory to practice and showed learners the value of topics being covered in order to address this key aspect of meeting these adult learner needs.

Effective teaching and learning for adult learners 69

Learners' self-concept: Adults need to be responsible for their decisions on education

Knowles et al. (2015, p. 44) stated that adults have a self-concept of being responsible for their own decisions, their own lives, and a need to be treated, and seen by others, as capable of self-direction. Further, they could resent/resist situations where others are imposing their will on them. This can create tensions in adult education as learners could revert to a dependency approach, which they could have experienced whilst at school. Adult educators, therefore, need to help the transition from direction to self-direction (ibid.).

This Chapter (see The Andragogical Model within Online and Blended Learning Contexts Section) has highlighted the difficulty of learners moving into HE given previous educational experiences. Many of the learners featured in Youde's (2014, 2018) study were engaging in HE for the first time and may have had perceptions of education rooted in their experiences at school. They may have been more comfortable in passive learning environments, but this would be challenged by an adult's desire to be self-directing (Knowles et al., 2011, p. 63). This challenge may have been enhanced as the learning context under investigation was markedly different from school experiences as, for example, courses had vocational relevance, there was application to work contexts and, importantly, there was a change in delivery model. Further, adults often have competing pressures as they balance study with work and family life. The move into such a different learning context has to be managed by tutors to meet adult learner needs and requires a number of skills, qualities and competences that tutors exhibited across modules, but particularly by those achieving higher scores on the learner survey (CEQ).

All the modules investigated allowed aspects of learner self-direction with learner autonomy (Moore, 1997), but with appropriate structure and support present. Learners had choice over the focus of module assessment, evaluating the implications of an aspect of law on their employing institution being a relevant example. As there was choice in the scope of assessments, learners had some responsibility for their decisions, thus suggesting congruence with the learners' self-concept core principle. Further, learners studied independently outside face-to-face sessions, predominantly on assessment requirements, with this highlighting their responsibility for decisions on learning. To support this, modules were structured around assessment requirements and, with the predominance of asynchronous communication, this allowed learners to manage competing pressures. Feedback was valued by learners (as indicated by the high Good Teaching Feedback CEQ scale score, 3.73, see Chapter 3, Table 3.2) with tutor support available throughout modules and, if used effectively, this would support the development of student-centred learning.

Meeting adult learners' self-concept is potentially demanding for tutors in online and blended contexts, but a range of skills, qualities and competences appear important in meeting this principle. Youde (2014, 2018) found

70   Effective teaching and learning for adult learners

that tutors achieving higher CEQ scores were more proactive in supporting learners and created space for learning on modules. They were empathic to adult learner needs with some describing strategies to encourage autonomous learning. These skills and qualities were supported with relevant tutor emotional competences (ECs), which were outlined in Chapter 4. These included Self-management and Relationship Management emotional competences (Goleman, 2001), for example, Conscientiousness in supporting learners with effective Communication (Youde, 2016).

To summarise, Youde's (2014, 2018) study found that there was evidence of learner self-direction across modules and this appeared particularly important on vocational courses for those with competing pressures. This was facilitated by an assessment driven structure with available tutor support. Importantly though, the achievement of this principle was aided by a number of tutor skills, qualities and competences.

Role of learners' experiences: Adults use experiences as the basis for learning activities

Youde (2014, 2018) found that tutors engaged in a number of practices to integrate learner experiences into module teaching, learning and assessment, however, there was scope for potential improvements in addressing this principle. Tutors used a variety of teaching and learning methods in face-to-face sessions, which included group work activities. Individual learner experiences were also used throughout modules as there was choice over assessment focus with application to work contexts and roles. Assignments were problem-based and generally case-method within learners' organisations, with examples being action research and an evaluation of leadership and management structures.

Knowles et al. (2011, p. 65) argue that adult educators should "try to discover ways to help adults examine their habits and biases and open their minds to new approaches", which tutors did with the examples cited above. However, increased peer collaboration could encourage learners to overcome habits and biases in their work roles and be open to new approaches. All tutors adopted a facilitative teaching style with two tutors describing their learners as "the experts", which suggests there is value in peer collaboration when studying vocationally relevant courses. However, such peer collaboration was limited across formal module CMCs, but this did not prevent the general module success evident or learner satisfaction with their experience (see Chapter 3). This suggests this andragogical principle is important, but more could be done to encourage the sharing of learner experiences within online contexts. This notion of "experts" resonates with the discussion of experiential learning above and its democratic nature. Here, the tutors were positioning themselves alongside their learners rather than directing their learning.

Effective teaching and learning for adult learners 71

Readiness to learn: Adults are more interested in learning if there is an immediate relevance to work

This principle was addressed through the nature of teaching, learning and assessment common to all modules under investigation by Youde (2014, 2018). Modules generally mirrored the Individual Constructivist Perspective (Mayes & de Freitas, 2007; see Chapter 7 for further discussion about teaching, learning and assessment within the modules) with active discovery in work contexts a common approach across modules. Assessments were problem-based and generally case-method within learners' organisations. Further, learners had choice over assessment focus, which could be linked to their own interests and role. Knowles et al. (2015, p. 45) state that:

> Adults become ready to learn those things they need to know and be able to do so in order to cope effectively with their real life situations. An especially rich source of *readiness to learn* [original emphasis] is the development task associated with moving from one developmental stage to the next.

It could be argued that these learners were demonstrating *readiness to learn* by enrolling on vocationally relevant degrees as this suggests they are moving from one development stage to the next in relation to their careers (Youde, 2018, p. 266). Further, data analysis suggested students were intrinsically motivated with tutors describing committed and motivated learners (see Motivation to Learn Section for further discussion of learner motivation). Beyond this, there were limited data from Youde's study to support this core principle. However, actions are suggested that tutors can adopt to facilitate learners' knowledge to develop practice within a specific work context. These being tutors developing teaching and assessment strategies that have relevance to learners' work contexts. Such actions, though, are a narrower conception of this core principle than that which Knowles' et al. appear to describe above.

Orientation to learning: Adult learning is problem-centred rather than content orientated

Again, Youde (2018, p. 266) found that this principle was strongly addressed with the nature of teaching, learning and assessment common to all modules under investigation. Knowles et al. (2015, p. 46) note that adults are motivated to learn if they perceive the activity to be beneficial in dealing with tasks or life situations, or work situations in this context. Further, learning is enhanced when applied to real-life situations. Assessments were problem-based within learners' organisations. Learners also had choice over the assessment focus and, therefore, this should be beneficial to their work role.

Motivation to learn: Adults' most potent motivators are intrinsic

This Section utilises examples from Youde's (2014, 2018) research to illustrate learners' intrinsic motivation to study, but argues there are other important extrinsic motivators that influenced their perceptions of module quality. Tough (1979) notes that intrinsic motivators can be blocked by barriers such as negative self-concept as a student and time constraint. Such barriers can be lowered by tutors but require certain skills, qualities and competences to be actioned effectively. Further, this Chapter has noted that some learners undertake study for instrumental purposes, such as to increase promotional opportunities, with this described by one tutor as an issue encountered on her module. This, and the effect of tutors, indicated influencing extrinsic motivators, which are considered within this Section.

Learner intrinsic motivation

The learners investigated by Youde (2014, 2018) predominantly adopted Deep over Surface approaches to study, indicating some intrinsic motivation. Tutor interviews outlined a consensus opinion of learners being motivated, engaged in their study, and producing good quality work. One tutor's module provided a clear example of learners' intrinsic motivation when achievement was broadly similar to that of previous cohorts even though the module had been heavily disrupted. This module also highlighted a number of tutor skills, qualities and competences that appeared to enhance the learners' experience.

Extrinsic motivations influencing learner perceptions of quality

Biggs and Tang (2007, p. 32) argued that learners seeing value in the area of study and expecting success were key factors for tutors to encourage learning, and these points highlighted issues relevant to all modules in Youde's (2014, 2018) research. The discussions above regarding the andragogical principles; *need to know, role of learners' experiences,* and *readiness to learn,* demonstrate that learners saw value in studying these modules. Learners 'expecting success' was evidenced through formative assessment procedures across modules. Each module outlined detailed formative assessments that included feedback on assignment plans and drafts with tutors indicating high uptake across modules. This was supplemented with assessment briefs and, in some cases, exemplar work. This feedback is likely to have reassured learners that they could 'expect success' on modules whilst helping to contextualise learning in practice.

Biggs and Tang (2007, p. 34) further highlighted the importance of tutors building fascination for the subject area as an extrinsic motivator of learners

Effective teaching and learning for adult learners   73

and this was apparent across all modules in Youde's (2014, 2018) study. Tutors described strategies within face-to-face sessions to motivate learners for the module duration, including adopting a variety of learning activities. This was enhanced, in some cases, with enthusiasm for the subject area and a general commitment to supporting learners through the assessment process.

A number of tutor extrinsic motivators were apparent throughout modules, evidenced through differing scores on a learner survey (as measured by the CEQ, see Chapter 3, Table 3.2), which indicated important skills, qualities and competences. This Section notes the influence of the following factors as influential in learner perceptions of quality:

- tutor support for formative assessments
- proactive tutor communication with learners
- tutor's previous relationships with learners prior to the module
- tutor communication with learners prior to the module commencing (Youde, 2018, p. 268).

Structuring modules by the assessment strategies allowed greater learner autonomy than a content driven approach, however, mechanisms were in place for tutors to support learners (Youde, 2018). Online and blended PT courses need to be flexible in terms of meeting learning outcomes, but have sufficient structure in their delivery for learners with competing pressures from work and family life. This was evident from all the modules, particularly around assessment, but was enhanced with learner support mechanisms. All tutors emphasised commitment to supporting learners through assessments, which was exemplified through response times. One tutor illustrated this when stating, "the response times were really good this year, often in the morning that it arrived". These learners appear to require a minimum level of support, which involves timely and constructive feedback to formative assessments. Five tutors, receiving the higher CEQ scores, outlined similar proactive strategies to support and encourage learners in meeting the formative and summative assessment requirements of modules. Formative assessment processes were monitored closely with e-mail, phone calls or "quick chats" within face-to-face sessions used to prompt learners and encourage dialogue.

The student support mechanisms experienced by participants in Youde's (2014, 2018) research appeared most effective when facilitated by e-mail and not by other forms of CMCs, such as wikis and discussion boards. Whilst this may be expected given e-mail's requirement of a personal response there appeared to be other factors influencing learner perceptions. The two tutors receiving the highest CEQ scores both spoke enthusiastically about being available for learners, sending e-mails to check on progress and responding in a timely manner. They found the use of e-mail motivational to learners as it provided immediacy and intimacy. Similar feedback was received

74   Effective teaching and learning for adult learners

from other tutors about the value of e-mail in prompting and encouraging learners, however, other communication media were less effective with both tutors and learners influencing this. VLE content analysis revealed that one tutor established a wiki and two tutors included discussion boards for learners to showcase elements of practice and outline plans for assessment. These methods were included to elicit peer support and collaboration in the assessment process and allow peers to validate assignment plans. In each case, contributions were not part of the summative mark received for the module and limited learner engagement was evident. Further, on module discussion boards, two tutors had not contributed or commented on the uploaded assignment plans. So, although both had commented on learners' assignment work via e-mail, they were 'invisible' in this communication media with both receiving below average CEQ scores.

A tutor's previous relationship with learners appeared significant in their perception of module quality (Youde, 2014, 2018). This was apparent with the three tutors receiving the highest CEQ scores who had either taught the learners on a previous module or had carried out the degree course induction. These tutors also communicated with learners prior to their module commencing with a welcome e-mail and a plan for the first face-to-face teaching day. For example, one tutor's learners were sent a plan of the day prior to attending, and tutorials were available when teaching was completed. It appears that effective tutors, in learners' eyes, were mindful of proactive communication and support throughout the whole duration of a module.

A number of tutor extrinsic motivators appeared influential evidenced through differing CEQ scores (Youde, 2018). Those receiving higher CEQ scores were more likely to have engaged in greater online interactions, were more proactive in learner support, communicated with groups prior to the first face-to-face session, and created more space for learning by keeping the focus on module assessment. Therefore, Youde's (2014, 2018) data suggested extrinsic motivators influence learner perceptions of the teaching, learning and assessment. Consequently, the data suggest extending the angragogical model's core principle, *motivation to learn*, to include extrinsic motivators (see Appendix 1). These actions required a number of tutor skills and qualities and exhibited a range of emotional competences, such as Self-awareness and Self-management (Goleman, 2001; Youde 2018), which were outlined in Chapter 4.

A proposed andragogical model for blended learning contexts

Within Youde's (2014, 2018) research, the andragogical model offered an analytical lens that was valuable as it provided a number of actions appearing to influence learner perceptions of quality, which can support practice for tutors and HE institutions in similar contexts. This Chapter has

Effective teaching and learning for adult learners 75

highlighted the flexible application of this model and value in noting strengths and weaknesses in specific contexts. This has allowed the proposal of an andragogical model to meet the needs of adult learners studying PT vocationally relevant degrees at a distance (Youde, 2014, 2018). The vocational nature of the courses was significant in highlighting the similarities with practices evident on the modules with Knowles et al.'s (2011) model. Youde argued that the predominant approaches to teaching and assessment adopted by tutors were mainly congruent with the model's core principles, which was largely due to the structured, assessment driven learning environment, and the type of problem and case-based assessments undertaken by learners on the courses investigated. Consequently, the angragogical model proposed by Youde maintains the six core principles, however, the analysis highlighted the importance to tutors of providing extrinsic motivators, with this also added to the model. The research highlighted important factors for adults, with appropriate assessment strategies, based on andragogical principles, appearing important for encouraging self-directed experiential learning.

In addition, factors are provided for each principle to potentially operationalise the model for online and blended learning practitioners within similar contexts (Youde, 2014, 2018). These factors are outlined under each core principle in Appendix 1. The factors were predominantly constructivist in orientation and were significant in the development of a conceptual model for understanding the data presented within Youde's (2014) study. This model represents an interpretation of effective practice in a blended learning context and is presented, together with a rationale, in Chapter 11.

In summary

This Chapter has presented data for two purposes. Firstly, to explore effective tutoring in online and blended learning contexts for adult learners using the andragogical model's constituent core principles (Knowles et al., 2015) as a lens for the analysis. It has suggested a new way of analysing and understanding online and blended learning, potentially reviving the andragogy model within this context (Youde, 2018). Secondly, it builds on the existing body of knowledge regarding the importance of extrinsic motivation for adult learners, contributing to current debates about adult learner motivations for study. Although reporting on a small-scale research study, this Chapter has taken tentative steps to present an empirical base to Knowles' Model (Youde, 2018). Common themes are emerging from the exploration of andragogy and approaches to study that promote actions tutors can take to encourage adoption of deep approaches in learners. These were then contextualised within the Chapter for online and blended learning contexts and provide an overview of effective tutors and tutoring to meet adult learner needs.

76 Effective teaching and learning for adult learners

A range of issues have been raised within this Chapter around effective tutors and tutoring that are explored further in this book. These include:

- the tutor providing a structured learning experience that encourages reflection on previous experiences
- clear goals being outlined as the module commences, thus establishing the relevance of the subject area as well its purpose and value. As part of this process tutors can stimulate learner interest and build fascination for the subject area
- learners' approaches to study can be influenced by tutors, however, during the operation of a module, the impact of this is questionable
- adult learners are frequently intrinsically motivated in their study, but can be undertaking courses for instrumental reasons or be influenced by competing demands of their professions and family life
- tutors have to manage learners' competing pressures as well as their own as academics
- assessment methods, both formative and summative, should allow students to contextualise learning within their work setting and integrate their experiences, but also be manageable and enable a depth of analysis
- the tutor has an important role in providing extrinsic motivators to encourage their learners' belief that they can be successful with structured student support mechanisms and detailed, timely feedback on assessments being integral to achievement.

Youde's (2014, 2018) proposed model (see Appendix 1) could aid teaching, assessment and learner support and assist course leaders in the design and development of online and blended learning programmes. Knowles et al.'s, (2015) andragogical model, and the six core principles on which it is based, have relevance in contemporary online and blended learning contexts for PT learners undertaking vocationally relevant degrees.

The book now moves onto explore theories of learning that emerged before the andragogical model in relation to distance education discourse to argue that emotional competences have underpinned thinking and practice in this area for a longer number of years than is generally recognised.

References

Ausburn, L. J. (2004). Course design elements most valued by adult learners in blended online education environments: An American perspective. *Educational Media International, 41*, 327–337. doi: 10.1080/0952398042000314820.

Bailey, C. J., & Card, K. A. (2009). Effective pedagogical practices for online teaching: Perception of experienced instructors. *Internet and Higher Education, 12*(3-4), 152–155.

Biggs, J. B., Kember, D., & Leung, D.Y. P. (2001). The revised two-factor study process questionnaire: R-SPQ-2F. *British Journal of Educational Psychology, 71*, 133–149.

Biggs, J., & Tang, C. (2007). *Teaching for quality learning at university* (3rd ed.). Maidenhead: Open University Press.

Blondy, L. C. (2007). Evaluation and application of andragogical assumptions to the adult online learning environment. *Journal of Interactive Online Learning, 6*(2), 116–130.

Brookfield, S. D. (1986). *Understanding and facilitating adult learning.* San Francisco, CA: Jossey-Bass.

Creanor, L. (2002). A tale of two courses: A comparative study of tutoring online. *Open Learning, 17*(1), 57–68.

Dewey, J. (1938). *Experience and education.* New York, NY: McMillan.

Entwistle, N. J., & Ramsden, P. (1983). *Understanding student learning.* London: Croom Helm.

Feinstein, L., Anderson, T. M., Hammond, C., Jamieson, A., & Woodley, A. (2007). *The social and economic benefits of part-time, mature study at Birkbeck College and the Open University.* Milton Keynes and London: Open University. Retrieved from http://s3.amazonaws.com/academia.edu.documents/42366787/surveyone.pdf?AWSAccessKeyId=AKIAIWOWYYGZ2Y53UL3A&Expires=1491989775&Signature=fJQUxUXvYsz3V05G5aXo1NKZsJE%3D&response-content-disposition=inline%3B%20filename%3DThe_Social_and_Economic_Benefits_of_Part.pdf

Gibbs, G. (1992). *Improving the quality of student learning.* Bristol: Technical and Educational Services.

Goleman, D. (2001). An EI-based theory of performance. In C. Cherniss & D. Goleman (Eds.) *The emotionally intelligent workplace: How to select for, measure, and improve emotional intelligence in individuals, groups, and organization* (pp. 27–44). San Francisco, CA: Jossy-Bass.

Grace, A. P. (1996). Striking a critical pose: Andragogy - missing links, missing values. *International Journal of Lifelong Education, 15*(5), 382–392.

Gregory, J. (2002). Principles of experiential education. In P. Jarvis (Ed.) *The theory and practice of teaching* (pp. 94–107). London: Kogan Page.

Hartree, A. (1984). Malcolm Knowles' theory of andragogy: A critique. *International Journal of Lifelong Education, 3*(3), 203–210.

Jarvis, P. (1985). *The Sociology of Adult and Continuing Education.* London: Croom Helm.

Jarvis, P. (2012). Adult learning: Andragogy versus pedagogy or from pedagogy to andragogy. In P. Jarvis & M. Watts (Eds.) *The Routledge international handbook of learning* (pp. 134–143). Abingdon: Routledge.

Kember, D. (2007). *Reconsidering open and distance learning in the developing world: Meeting students' learning needs.* Abingdon: Routledge.

Kember, D., Leung, D.Y. P., & McNaught, C. (2008). A workshop activity to demonstrate that approaches to learning are influenced by the teaching and learning environment. *Active Learning in Higher Education, 19*(1), 43–56.

Knowles, M. S. (1984). *Andragogy in action: Applying modern principles of adult learning.* San Francisco, CA: Jossey-Bass.

Knowles, M. S., Holton, E. F., & Swanson, R. A. (2011). *The adult learner: The definitive classic in adult education and human resource development* (7th ed.). Woburn: Butterworth Heinemann.

Knowles, M. S., Holton, E. F., & Swanson, R. A. (2015). *The adult learner: The definitive classic in adult education and human resource development* (8th ed.). Abingdon: Routledge.

Kolb, D. (1981). Learning styles and disciplinary differences. In A. W. Chickering (Ed.) *The modern American college* (pp. 232–255). San Francisco, CA: Jossey-Bass.

Kolb, D. A. (1984). *Experiential learning: Experience as the source of learning and development.* Englewood Cliffs, NJ: Prentice Hall.

78 Effective teaching and learning for adult learners

Kolb, D., & Fry, R. (1975). Towards an applied theory of experiential learning. In C. Cooper (Ed.) *Theories of group processes* (pp. 33–57). London: Wiley.

Marton, K., & Säljö, R. (1976). On qualitative differences in learning: I - Outcome and process. *British Journal of Educational Psychology*, *46*, 4–11.

Maslow, A. (1968). *Toward a psychology of being* (2nd ed.). New York, NY: D Van Nostrand Company.

Mayes. T., & de Freitas, S. (2007). Learning and e-learning: The role of theory. In H. Beetham & R. Sharpe (Eds.) *Rethinking pedagogy for a digital age: Designing and delivering e-learning* (pp. 13–25). Abingdon, Oxfordshire: Routledge.

McDonald, P. L. (2014). Variation in adult learners' experiences of blended learning in higher education. In A. G. Picciano, C. D. Dziuban, & C. R. Graham (Eds.) *Blended learning: Research perspectives* (Vol. 2, pp. 215–234). New York, NY: Routledge.

Mclay, M., Mycroft, L., Noel, P., Orr, K., Thompson, R., Tummons, J., & Weatherby, J. (2019). Learning and learners. In J. Avis, R. Fisher, & R. Thompson (Eds.) *Teaching in lifelong learning: A guide to theory and practice* (3rd ed., pp. 81–107). Maidenhead: Open University Press.

Merriam, S., & Caffarella, R. S. (1999). *Learning in adulthood* (2nd ed.). San Francisco, CA: Jossey-Bass.

Moore, M. G. (1997). Theory of transactional distance. In D. Keegan (Ed.) *Theoretical principles of distance education* (pp. 22–38). New York, NY: Routledge.

Murphy, L. M., Shelley, M. A., White, C. J., & Baumann, U. (2011). Tutor and student perceptions of what makes an effective distance language teacher. *Distance Education*, *32*(3), 397–419.

Prensky, M. (2001). *Digital natives, digital immigrants*. Retrieved from: http://www.marcprensky.com/writing/Prensky%20-%20Digital%20Natives,%20Digital%20Immigrants%20-%20Part1.pdf

Ramsden, P. (1991). A performance indicator of teaching quality in higher education: The course experience questionnaire. *Studies in Higher Education*, *16*, 129–150.

Savicevic, D. (2008). Convergence or divergence of ideas on andragogy in different countries. *International Journal of Lifelong Education*, *27*(4), 361–378. doi:10.1080/02601370802051504.

Smith, A. (2004). "Off-campus support" in distance learning - how do our students define quality? *Quality Assurance in Education*, *12*(1), 28–38.

Smyth, S., & Houghton, C. (2012). Students' experiences of blended learning across a range of postgraduate programmes. *Nurse Education Today*, *32*(4), 464–468.

Swain, J., & Hammond, C. (2011). The motivations and outcomes of studying for part-time mature students in higher education. *International Journal of Lifelong Education*, *30*(5), 591–612.

Taylor, E. W., & Laros, A. (2014). Researching the practice of fostering transformative learning: Lessons learned from the study of andragogy. *Journal of Transformative Education*, *12*(2), 134–147.

Tough, A. (1979). *The adult's learning projects*. Toronto: Ontario: Institute for Studies in Education.

Vermetten, Y. J., Lodewijks, H. G., & Vermunt, J. D. (1999). Consistency and variability of learning strategies in different university courses. *Higher Education*, *37*, 1–21.

Wheeler, S. (2012). Digital learning futures. Retrieved from http://www.steve-wheeler.co.uk/2015/03/social-mobile-and-personal-learning.html#!/2015/03/social-mobile-and-personal-learning.html

Wheeler, S. (2015). *Learning with 'e's*. Carmarthen: Crown House Publishing.

Youde, A. (2014). *A Mixed Methods Exploration of Effective Tutors and Tutoring in Blended Learning Contexts* (Unpublished EdD Thesis, The University of Huddersfield, Huddersfield). Retrieved from http://eprints.hud.ac.uk/id/eprint/20351/

Youde, A. (2016). Tutor emotional competences valued by learners in a blended learning context. *European Journal of Open, Distance and E-Learning (EURODL)*, *19*(2), 81–97.

Youde, A. (2018). Andragogy in blended learning contexts: Effective tutoring of adult learners studying part-time, vocationally relevant degrees at a distance. *International Journal of Lifelong Education*, *37*(2), 255–272. doi 10.1080/02601370.2018.1450303.

Youde, A. (2019). The development of the course experience questionnaire and revised-study process questionnaire for part-time learners on blended, vocationally relevant, degree programmes. In EduLearn 2019 Proceedings: 11th International Conference on Education and New Learning Technologies, Palma, Majorca (pp. 10–17). doi 10.21125/edulearn.2019.0005.

Chapter 6

Analysis of prominent distance education theorisations to explore developing relations in online and blended learning

Introduction

This Chapter explores some key theories of distance education, particularly Moore's (1997) Transactional Distance Theory and Holmberg's (2003) theorisation of distance education, to argue that tutor emotional competence (EC) underpins their effective implementation in practice. As a prelude, Classical Humanist approaches to education are briefly outlined, particularly drawing on the foundational work of Rogers, Dewey and Maslow, to identify and theoretically situate some aspects personal relations relevant to e-learning contexts. The Chapter will highlight some emotionally competent traits that appear valuable for tutors as well as raising awareness of learner feelings whilst studying at a distance. Finally, there is an outline of practical measures that tutors can take to develop tutor/learner relations within a blended learning environment.

Humanist theories of learning

As stated in Chapter 5, Humanist theories of learning take a person–centred approach in which true learning comes from within (Mclay et al., 2019, p. 94). Such theories have commonly drawn on the work of Dewey (1938), particularly his consideration of experience and reflection within education. Although not exclusively, these ideas resonate with adult education. The works of Abraham Maslow and Carl Rogers are relevant to this discussion, particularly their promotion of student–centred learning (Mclay et al., 2019, p. 94). Maslow's (1968) construct of self-actualisation encourages a tutor to connect the learner's area of study to their own motives, interest and desires. This has clear synergies with Knowles' andragogical model (see Chapter 5), particularly with regard to *learners' self-concept* (adults need to be responsible for their decisions on education), *role of learners' experiences* (adults use experiences as the basis for learning activities), and *readiness to learn* (adults are more interested in learning if there is an immediate relevance to work; Knowles, Holton, & Swanson, 2015). Rogers espoused the importance of personal relations between tutors and learners, with these built on trust, respect and, as discussed throughout this Chapter, empathy (Rogers & Freiberg, 1994).

Analysis of prominent distance education theorisations 81

For such relations to develop, tutor EC is required to influence learner perceptions of quality (Youde, 2016).

Some theorisations of distance learning

A key consideration within online and blended learning is the importance of effective support strategies for adult learners with this Section highlighting elements of good practice from relevant empirical research and theorisations. Even though there is some face-to-face contact, blended learning delivery needs to consider learners' feelings when a significant proportion of their study is at a distance. This is an area rarely considered in online and blended learning discourses. This Section particularly focuses on engaging learners studying through electronic media at a distance from a university and includes guidance around aspects of teaching, learning and support that can be beneficial. This, again, forms a base from which to consider good practices in this context. Later in this Section, similarities are discussed between the tutor competences suggested by theorisations from distance education literature and the emotional competences (ECs) presented in Chapter 4.

To support teaching, learning and assessment in online and blended contexts student support strategies should be embedded within the programme structure (MacDonald, 2006; Stubbs, Martin, & Endlar, 2006; see Chapter 10 for a further discussion of learner support strategies). Orton-Johnson (2009) stresses this point with regard to adult learners by advising that they should be fully informed and supported when undertaking online and blended learning as students need clear aims to be able to see the relevance of their learning and to support them in achieving their goals.

To further explore effective teaching, learning and student support in online and blended contexts, analysis of dominant discourses in distance education is instructive. This is particularly apparent when evaluating constructivist approaches to learning and this Section argues the importance of tutor/learner dialogue in online and blended learning environments. These contexts have the benefit of utilising methods of communication media that afford a basis for improved peer collaboration and a number of models with a social constructivist flavour have emerged (see Chapter 7). These models, because of their focus on peer collaboration opportunities, have lost some attention to learner feelings when studying at a distance. To effectively foster interpersonal relationships with learners, tutor EC is required and this is an area where distance education theorisations are informative.

Holmberg's theory of distance education based on empathy

Holmberg was a pioneer of thinking in relation to distance education, in the era of paper-based, postal correspondence courses, long before the availability of online and blended learning technologies – although later work

82 Analysis of prominent distance education theorisations

considered his ideas within online contexts (e.g., see Holmberg, 1989). In his discussion of distance education theory and practice, Holmberg (1989, p. 163) states that "learning is encouraged by frequent communication with fellow humans interested in study". The feeling of belonging, to a course and/or an institution, is just as significant as the tutor/learner exchanges about the topics being studied. Further, and in agreement with Rogers above, Holmberg (1989, p. 162) regards empathy as an essential tutor trait when dealing with students and a significant consideration within distance education contexts.

Holmberg's theory of distance education has resonance for this book and the general consideration of effective tutoring in online and blended contexts. Firstly, the theory is focussed on those opting for alternatives to traditional face-to-face teaching, commonly working adults undertaking study for vocational or personal development (Holmberg, 2003, p. 81). Secondly, the theory's context is within a supporting organisation, such as a university, providing programmes of study with accompanying teaching, learning, support and administration. Finally, and of significance, is Holmberg's consideration of personal relations, where he states:

> Central to learning and teaching in distance education are personal relations between the parties concerned, study pleasure, and empathy between students and those representing the supporting organization. Feelings of empathy and belonging promote the students' motivation to learn and influence the learning favorably. Such feelings are fostered by lucid, problem-oriented, conversation-like presentations of learning matter expounding and supplementing the course literature; by friendly mediated interaction between students, tutors, counselors, and other staff in the supporting organization; and by liberal organizational-administrative structures and processes. Factors that advance the learning process include short turnaround times for assignments and other communications between students and the supporting organization, suitable frequency of assignment submissions, and the constant availability of tutors and advisers (Holmberg, 2003, p. 81–82).

Again, clear synergies are apparent with Rogers' consideration of personal relations, underpinned by tutor empathy for learners' educational experiences. Such personal relations require emotionally competent tutors to support effective practice when studying at a distance. There is alignment with humanist approaches to learning with Holmberg's consideration of student motivation, problem-orientated approaches and friendly interactions with all stakeholders forming part of the learner's experiences. Further, there is congruence with Biggs' Constructive Alignment Model (2003, p. 26; see Chapter 7 for a more detailed discussion), which posits that the climate teachers create through their interactions with students is integral to effective teaching and learning within higher education (HE). Again, tutor ECs are necessary to create such a climate in a way that is conducive to the nature of adult learners.

Analysis of prominent distance education theorisations   83

Moore's transactional distance theory

Moore's (1997) Theory of Transactional Distance has significance for those who teach with limited face-to-face contact as it considers the separation of tutors and learners and the effect of this on participants' behaviour. Even when there is some face-to face contact, such feelings of separation can be apparent and inhibiting. As Moore outlines:

> With separation there is a psychological and communication space to be crossed, a space of potential misunderstanding between inputs of instructor and those of the learner. It is this psychological and communications space that is the transactional distance (Moore, 1997, p. 22).

It is this psychological and communications space that online and blended tutors need to address by considering three teaching and learning variables that impact on the extent of the Transactional Distance; dialogue, structure and learner autonomy (Moore, 1997). In general, increased dialogue reduces the Transactional Distance, however, dialogue refers to more than just interactions between tutors, students and peers, as it should be of value to each party. The quality of dialogue is more important than the quantity of interactions. Laurillard (2002, p. 73) concurred with Moore's view by recommending a continuing iterative dialogue between tutor and student in e-learning contexts where learning goals are agreed and a discursive dialogue is promoted. Laurillard's prescription is constructivist in foundation, but with emphasis on the importance of feedback to aid the learner's development. Brindley, Blaschke, and Walti (2009) further stressed the value of timely, high quality feedback in online learning environments, particularly formative, to enhance student learning. Important tutor skills are required to maintain the quality of the relationship and continue the dialogue, particularly EC in relationship management (Youde, 2016). It is therefore important to explore the quality of dialogue between tutors and learners in both face-to-face and online environments to consider its role in supporting teaching, learning and assessment.

Generally, university tutors can exert influence over the structure and content of their units of study and they can encourage learner autonomy, particularly with regard to assessments. Therefore, Moore's (1997) conceptions of structure and learner autonomy can support tutor practices. Moore refers to structure as:

> the rigidity or flexibility of the programme's educational objectives, teaching strategies and evaluation methods. It describes the extent to which an educational programme can accommodate or be responsive to each learner's individual needs (Moore, 1997, p. 26).

Moore explains that Transactional Distance is lowered if the structure is more flexible, but there are tensions here with the needs of part-time students

84 Analysis of prominent distance education theorisations

who may be experiencing HE for the first time. Courses need to be flexible in terms of learning outcomes, but need to have sufficient structure in their delivery for students with competing pressures from work and family life. As students have limited face-to-face contact with their tutors, a clear structure to their learning may help, for example, through the provision of an appropriate spread of assessment deadlines throughout the academic (and work) year.

Discussions of structure provide an interesting consideration for Moore's final variable, learner autonomy. As Falloon (2011, p. 206) notes, too much structure can become an inconvenience to some and work against the reasons for choosing online and blended learning. Moore (1997, p. 31) describes learner autonomy as:

> the extent to which in the teaching/learning relationship it is the learner rather than the teacher who determines the goals, the learning experiences, and the evaluation decisions of the learning programme (Moore, 1997, p. 31).

Whilst this description implies the Transactional Distance is lowered if students are working with greater independence, my view of autonomy mirrored Shin's (2002, p. 127) when she argues it is "to what extent a student is able to exert his/her decision-making power over tasks related to their learning". Again, this view highlights tensions regarding the importance of a structured environment with clear goals, but this must allow for learners having choice in learning by, for example, being able to choose assessments relevant to their individual work practices. Similarities are evident here with Knowles, Holton, and Swanson's (2015) Andragogical Model outlined in Chapter 5 regarding appropriate assessment strategies for adult learners in online and blended learning environments.

There have been a number of empirical studies to evaluate the status of Moore's theory (e.g., see Bischoff, Bisconer, Kooker, & Woods, 1996; Chen, 2001), which generally outline its face validity as a framework to evaluate distance education. However, Gorsky and Caspi's (2005) review of empirical literature argued that the basic tenets of Transactional Distance Theory were not supported by the research findings, and they stated it was reduced to a single proposition regarding dialogue. This, they considered, was tautologous. Goel, Zhang, and Templeton (2012, p. 1123) argue that although the theory had by then been around for a number of years, it had high face validity but its empirical validity still required development. In addition, their empirical research found support for the influence of transactional distance factors on e-learning. Falloon (2011) agreed that Moore's theory was relevant for the digital world, but warned of the influence of factors affecting dialogue and learner autonomy, such as, broadband speeds, inadequate computer specifications and learner technical competence. However, the impact of such factors

Analysis of prominent distance education theorisations   85

should be diminished as technology and learners' digital skills continue to develop. Moore (2013) notes the contemporary relevance of his theory when advising the use of existing knowledge of distance education practices when developing massive open online courses (MOOCs) to ensure the preparation of appropriate teaching materials and to facilitate dialogue.

Shin's transactional presence theory

Whilst Moore (1997) and Laurillard (2002) discussed learner interaction with the course content and tutors, Shin (2002), developed this discussion further through consideration of their interaction with peers and the institution. She proposes the construct of Transactional Presence "to be concerned with the degree to which a distance student perceives the availability of, and connectedness with, teachers, peer students and institution" (Shin, 2002, p. 132). Here, "availability" is presented as needs and desires of learners being able to be met on request. "Connectedness" refers to the learner's belief or feeling that a reciprocal relationship exists with tutors, peers and the institution.

The connectedness students feel to the institution is important for distance learners as they are far more reliant on outward facing technologies, such as online enrolment systems and library interfaces, with personal contact often unavailable if systems are experiencing technical difficulties or if the user is unsure of their correct use. Individual module tutors' influence over the Transactional Presence between learners and the institution can be limited, but they are often the first contact and appropriate, timely advice when they are experiencing difficulties can help. This can be significant in learner perceptions of quality, particularly around notions of support.

The construct of tutor 'availability' provides some tensions if the literal definition is accepted. It requires tutors to be available and supportive of learners, whilst being mindful of their competing pressures and trying to develop capable, autonomous learners. Clear communication, adherence to standards, and quality dialogue are essential to mitigate such competing pressures, as well as learners' awareness of wider HE support structures.

Distance education theorisations and emotional competence

Research has highlighted the learner benefits of tutor Transactional Presence and Tutor Presence (Garrison, Anderson, & Archer, 2000; Salmon, 2011), both in online and blended learning contexts, although various similar constructs have emerged in e-learning literature. Garrison et al. (2000) conceptions of Social Presence and Tutor Presence being relevant examples (see Chapter 7 for a more detailed discussion of these conceptions). Sherratt (2008, p. 810) explored both tutors' and students' perceptions of the tutor in blended learning environments and found that students valued 'visibility' by tutors, which, she argued, helped to maintain trust and, I argue, has congruence with notions of Transactional Distance and Transactional Presence. Learner success is strengthened by a strong consistent tutor presence in online learning environments with increased satisfaction emerging from the level of engagement with peers, tutors and content (Ke, 2010; LeBaron & McFadden, 2008).

This analysis of prominent theorisations within distance education discourse has highlighted the importance of emotionally competent tutoring. Firstly, notions of empathic tutoring (Holmberg, 2003; Rogers & Freiberg, 1994) align with prominent trait-based models of EI, such as, Goleman's (2001) Framework of ECs and Bar-On's (2006) Model of Emotional-Social Intelligence (ESI). Further, Moore's notion of dialogue, a key factor in narrowing tutor/learner Transactional Distance, suggests both the importance of relationship management ECs (Goleman, 2001; Youde, 2016) and effective e-moderating (Salmon, 2011). This view complements Salmon's (2011, p. 104) opinion that emotional intelligence and the ability to influence others are important attributes, necessary when tutoring online. She argues that this includes motivation, with has resonance with Maslow's self-actualisation construction referred to earlier in this Chapter.

Improving personal relations within a blended learning environment

The consideration of theory advocating the importance of developing tutor/learner relations has highlighted the converging views of a range of authors. However, what has not been discussed yet are practical examples of how personal relations can be developed in the current e-tutoring context (see Chapter 1). Research is now presented, from within an educational disciplinary area, that noted tutor actions that appeared to both influence learner perceptions of quality, and developed and maintained relations (Youde, 2014, 2017, 2019). Learner feedback on an attitude survey (see Chapter 10 for a discussion of the survey's development), which included questions about clear communication, motivational comments to improve work, and tutors making the subject interesting, suggested the centrality of good tutor communication (Ramsden, 1991).

Youde (2014) provided examples of how tutors can develop and maintain relations with their learners within a blended learning environment. An interesting finding was that personal relations appeared to be developed by some tutors even though minimal interactions were found within the course virtual learning environment (VLE). This, however, could have been due to the nature of the adult learners under investigation and their learning preferences in this e-tutoring context. Therefore, the research explored how tutors were communicating with their learners. The Section is structured in two parts, firstly, learner support is explored before the quality of tutor/learner dialogue

Analysis of prominent distance education theorisations   87

is considered. Following this, these findings are considered in relation the prominent distance education theorisations outlined earlier in this Chapter.

Tutors' support of learners

Literature discussed earlier in this Chapter stated that in order to sustain the chosen teaching, learning and assessment, effective student support strategies need to be embedded within the programme structure (MacDonald & McAteer, 2003; Stubbs et al., 2006). In Youde's (2014) study the design of such support was structured around the assessment strategies within the modules investigated. Effective tutors, in learners' eyes, enhanced this with active management of support, predominantly facilitated by e-mail. These tutors outlined similar proactive strategies to support and encourage learners in meeting the formative and summative assessment requirements of modules. Formative assessment processes were monitored closely, with e-mail, phone calls or discussions at face-to-face sessions used to prompt learners and encourage dialogue. Common across all modules was learner support through feedback on formative assessments.

Tutors emphasised a commitment to supporting learners through assessments, which was exemplified through response times. One tutor illustrated this when stating, "the response times were really good this year, often in the morning that it arrived". The learners under investigation appeared to require a minimum level of support, which involved timely and constructive feedback to formative assessments, however, some tutors were more proactive in communicating. This level of support was exemplified by a tutor, who stated:

> I don't know if I am soft but when I tutor with blended [learning] I do regularly send students emails and try to keep regular contact and I also make it very clear that it is their responsibility to actually contact me.

Whilst illustrating a high level of support this comment highlights expectations of tutor and learner roles set throughout the module, and the value of e-mail in online and blended learning. Such attention to response times has resonance with Holmberg's recommendation of the "constant availability of tutors and advisers" (Holmberg, 2003, pp. 81–82) and Shin's notion of "availability" (Shin, 2002, p. 132), where the "needs and desires of learners being able to be met on request". Earlier, these notions were challenged as potentially creating tensions between tutors' teaching commitments and the other demands placed on their time. However, it appears that effective tutors, in their learners' eyes, were managing to meet their requests for support in a timely manner.

Student support mechanisms appeared most effective when facilitated by e-mail and not by other forms of computer mediated communications (CMCs) such as wikis and discussion boards. Whilst this may be expected

88 Analysis of prominent distance education theorisations

given e-mail's requirement of a personal response, there appeared to be other factors influencing learner perceptions. Two tutors spoke enthusiastically about being available for learners, sending e-mails to check on progress and responding in a timely manner. This support was facilitated by e-mail, which provided immediacy and intimacy, which they found motivating for learners. Similar feedback was received from other tutors about the value of e-mail in prompting and encouraging learners, however, other communication media were less effective with both tutors and learners influencing this. One tutor established a wiki and two discussion boards for learners to showcase elements of practice and outline plans for assessment. These methods were included to elicit peer support and collaboration in the assessment process and allow peers to validate assignment plans. In each case, contributions were not part of the summative mark received for the module and limited learner engagement was evident. Further, on both discussion boards, the tutors had not contributed or commented on individual plans or made general comments about submissions that could guide others. Although both tutors commented on learner's assignment work via e-mail, they were 'invisible' in module discussion boards. Again, this discussion highlights the challenges of engaging adult learners to communicate and collaborate within formal university online environments and corresponds with the findings of Boelens, De Wever and Voet (2017), in their systematic literature review of blended learning environment design, who identified stimulating peer-to-peer interaction as a key challenge. This could be due to tutors responding to requests via e-mail, or it could be due to the pressures of work and family life preventing full engagement in a programme of study. Further, students could be drawing on their personal learning networks (Wheeler, 2015), external to the university, to support their studies.

In a similar way to that outlined in Chapter 5, this Section points to the importance of a simple programme structure, focussed around module assessment requirements, supported by active and available student support. Some tutors were more proactive in engaging with learners, particularly around formative assessment requirements. Further, this Section has raised the issue of tutor visibility to learners, which is considered below together with its impact on tutor/learner dialogue.

The extent and quality of tutor/learner dialogue

This Chapter has discussed how tutor 'availability' (Shin, 2002, p. 132) and 'visibility' (Sherratt, 2008, p. 810) are central to fostering a tutor/student dialogue, which, it was argued, are crucial for effective learning in HE at a distance (Laurillard, 2002; Moore, 1997). As stated earlier, learner feedback highlighted clear communication, motivational comments to improve work, and tutors making the subject interesting as important factors (Youde, 2014). These areas suggest available and visible tutors who have engaged in

Analysis of prominent distance education theorisations 89

dialogue with learners and this Section explores this further. The analysis in this Section was limited as minimal interactions were found within the course VLE. Further, access to actual tutor e-mails was not available, so the examples outlined below are largely from tutors' description of their practice. This limits the analysis of 'quality' dialogue, with a greater focus given to tutor availability and visibility.

Availability, visibility and dialogue were evident throughout the modules, as described in the previous Section, around proactive communications with learners and discussions of learners' formative assessments. Further examples include one tutor creating space each week to be available for learners and manage the module's online elements, with another providing web conferences at regular intervals. Three forwarded hyperlinks to access additional reading which, again, used e-mail as a means of promoting dialogue, thereby appearing 'visible' to learners. Within all modules, however, the extent of dialogue was driven by formative assessments, through learners discussing tutor feedback. All tutors described limited discussions beyond formative assessments, for example, around module content, and, as outlined earlier, there was little dialogue evident in online environments.

Significant influences on the visibility of tutors appeared to be communications sent to learners before the first face-to-face teaching session. Examples of communications included a detailed plan of the first session, copies of all materials to be used, and some reading to be discussed at the class. One tutor established a group on a social networking site and provided information about herself and the module with learners contributing images and brief biographies. Each of these measures offered an opportunity for dialogue and appeared to influence learner perceptions of availability and visibility. Previous relationships with learners appear to have a strong influence on the availability and visibility of tutors. Tutors receiving the three highest scores on the learner attitude survey each had management responsibilities on learners' courses and two had taught earlier modules. It is reasonable to assume, learners knew these tutors were available and that trust had emerged through positive exchanges and this led to a lowering of Transactional Distance (Moore, 1997).

Examples of practice were evident that could have potentially limited availability and visibility. Two tutors highlighted the time pressured nature of blended learning as a barrier in developing relationships with learners. This also suggested a greater focus on content delivery in face-to-face sessions rather than a more facilitative approach. For example, one comment illustrated issues that could be preventing a dialogue to foster:

> I think in actual fact where I have struggled with blended learning provision is you have got the same amount of content that you need to do for the module, but I have got two full days. I haven't got enough time so I need to be more adept at communicating and getting them to do things themselves.

To summarise, Youde (2014, 2017, 2019) found that assessment strategies drove a good quality dialogue between tutors and some learners during the modules. Formative assessment procedures (plans and drafts) encouraged a dialogue if learners chose, with all tutors indicating a high uptake. This level of interaction, whilst limited to assessment, appears to be sufficient for these adult learners to be successful in a blended learning context. Tutors receiving higher scores on a learner attitude survey outlined a greater number of strategies to be 'available' and 'visible' to learners, which offered increased opportunities for dialogue. This was enhanced as these tutors were more proactive in contacting learners who had potentially become disengaged. In addition, tutors' previous relationships with learners appeared to influence perceptions of quality.

Key tutor actions to develop tutor/learner relations

The discussion in this Section has outlined a number of practical measures tutors can take to develop tutor/learner personal relations within a blended learning environment (Youde, 2014, 2017, 2019). These could support tutors in similar contexts, and include:

- assessments are developed to encourage tutor 'availability' and 'visibility' and form the basis of tutor/learner dialogue
- tutors are empathic to adult learner needs and mindful of their competing pressures
- tutors provide proactive learner support
- tutors provide proactive communications such as communication before the first face-to-face session
- tutors should teach learners at multiple points during courses when practical, thereby encouraging relationships to develop
- tutors should use e-mail effectively.

Consideration of Youde's findings in relation to prominent distance education theorisations

This Section synthesises distance education theorisations to consider the quality of experience for the adult learners investigated by Youde (2014, 2017, 2019). It evaluates the modules with which they engaged to establish their suitability for those studying predominantly at a distance and argues that there was effective practice across modules, which supported the general success of the provision observed. All the modules demonstrated important features of Transactional Distance Theory (Moore, 1997), and Transactional Presence (Shin, 2002), with some congruence with core principles of the andragogical model (Knowles et al., 2011), indicating effective practice for adult learners studying part-time at a distance. In demonstrating important features of these

Analysis of prominent distance education theorisations 91

theorisations, a number of Social Awareness and Relationship Management ECs were evident, which contribute to a conceptual framework of effective tutoring in online and blended learning environments (see Chapter 11).

Dialogue, structure and learner autonomy are the key variables (Moore, 1997) necessary to reduce Transactional Distance between tutors and learners, and they were demonstrated in all modules. As outlined in the previous Section, and appropriate for these learners, modules were structured around assessment strategies. Moore (1997, p. 26) refers to structure as "the rigidity or flexibility of the programme's educational objectives, teaching strategies and evaluation methods", and there appeared sufficient flexibility for learners, who could tailor modules to their vocational context and adopt preferred approaches to study. The modules could accommodate learner's individual needs (Moore, 1997, p. 26) particularly with regard to choice of assessment, which indicates learner autonomy. Further, learners determined assessment goals as they had choice of topic and were largely responsible for learning experiences. This responsibility could have fostered constructivist approaches to learning by the achievement of understanding through active discovery where learners construct new ideas. The presence of key features of Transactional Distance Theory suggests that these learners were also experiencing elements of a Transactional Presence (Shin, 2002) whilst undertaking modules.

A Transactional Presence was apparent between some learners and tutors with this indicating effective practice in supporting distance learning. Tutors emphasised the role of the first face-to-face session in forming relationships if they had not previously taught learners. The extent of tutor support, contact prior to first face-to-face session, extent of dialogue, and 'visibility' of some tutors, were key factors that indicate a Transactional Presence between some tutors and learners. This suggested that some tutors were 'available' to meet the needs and desires of learners, who also felt 'connected' as a reciprocal relationship existed. Further, analysis of the Four-Branch Model's Understanding Branch (see Chapter 2) emphasised the importance of tutor/learner relationships developing over time in understanding the impact of external events on individual's emotional responses. The development of a tutor/learner Transactional Presence indicates a number of Social Awareness and Relationship Management ECs were demonstrated by the most effective tutors (Youde, 2016). As relationships develop, learners are more likely to perceive tutors as available and that a connection exists.

The discussion of Transactional Distance Theory and the Transactional Presence construct within this Section has revealed congruence with the andragogical model (see Chapter 5). Learners' self-concept, which refers to adults' need to be responsible for their decisions in education, provides an interesting consideration in relation to Moore's (1997) concepts, structure and learner autonomy. Modules were sufficiently structured to support mature PT learners managing the influence of daily events, together with the pressures and time constraints of their employment (Creanor, 2002; Smyth &

Houghton, 2012), however, choice of assessment topic and responsibility for learning experiences, given the limited face-to-face teaching, allowed decisions on their study strategies to be made. These factors appear similar to the role of learners' experiences and readiness to learn core principles, as adults are more interested in learning if there is an immediate relevance to work, which further suggests overlap with Moore's concept of learner autonomy.

In summary

This Chapter has presented an overview of humanist and distance education theorisations to highlight the importance of personal relations within online and blended learning environments. Some practical measures have been suggested to support such relationship development. Tutor ECs that can help have been identified, particularly empathy for adult learners undertaking vocationally relevant qualifications whilst in full-time employment. The next Chapter further considers effective teaching, learning and assessment for these particular learners.

References

Bar-On, R. (2006). The Bar-On model of emotional-social intelligence (ESI). *Psicothema, 18*, 13–25.

Biggs, J. (2003). *Teaching for quality learning at university* (2nd ed.). Maidenhead: Open University Press.

Bischoff, W., Bisconer, S., Kooker, B. M., & Woods, L. C. (1996). Transactional distance and interactive television in the distance education of health professionals. *American Journal of Distance Education, 10*(3), 4–19.

Boelens, R., De Wever, B., & Voet, M. (2017). Four key challenges to the design of blended learning: A systematic literature review. *Educational Research Review, 22*, 1–18. doi: 10.1016/j.edurev.2017.06.001.

Brindley, J., Blaschke, L. M., & Walti, C. (2009). Creating effective collaborative learning groups in an online environment. *The International Review of Research in Open and Distributed Learning, 10*(3), 1–18.

Chen, Y. J. (2001). Dimensions of transactional distance in world wide web learning environments: A factor analysis. *British Journal of Educational Technology, 52*(4), 327–338.

Creanor, L. (2002). A tale of two courses: A comparative study of tutoring online. *Open Learning: The Journal of Open, Distance and e-Learning, 17*(1), 57–68.

Dewey, J. (1938). *Experience and education*. New York: McMillan.

Falloon, G. (2011). Making the connection: Moore's theory of transactional distance and its relevance to the use of a virtual classroom in postgraduate online teacher education. *Journal of Research on Technology in Education, 43*(3), 187–209.

Garrison, D. R., Anderson, T., & Archer, W. (2000). Critical inquiry in a text-based environment: Computer conferencing in higher education model. *The Internet and Higher Education, 2*(2-3), 87–105.

Goel, L., Zhang, P., & Templeton, M. (2012). Transactional distance revisited: Bridging face and empirical validity. *Computers in Human Behaviour, 28*(4), 1122–1129.

Analysis of prominent distance education theorisations 93

Goleman, D. (2001). An EI-Based theory of performance. In C. Cherniss & D. Goleman (Eds.) *The emotionally intelligent workplace: How to select for, measure, and improve emotional intelligence in individuals, groups, and organization* (pp. 27–44). San Francisco, CA: Jossy-Bass.

Gorsky, P., & Caspi, A. (2005). A critical analysis of transactional distance theory. *The Quarterly Review of Distance Education, 6*(1), 1–11.

Holmberg, B. (1989). *Theory and practice of distance education.* London: Routledge.

Holmberg, B. (2003). A theory of distance education based on empathy. In M. G. Moore. & W. G. Anderson (Eds.) *Handbook of distance education* (pp. 79–86). Abingdon: Routledge.

Ke, F. (2010). Examining online teaching, cognitive, and social presence for adult students. *Computers & Education, 55*(2), 808–820.

Knowles, M. S., Holton, E. F., & Swanson, R. A. (2011). *The adult learner: The definitive classic in adult education and human resource development* (7th ed.). Woburn: Butterworth Heinemann.

Knowles, M. S., Holton, E. F., & Swanson, R. A. (2015). *The adult learner: The definitive classic in adult education and human resource development* (8th ed.). Abingdon: Routledge.

Laurillard, D. (2002). *Rethinking university teaching: A framework for the effective use of learning technologies* (2nd ed.). Abingdon, Oxfordshire: RoutledgeFalmer.

LeBaron, J., & McFadden, A. (2008). The brave new world of e-learning: A department's response to mandated change. *Interactive Learning Environments, 16*(2), 143–156.

MacDonald, J. (2006). *Blended learning and online tutoring: A good practice guide.* Aldershot: Gower.

MacDonald, J., & McAteer, E. (2003). New approaches to supporting students: Strategies for blended learning in distance and campus based environments. *Journal of Educational Media, 28*(2-3), 129–145.

Maslow, A. H. (1968). *Toward a psychology of being.* New York, NY: Van Nostrand.

Mclay, M., Mycroft, L., Noel, P., Orr, K., Thompson, R., Tummons, J., & Weatherby, J. (2019) Learning and learners. In J. Avis, R. Fisher, & R. Thompson (Eds.) *Teaching in lifelong learning: a guide to theory and practice* (3rd ed., pp. 81–107). Maidenhead: Open University Press.

Moore, M. G. (1997). Theory of transactional distance. In D. Keegan (Ed.) *Theoretical principles of distance education* (pp. 22–38). New York, NY: Routledge.

Moore, M. G. (2013) *Michael G Moore in interview with Steve Wheeler.* Retrieved from http:// www.youtube.com/watch?v=8OJuvcLGZz0.

Orton-Johnson, K. (2009). I've stuck to the path I'm afraid: Exploring student non-use of blended learning. *British Journal of Educational Technology, 40*(5), 837–847.

Ramsden, P. (1991). A performance indicator of teaching quality in higher education: The course experience questionnaire. *Studies in Higher Education, 16*, 129–150.

Rogers, C. R., & Freiberg, H. J. (1994). *Freedom to learn* (3rd ed.). Columbus, OH: Merrill-MacMillan.

Salmon, G. (2011). *E-moderating: The key to teaching & learning online* (3rd ed.). London: RoutledgeFalmer.

Sherratt, C. (2008). Working together: Perceptions of the role of the tutor in a postgraduate online learning programme. In International Conference on Networked Learning, Halkidiki, Greece. Retrieved from http://www.networkedlearningconference.org.uk/past/nlc2008/abstracts/PDFs/Sherratt_803-810.pdf

Shin, N. (2002). Beyond interaction: The relational construct of 'transactional presence'. *Open Learning, 17*(2), 121–137.

Smyth, S., & Houghton, C. (2012). Students' experiences of blended learning across a range of postgraduate programmes. *Nurse Education Today, 32*(4), 464–468.

Stubbs, M., Martin, I., & Endlar, L. (2006). The structuration of blended learning: Putting holistic design principles into practice. *British Journal of Educational Technology*, *37*(2). 163–175.

Wheeler, S. (2015). *Learning with 'e's*. Carmarthen: Crown House Publishing.

Youde, A. (2014). *A mixed methods exploration of effective tutors and tutoring in blended learning contexts* (Unpublished EdD Thesis, The University of Huddersfield, Huddersfield). Retrieved from http://eprints.hud.ac.uk/id/eprint/20351/

Youde, A. (2016). Tutor emotional competences valued by learners in a blended learning context. *European Journal of Open, Distance and E-Learning (EURODL)*, *19*(2), 81–97. doi: 10.1515/eurodl-2016-0008.

Youde, A. (2017). I don't need peer-support: Effective tutoring in blended learning environments for learners studying vocationally orientated degrees. In INTED 2017 Proceedings: 11th International Technology, Education and Development Conference, Valencia, Spain (pp. 1552–1561). doi 10.21125/inted.2017.0499

Youde, A. (2019). I don't need peer support: Effective tutoring in blended learning environments for part-time, adult learners. *Higher Education Research & Development*. doi:10.1080/07294360.2019.1704692.

Chapter 7

Effective teaching in online and blended learning environments

Introduction

This Chapter outlines prominent models and frameworks for effective e-tutoring within Higher Education (HE) and argues that these provide a sound theoretical basis for how to teach. However, they say little about the skills and competences e-tutors should possess to deliver effective practice in this context. Firstly, Mayes and de Freitas's (2007) three broad theoretical perspectives to inform online and blended learning design are outlined, which draw on Biggs' Constructive Alignment Model (2003). Then, key models and frameworks that have encouraged tutor/peer and peer-to-peer interaction are discussed. Garrison, Anderson, and Archer's (2000) conception of Social Presence builds from the discussion in the previous Chapter regarding distance education theorisations. Later models, such as Laurillard's Conversational Framework (2002) and Salmon's Five-Stage Model (2011), are critiqued regarding their suitability going forward given 'new' learner's and their personal learning networks (PLN) (Wheeler, 2015). This discussion is then developed to consider prominent theories of learning developed for the digital age – Connectivism, Heutagogy and Paragogy. Research is presented that adopted Mayes and de Freitas's (2007) perspectives to analyse blended learning provision with actions suggested to support effective tutoring in this context. This discussion is developed to explore effective teaching and learning on formal university courses for adults in the digital age.

Effective teaching in higher education

This Section outlines the findings of a literature review undertaken to develop an overview of effective teaching in HE. This provided the basis of a more detailed exploration of literatures that underpin the development of this and the next Chapter. They explore:

- effective teaching, learning, assessment and support in online and blended contexts (this Chapter)
- tutors' personal qualities and skills that support effective teaching in online and blended learning contexts (Chapter 8).

96 Models and frameworks for effective e-tutoring

In order to establish a broad list of competences necessary for successful tutoring in HE a scope of relevant literatures was undertaken, which were mainly promoting good practice in traditional delivery patterns. These sources included Biggs and Tang (2007), Carnell (2007), Devlin and Samarawickrema (2010), Ellington (2000), Kember and McNaught (2007), Minton (2005), and Nicoll and Harrison (2003), and they outlined key areas to explore when discussing effective online and blended tutors. The following competences and knowledge were discerned:

- an understanding of student learning and motivation
- the use of effective teaching and learning methods
- the use of effective assessment methods
- feedback on student work and monitoring their progress
- reflection on practice
- a commitment to continuing professional development
- to be organised
- the ability to work within available resources.

There are pertinent overlaps here with Youde's (2014, 2016) group of emotional competences contributing to the effectiveness of tutors within blended learning environments (see Chapter 4). Following data analysis, this was adapted from the prominent trait-based model of emotional intelligence (EI), Goleman's (2001, p. 1) Framework of Emotional Competence. Youde (2016) suggested an addition to Goleman's Self-Management competences to include Organisation, defined as the ability to plan work activities efficiently and to prioritise. The ability to work within available resources has resonance with prominent trait-based models of EI. This ability would be supported by Goleman's Self-management competences, Adaptability and Initiative, and Bar-On's (2006) Adaptability component, which is comprised of both Problem Solving and Flexibility competences. When considering a commitment to continuing professional development, again, there is resonance with these models, however, trait-based models suggest a greater drive for improvement than was unearthed in the literature review. This commitment suggests it would be underpinned by Goleman's Achievement Drive and Bar-On's Self-actualisation competences. Goleman (2001) defined Achievement Drive as tutors having an optimistic striving to continually improve performance, which does not align with the findings of the literature review as it advocated keeping up-to-date with relevant continuous professional development (CPD) activities. However, for deeply committed tutors, these competences could underpin a tutor's actions in achieving all the points listed above, for example, adopting new teaching and learning approaches to continually work towards and improve learner outcomes.

This Chapter now considers the teaching, learning and assessment elements above regarding effective practice within online and blended environments.

Effective teaching, learning and assessment in online and blended learning environments

This Section outlines a number of elements of effective practice in online and blended learning contexts, but particularly focuses on the 'alignment' of teaching, learning and assessment. In order to evaluate such practice, reference is made to Biggs' Constructive Alignment Model (2003) in which all components of teaching and learning are congruent or aligned. This approach is still significant in underpinning course design (Ruge, Tokede, & Tivendale, 2019). Mayes and de Freitas (2004, p. 7) draw on Biggs' Model (2003) when they present three broad theoretical perspectives to inform online and blended learning design. The perspectives have their origin in established education theory traditions (Mayes & de Freitas, 2004, p. 7), which further strengthen their value in evaluating learning designs. The HE student learning context involves networks of users sharing content and tools (Salmon, 2011; Wheeler, 2015), and Web 2.0[1] technologies affording greater collaboration (Beetham & Oliver, 2010, p. 157) in both formal and informal computer-mediated communications (CMCs). Further, effective teaching within HE has been broadly understood as focussed on students and their learning (Devlin & Samarawickrema, 2010, p. 112), and both Biggs' and Mayes and de Freitas' recommendations are consistent with this view and relevant for the student context.

Constructivist learning theory underpins Biggs' (2003) Model to indicate the level of understanding that is anticipated from a teaching experience. For example, is the aim for memorisation or analysis of a particular issue? Whatever the aim, it is important that learners construct their own understanding, and in their own way, for a teaching experience to be considered effective (Biggs, 2003, p. 27). Biggs (2003, p. 26) argues that when the following components are aligned, teaching is likely to be more effective:

- curriculum
- teaching methods
- assessment
- the climate teachers create with their interactions with students
- institutional climate.

An imbalance between these components can lead to poor teaching and Surface approaches to study, where learners complete only the required activities in order to achieve desired outcomes (Biggs, Kember, & Leung, 2001, p. 138). When all components are working towards a common goal, it is more likely that Deep approaches are adopted where learners use the highest level of learning activities (Biggs et al., 2001, p. 138; see Chapter 5 for a more detailed discussion of Deep and Surface approaches to study). For example, lectures may not be the most appropriate way to encourage trainee teachers

98 Models and frameworks for effective e-tutoring

to see the value of small group work. A more suitable approach to achieve the session's aims and encourage deeper approaches to study may be participation in group work activities with reflection on the experience afterwards (Biggs, 2003, p. 27).

Effective teaching must continue to evolve so it reflects and responds to the context in which the teaching and learning is occurring (Devlin & Samarawickrema, 2010, p. 111). As stated above, when aligned, teaching is likely to be more effective (Biggs, 2003, p. 26) and Mayes and de Freitas' (2004, p. 7) perspectives suggest suitable approaches to online and blended learning contexts. Their three broad theoretical perspectives on learning are:

- the associationist/empiricist perspective (learning as activity)
- the constructivist perspective[2] (learning as achieving understanding through individual or social approaches)
- the situative perspective (learning as social practice).

Mayes and de Freitas (2007, p. 20) state, "most implementations of e-learning will include online and blended elements that emphasise all three levels: learning as behaviour, learning as the construction of knowledge and meaning, and learning as social practice", and this may be expected when delivering a larger unit of study in HE, such as a module. These perspectives are now outlined with discussion of their 'alignment', particularly with regard to teaching, learning and assessment.

The Associationist Perspective regards learning as acquiring competence through learners obtaining knowledge by building associations using different concepts, with skills being developed as a result of increasingly complex actions. The pedagogy aligning with this perspective includes consideration of competences, organised activities, progressive difficulties with clear goals and feedback, including repetition and Socratic dialogue (Laurillard, 2002, p. 87), with assessments requiring accurate reproduction of knowledge or skill. An e-learning example of this perspective would be a competency-based software programme commonly used in HE around areas of compliance. The user navigates through screens of information, around data protection for example, and then completes a test at the end. This has to be passed for the HE organisation to prove that it has conducted necessary training and it has been, in their view, effective. Within HE learning contexts this perspective could be valuable when it is necessary to know (or transmit) key information within a disciplinary area from the teacher to the learner, for example, key legislation for Law students and safeguarding procedures for teachers.

The Constructivist Perspective has both an individual and social focus that advocates learning as achieving understanding in individual and collaborative contexts (Beetham & Sharpe, 2007, p. 220). Fox (2001, p. 31) argues that it is important for tutors to realise students are always trying to make sense

Models and frameworks for effective e-tutoring 99

of their study in terms of what they already know. This is relevant for adult learners who are trying to apply their learning to work practices, organisational issues and a turbulent external environment (Beetham, 2012, p. 8). Such learners are professionals and bring a breadth of existing knowledge, understanding and experiences to the classroom (Fox, 2001, p. 29), and this highlights the relevance of exploring constructivist learning theory when exploring effective online and blended learning for adult learners.

The Individual Constructivist Perspective (ICP) highlights the achievement of understanding through active discovery where learners construct new ideas by hypothesis testing (Mayes & de Freitas, 2007). The pedagogy aligning with this perspective includes interactive environments for knowledge expansion, cognitive scaffolding, experimentation with the discovery of principles, adaptation of teaching to existing student understanding, and support for reflection, analysis and evaluation. Assessment strategies aligning with this perspective encourage experiential learning, experimental learning, problem-based learning, case-based learning and self-evaluation, and autonomy in learning. Within online and blended learning contexts, I consider this perspective as one which primarily focuses on students learning independently from tutors and peers. However, tutors provide support to learners, engage in dialogue regarding learning and assessment, but with limited peer interaction and collaboration occurring outside any face-to-face classes.

The Social Constructivist Perspective (SCP) highlights the achievement of understanding through collaboration and dialogue (Mayes & de Freitas, 2007). The pedagogy aligning with this perspective includes interactive and collaborative environments leading to conceptual development; support for reflection, peer review and evaluation; and experimentation with shared discovery. Assessments aligning with this perspective are common to the IPC, however, include consideration of collaborative activities, participation, peer review and shared responsibility. Within online and blended learning contexts, I consider this perspective includes a far greater focus on peer collaboration throughout teaching, learning and assessment, particularly outside any face-to-face classes and within online learning environments.

The Situative Perspective has grown in prominence within online and blended learning discourse to consider the social and cultural setting of the learning environment (Mayes & de Freitas, 2007, p. 18). Here, learning is understood as developing practice in a particular community (Lave & Wenger, 1991). The structural characteristics of a community of practice include a domain of knowledge, a notion of community, and a practice (Wenger, McDermott, & Snyder, 2002). The domain of knowledge creates common ground, such as topic of study in HE, inspires members to participate, guides their learning and gives meaning to their actions. The community creates the social environment for that learning, encouraging a sharing of ideas, collaboration and interaction. The practice is the focus around which the learning and subsequent knowledge is developed, commonly through the above community interactions (Wenger et al., 2002).

Situative learning extends social constructivist theory by emphasising the context being close or identical to the situation in which the learner practices, with common examples in educational contexts including work-based learning, continuing professional development, and apprenticeships (Mayes & de Freitas, 2007). Relevant pedagogic approaches to support situative learning include participation in social practices of enquiry and learning; facilitation of the development of skills, identities and professional relationships; and dialogue to support the development of learning relationships. Appropriate assessment strategies aligning with the Situative Perspective include extending performance in a variety of contexts and the authenticity of practice. The potential vocational orientation of online and blended courses for adult learners promote the relevance of this perspective within these contexts. Teaching may occur within face-to-face and online environments, but learning and assessment could exhibit Situative Perspective characteristics.

Fox (2001, p. 29) warns against adopting extreme statements about learning such as "all knowledge is socially constructed", providing a reminder that individual and social approaches co-exist. When evaluating online and blended practices tutors should be mindful of this and use these categories as broad indicators of the overall approaches being adopted. However, these perspectives articulate an 'aligned' approach to teaching, learning and assessment that can lead to effective practice within online and blended HE courses, particularly at unit or modular level.

Prominent e-learning frameworks and models

As the affordances of online and blended learning became apparent at the start of the twenty-first century, a range of models and frameworks emerged that aimed to understand, guide and enhance HE practice. This Section considers the most prominent of these by outlining their key features and discussing their relevance in the current e-tutoring context. Although there were notable exceptions (for example, e-training models discussed below), these models and frameworks tended to be social constructivist in orientation, in that, understanding is achieved through collaboration and dialogue (Mayes & de Freitas, 2007).

E-training models

Mclay et al., (2019, p. 88) note that "behaviourism attempts to approach learning scientifically, with an accumulation of knowledge based on repeatable and verifiable experiments", and this theory of the learning process underpins a range of approaches to e-learning. Mayes and de Freitas (2004, p. 28) conclude that a range of e-learning applications have emerged, driven by organisational training needs, and rooted in an instruction systems design perspective (ISD). These models' defining characteristics are:

- the identification of clear learning outcomes in terms of the subject matter or skill to be mastered
- the instructional method involves achieving the learning outcomes in a hierarchical 'bottom-up' analysis of the domain or skill
- the role for technology will usually involve a simulation of a process and the automatic presentation of problems or routines that have been carefully graded in difficulty
- assessment may be automated: both for progress through the stages of the required mastery, and for summative performance measures (Mayes & de Freitas, 2004, p. 28).

Mayes and de Freitas' (2007) Associative Perspective has roots in this approach to both teaching and learning, and the affordances to online and blended tutors are similar to those described in that Section above. E-training models' key utility is when the transmission of information is required from tutor to learner.

Salmon's five-stage model (e-tivities approach)

This model aids the design of online courses or units, as well as, describing the stages of learning, interactivity and socialisation through which learners and tutors may progress as they undertake their study (Salmon, 2011). The stages include roles and actions for tutors and, within HE, are usually developed around a virtual learning environment (VLE) with asynchronous communication facilities. Given the suggested interaction between tutors and peers, the Model would be considered social constructivist in orientation, particularly when used with adult learners who are likely to be drawing on past experiences as part of their study. Other educational technologies such as synchronous online conferences, blogs, wikis and e-portfolios can be incorporated into a unit or course designed around this Model. The five stages are:

- access and motivation
- online socialisation
- information exchange
- knowledge construction
- development.

The Model promotes tutor-learner dialogue and peer collaboration to encourage learning and understanding. Its early stages focus on preparing students for online learning by considering access, motivation and introductions to their peers. Following this, deeper learning approaches are encouraged as

102   Models and frameworks for effective e-tutoring

information is exchanged, knowledge constructed through discussion and, finally, a metacognitive process that "promotes integration and application of learning experiences" (Salmon, 2011, p. 48). At the later stages it is natural for the students to reflect, both on their learning throughout the course, but also on the online learning experience.

A limitation of Salmon's Model is the assumption that any tutor can be effective by following the stages and suggested actions. However, interpersonal and intrapersonal skills are required in the tutor to motivate and engage learners in online environments (Salmon, 2011). Chapter 10 suggests practical online tutoring methods that can support tutor engagement and enhance the actions suggested by this Model.

Laurillard's conversational framework

This Framework (Laurillard, 2002) was designed for HE and, given its promotion of tutor/learner dialogue, appears social constructivist in orientation. Its key focus is guidance for tutors when teaching individual learners; however, it has a much broader scope. The Framework characterises the teaching-learning process as an iterative conversation in a similar fashion to Kolb's (1984) Experiential Learning Cycle (see Chapter 5). It outlines the dialogic relationships between the teacher and student, and includes (Laurillard, 2002, p. 86):

- discursive processes – description of topic goal
- adaptive processes – internal to both teacher and student, adapts actions to task level
- interactive processes – activities to achieve task goal
- reflective processes – internal to both teacher and student, reflect on activity's achievement of topic goal.

The Framework represents both a design model for online and blended educational environments, and a theory of learning. It includes twelve types of interactions (see Figure 7.1 for an outline), which are seen as essential to the learning process and are based around the four process types outlined above.

This approach provides a framework for engaging learners in online discussions and allows a tutor to evaluate the scope and variety of communications in a course (Bennett & Youde, 2010). However, in a similar criticism to that made of Salmon's Model above, there is the assumption implied that any tutor can be effective using this approach. Laurillard (2002) emphasises the importance of student feedback in the learning process, but notes that it can be limited in HE environments. More generally, the Conversational Framework requires a level of dialogue and feedback that can be difficult to maintain with the large groups commonly found in HE (Bennett & Youde, 2010).

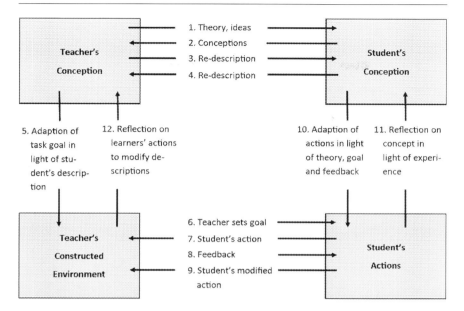

Figure 7.1 Laurillard's (2002, p. 87) conversational framework.

Community of inquiry framework

Unlike Salmon's and Laurillard's approaches that provide guidance to tutors communicating with learners, Garrison et al. (2000) Community of Inquiry Framework's (see Figure 7.2) 'raison d'être' is to evaluate online learning environments. Like Knowles' theory of Andragogy (Knowles, Holton, & Swanson, 2015) described in Chapter 5, this Framework has its origins in the work of Dewey and aligns with constructivist approaches to learning in HE (Garrison & Arbaugh, 2007, p. 158).

The Framework suggests three key elements that are required for effective online learning:

- cognitive presence – "the extent to which the participants in any particular configuration of a community of inquiry are able to construct meaning through sustained communication" (Garrison et al., 2000, p. 89)
- social presence – "the ability of participants in the Community of Inquiry to project their personal characteristics into the community, thereby presenting themselves to the other participants as 'real people'" (Garrison et al., 2000, p. 89)
- teaching presence – "the design, facilitation, and direction of cognitive and social processes for the purpose of realizing personally meaningful and educationally worthwhile learning outcomes" (Garrison & Arbaugh, 2007, p. 163).

104 Models and frameworks for effective e-tutoring

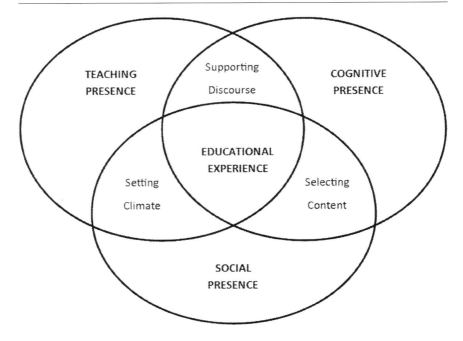

Figure 7.2 Community of inquiry framework (Garrison et al., 2000, p. 88).

All three elements must be evident within online environments for significant learning outcomes to be achieved (Garrison et al., 2000). However, limited suggestions are made regarding the skills, qualities and attributes that are required of the tutor to ensure such achievement. For example, Garrison and Arbaugh (2007, p. 160) state "a clear understanding of how social presence shifts or evolves in a purposeful online community is required". Do all tutors possess the required inter and intra-personal skills to facilitate this? This conception of social presences builds on the discussion of prominent distance education theories (see Chapter 6) as it goes some way to bridge the Transactional Distance that can be experienced between tutors and their learners (Moore, 1997).

Garrison and Arbaugh (2007, p. 163) cite a range of sources to argue that "teaching presence is a significant determinant of student satisfaction, perceived learning, and sense of community". This element is comprised of three dimensions (Garrison & Arbaugh, 2007):

- instructional design and organisation
- facilitating discourse
- direct instruction.

Key tutor competences are implied in these dimensions. Regarding instructional design and organisation, competence at structuring learning environments and

Models and frameworks for effective e-tutoring   105

planning interaction is required. Again, key inter and intra-personal skills are required to facilitate discourse as Garrison and Arbaugh (2007, p. 164) state this role "is associated with sharing meaning, identifying areas of agreement and disagreement, and seeking to reach consensus and understanding". Further, these skills are required to know when direct instruction is required that is both purposeful and motivational. This aligns with the findings from Chapter 5 that argued that for effective teaching in online and blended learning environments some transmission of key information was required from tutors.

This discussion of the teaching presence dimension highlights the complexity of tutoring in this area and the demands placed on the tutor to deliver an effecting learning experience. Chapter 4 noted the self-management competences required to underpin effective practice, such as trustworthiness, conscientiousness, adaptability, organisation, coping potential and initiative (Youde, 2016). Such competences are underestimated by the Community of Inquiry Framework. This, coupled with the understanding required regarding cognitive and social presence, highlight the range of skills, competences and attributes needed when e-tutoring. Chapter 8 develops this area further when considering tutor competences, skills and beliefs supporting effective teaching in online and blended learning contexts.

Drawing on the work of Cleveland-Innes and Campbell (2012) and Stenbom, Cleveland-Innes, and Hrastinski (2014), Rienties and Rivers (2014) suggest an extension to Garrison et al., (2000) Community of Inquiry Framework to include emotional presence. This is defined as "the outward expression of emotion, affect, and feeling by individuals and among individuals in a community of inquiry, as they relate to and interact with the learning technology, course content, students, and the instructor" (Cleveland-Innes & Campbell, 2012, p. 283). This growing body of research considering emotional presence highlights the importance of tutor EI to, for example, accurately appraise and express emotion; and the ability to understand emotion and emotional knowledge (Mayer & Salovey, 1997, p. 10). Emotions can occur at any time in the learning process, they can vary in responses from learner to learner, and, therefore, are a clear and distinct aspect of the Community of Inquiry Framework (Rienties & Rivers, 2014, p. 6). This promotes the significance of EI when tutoring in online and blended learning environments. Practical tutor actions are presented in Chapter 10 to help understand and manage learner emotions, and consider in greater depth issues arising from the above definition of emotional presence.

Challenges to social constructive approaches to teaching and learning within online and blended environments

There are challenges to tutors when adopting the above perspectives, models and frameworks in their teaching, and this Section now moves on to consider some of these, and in particular, the influence of competing demands of work and family on part-time (PT) learners.

Social constructivist approaches can be challenging to implement in online and blended learning contexts, given the limited face-to-face contact and the difficulties of collaborating through CMCs. Mason (2006, p. 131) considers collaborative learning as time consuming and inefficient, which is particularly relevant for adult learners studying at a distance. Learner participation can be challenging, given competing demands, but this can be aided when communication media are asynchronous. However, such participation and collaboration requires demanding skills of the online tutor with regard to what Feenberg (1989, cited in Salmon, 2003, p. 42) termed "weaving", which is the act of pulling the debate together, and can include summarising general themes, linking similar viewpoints, and relating personal experiences back to theories previously studied. Tutors developing a 'sense of community' amongst peers can overcome some of the challenges learners feel when studying online or at a distance (as discussed in Chapter 6), such as isolation (Abdous, 2011; Bernard, et al., 2009; Brindley, Blaschke, & Walti, 2009). However, online collaboration can lead to limited, superficial discussions, which can be grade-driven rather than purposeful collective inquiry (Ke, 2010), and can be challenging for tutors to facilitate. Finally, are such frameworks promoting socially constructivist approaches fit for adults learning in the digital age?

Learning theories for twenty-first century adults

This book has outlined the current e-learning context that online and blended tutors now practice within (see Chapter 1), and particularly in relation to the needs of adult learners (see Chapter 5). The previous Section argued that frameworks promoting social constructivist approaches within the formal confines of a HE course or unit of study, may not be appropriate for 'new' learners (see Chapter 1), with their self-directed learning, commonly undertaken through their personal and profession learning networks (Wheeler, 2015). Given the proliferation of resources on the internet, coupled with a growth in mobile devices and social media becoming integral to student learning as a communication channel, a number of learning theories have emerged for the digital age (Wheeler, 2015). Three prominent theories, Connectivism, Heutagogy and Paragogy, are now outlined before a discussion of their relevance for tutors within online and blended learning is presented. The Section concludes with a proposed approach that is supportive of learners, but affords the benefits suggested by these 'new' learning theories.

There are two key aspects of commonality between these theories, non-linearity and learner self-direction. Traditional teaching contexts, like a unit of study in HE, are commonly quite linearly structured. Learners are typically taken through a series of lectures, the content of which is decided by the tutor, with the summative assessment occurring near the end. Within online contexts, the E-training Models discussed earlier in this Chapter are relevant examples of such a linear approach. However, learning in the digital age is less structured, particularly in informal contexts, as adults drive exploration of their study through online resources and personal networks. This requires self-direction with learners having the appropriate digital literacies to find, critique, evaluate, adapt and use information for their specific learning need, whilst understanding their own strengths and weaknesses throughout this process.

Ausburn's (2004) study explored the course design elements most valued by 67 adult learners, with learner self-direction one of the key aspects identified. However, within formal education environments, such self-direction, particularly for adult learners returning to study, can be challenging. Chapter 5 introduced Knowles' theory of Andragogy and its constituent core principles (Knowles et al., 2015), which included the learners' self-concept: adults need to be responsible for their decisions on education. However, the Chapter argued that adults often want to be passive in the learning process (Knowles, Holton & Swanson, 2011, p. 63), but treating them in such a manner can cause tensions considering their need for self-direction. Some HE learners are non-traditional university entrants, who may not have experienced formal education since school and may feel more comfortable in passive learning environments. Effective tutors can develop learning structures that support adults in making the transition from dependent to self-directing learners (Knowles et al., 2011, p. 65). The approach suggested at the end of this Section includes the benefits of both structure and support, but allows for learner self-direction within the learning process.

Connectivism

This learning theory considers the impact of digital technologies and the new opportunities these create for learning and developing personal connections (Siemens, 2005). Although more focussed on informal and lifelong learning contexts, its relevance for this book is in developing understanding of the learning process adult learners may be undertaking while undertaking formal HE courses. The principles of Connectivism are:

- learning and knowledge rests in diversity of opinions
- learning is a process of connecting specialised nodes or information sources
- learning may reside in non-human appliances
- capacity to know more is more critical than what is currently known
- nurturing and maintaining connections is needed to facilitate continual learning
- ability to see connections between fields, ideas and concepts is a core skill

- currency (accurate, up-to-date knowledge) is the intent of all connectivist learning activities
- decision-making is itself a learning process. Choosing what to learn and the meaning of incoming information is seen through the lens of a shifting reality. While there is a right answer now, it may be wrong tomorrow due to alterations in the information climate affecting the decision (Siemens, 2005).

The principles encapsulate the range and variety of information sources available to adult learners, both contained in databases of information and other human beings around the world. They further suggest digital literacies (see Chapter 1) necessary for effective learning in this context. As Wheeler (2015, p. 37) states "Connectivism places the onus firmly upon individual students to develop their own personalised learning tools, environments, learning networks and communities, where they can 'store their knowledge'".

Heutagogy

Wheeler (2015, p. 39) notes that Heutagogy and the conceptualisation of self-determined learning embrace both formal and informal education contexts, hence their relevance for this book. It is defined as "self-determined learning", with a focus on what the learner wants to learn, and not what is taught (Hase & Kenyon, 2013, p. 7). This definition and focus naturally encompass most forms of informal learning where learners' hobbies and interests drive the study. However, Hase and Kenyon (2013, p. 8) cite an example of Heutagogy within a formal HE context. Here the learner has:

- a guided choice of topic
- a guided approach to the proposed learning
- agreement on reporting progress
- agreement on the content and method of final assessment.

These have to be discussed and agreed with a course or unit tutor.

Heutagogy, within formal learning environments, brings both benefits and challenges, although, the benefits are more greatly felt by the learner and the challenges by the provider. The learners are more active in the process, they develop skills in becoming self-directing, and they tend to be more satisfied given they are driving the study (Hase & Kenyon, 2013, p. 14). For universities, the negotiations outlined above between tutors and learners take time and need to be recorded. Assessments would need some comparability with others undertaking the unit to ensure equity. Finally,

Models and frameworks for effective e-tutoring 109

there are potential cultural tensions from adopting this approach as universities shift practices regarding teaching and move from a position of providing information and experiences to the learner (Hase & Kenyon, 2013, p. 14). Wheeler (2015, p. 39) states the central tenet of Heutagogy is that, inherently, learners know how to learn, however, this can be a challenge as adults arrive at university, a potentially unfamiliar environment to them (as it is to all new undergraduates).

Paragogy

This is a theory of peer-to-peer teaching and learning (Corneli & Danoff, 2011). Chapter 1 outlined an e-tutoring context, including the pervasiveness of mobile technologies and technological convergence (Wheeler, 2012, 2015), which would enable effective peer-to-peer collaboration in online and blended learning environments. Corenli and Danoff's theory was developed from their teaching of two online courses and from their consideration of Knowles' theory of Andragogy and its core principles (Knowles et al., 2015). They were particularly influenced by Blondy's (2007) evaluation and application of andragogical assumptions to adult online learning environments. When comparing Paragogy with Andragogy, Corenli and Danoff draw on Blondy's work to argue the challenge of learner self-direction, particularly regarding a lack of understanding of learning, and, therefore, learners need guidance and encouragement throughout the process. Such a facilitator, as stated necessary by Knowles, is not always required in peer-based settings where the "task of facilitation is shared among all participants or even encoded in the learning materials or supportive technologies" (Corneli & Danoff, 2011, p. 4).

This book has argued that effective peer-to-peer collaboration is challenging within online and blended learning environments. Whilst Corneli and Danoff's (2011) theory outlines a more complex process than just collaboration, two significant literature reviews of effective blended learning have both found stimulating effective peer-to-peer interaction as difficult (Boelens, De Wever, & Voet, 2017; Smith & Hill, 2019). Learners may have competing pressures, such as work and family commitments, and may be undertaking study for instrumental purposes, such as for promotion opportunities. Further, peer-collaboration can be limited when it does not form part of the summative assessment (Youde, 2014, 2017). Wheeler (2015, p. 40) considers quality, reliability and provenance of content as significant issues for Paragogy within formal education contexts, whilst citing Corneli and Danoff regarding the challenge this theory presents to the "privileged knowledge and power structures many formal education institutions continue to hold dear". Each of these factors could be influencing collaboration within online and blended learning environments. However, technologies and software

110 Models and frameworks for effective e-tutoring

allowing co-production of resources, asynchronously, at a distance, should see this challenge fading in the future.

An approach to effective teaching, learning and assessment within a blended learning environment

This Section proposes a module approach to teaching, learning, assessment and support for learners undertaking part-time, vocational degrees (Youde, 2014, 2017, 2019). Constructivist models of e-learning predominantly promote opportunities for peer interaction within formal, online university learning environments. Given the rise of social media engagement within society (Dabbagh & Kitsantas, 2012), new learning theories for the digital age, and PLNs (Wheeler, 2015), there are challenges for tutors in online and blended contexts to provide such opportunities for social constructivist learning experiences. As a result, Youde (2014, 2019) proposed an alternative approach for a social media rich external environment.

Youde's (2014, 2019) research noted that effective teaching was associated with the congruent nature of teaching, learning and assessment suggested by the Individual Constructivist Perspective (Mayes & de Freitas, 2007), which appears appropriate for learners studying PT vocationally relevant degrees at a distance. This Perspective highlights the achievement of active discovery where learners construct new ideas through hypothesis testing. This was apparent from the 'facilitative' teaching style adopted by all tutors within face-to-face contexts, but was further evidenced through the problem-based and case-method assessments adopted on the modules. The extent of learners working independently, particularly on module assessments, outside face-to-face contexts, resonated with individual constructivism as they were student-centred, encouraging experimentation and application of theory to practice. This led to a predominant module approach of individual student-centred pedagogy aligned with problem-based learning and assessment. In addition, modules were generally structured around assessment requirements, both formative and summative (see Chapter 5 for a more detailed discussion of module assessment). Clear goals and standards were apparent in detailed assessment briefs, some exemplar material, with dates set for both formative and summative aspects, commonly structured around face-to-face sessions. This level of structure appeared appropriate for PT, mature learners managing the influence of daily events, together with pressures and time constraints of work. Further, available and proactive tutor support was associated with module success.

This approach to teaching provides some structure and tutor facilitation, hence supporting adults in making the transition from dependent to self-directing learners (Knowles et al., 2015). However, there is scope for the learners' self-concept: adults need to be responsible for their decisions on education (Knowles et al., 2015). This was particularly evident in learners having choice over assessment focus, with assignment work rooted in work problems, and their ability to work independently between face-to-face sessions. When considering Hase and Kenyon's (2013, p. 8) Heutagogical approach within a HE context (see Heutagogy Section), there are commonalities with the effective teaching suggested by Youde (2014, 2019). Learners had a choice of topic for their assessment and the assessment structure provided a guided approach to the proposed learning. However, this structure provided the agreement on reporting progress, which learners had little choice over. Further, there was agreement on the content of the assessment, as suggested above to provide learner choice in this area, but there were no discussions regarding the summative assessment method.

Although the modules were found to be successful, there was minimal peer engagement evident, particularly within the course VLE (Youde 2014, 2019). The research found challenges for tutors to encourage learners to participate in online peer activities with the VLE analysis noting limited engagement on all modules. This does not mean, however, that learners are not communicating with peers, given the affordances of communication and social media technologies. Or that learners need to be communicating with their peers at all as support may be available through other networks, particularly as these learners are generally in work and undertaking study and assignments relevant to their professional contexts. These findings beg the following question: if learners are not engaging with peers within the formal module confines, who are they engaging with to support their degree studies? PT learners undertaking vocationally relevant qualifications could be drawing on their Personal or Professional Learning Networks (Wheeler, 2015) quite extensively to support their studies, hence, not requiring engagement with peers within online elements of university study. Such interactions could be more valuable than discussing the issue with course peers given the increased knowledge base available from, for example, a specific professional network. Siemens' (2005) assertion that "formal education no longer comprises the majority of our learning. Learning now occurs in a variety of ways – through communities of practice, personal networks, and through completion of work-related tasks", appears relevant for adult learners studying in online and blended contexts.

In today's social media rich society, Individual Constructivist Perspective approaches (Mayes & de Freitas, 2007) could be a suitable to allow time for learners to draw further on their own learning networks (Wheeler, 2015). They allow self-direction and a non-linear approach to learning, as suggested by Connectivism and Heutagogy, and access to a wealth of resources on the internet and in networks. Further, the ICP provides some structure and support for learners, which can help mitigate Wheeler's (2015, p. 40) concern regarding the quality, reliability and provenance of content of information found in such environments. The tutor's role in developing both digital

112 Models and frameworks for effective e-tutoring

literacies and traditional academic skills, such as evaluating a source's validity, are vital when adopting this teaching approach (Youde, 2019).

The ICP approach contradicts the recommendations of social constructivist models of e-learning, which commonly promote opportunities for peer interaction within online, formal university learning environments, The Five-Stage Model (Salmon, 2011), for example. Youde's (2014, 2019) research found learners' peer support and collaboration occurred mainly at face-to-face sessions with tutors having limited success in encouraging this interaction within formal online communication media. Online strategies to encourage peer interaction included synchronous conferencing, wikis and discussion boards to showcase elements of practice and outline plans for assessment, with tutors and VLE analysis identifying limited learner engagement.

In summary

This Chapter has presented a framework for the effective tutoring of adult learners undertaking PT vocationally related, HE qualifications within a blended learning environment. The framework is rooted in an appropriate theoretical base and provides tutors with an approach to teaching, learning and assessment that is relevant for today's learners. Learner perceptions of quality were found to be influenced by proactive support, with the following Chapter further considering the necessary skills, competences and roles of effective tutors in online and blended contexts.

Notes

1. When discussing e-learning, the labels web 1.0, web 2.0 and web 3.0 are commonly cited. Web 1.0 refers to a time when the web was largely 'read only' with limited interaction between users and sites. As users could increasingly interact with websites, the 'write' phase or web 2.0 emerged. Participation, sharing and collaboration now became common as, for example, videos were shared with their content discussed below. Co-production of content grew, the Wikipedia online encyclopaedia being a prominent example. As mobile technologies became common alongside smart applications and personalised content, web 3.0 was born. Websites can introduce tailored and selected content to users by monitoring their online habits and behaviours.
2. Mayes and de Freitas (2004) originally termed this the cognitive perspective but this has since been developed in the course of work in e-learning and pedagogy funded by Jisc.

References

Abdous, M. (2011). A process-oriented framework for acquiring online teaching competencies. *Journal of Computing in Higher Education, 23*(1), 60–77.

Ausburn, L. J. (2004). Course design elements most valued by adult learners in blended online education environments: An American perspective. *Educational Media International, 41*, 327–337. doi: 10.1080/0952398042000314820.

Bar-On, R. (2006). The Bar-On model of emotional-social intelligence (ESI). *Psicothema*, *18*, 13–25.

Beetham, H. (2012). *Institutional approaches to curriculum design: Full synthesis report.* Retrieved from http://repository.jisc.ac.uk/5081/1/JISC_Curriculum_Design_Final_Synthesis_i1.pdf

Beetham, H., & Oliver, M. (2010). The changing practices of knowledge and learning. In R. Sharpe, H. Beetham, & S. de Freitas (Eds.) *Rethinking learning for a digital age* (pp. 155–169). Oxford: Routledge.

Beetham, H., & Sharpe, R. (2007). An introduction to rethinking pedagogy for a digital age. In H. Beetham & R. Sharpe (Eds.) *Rethinking pedagogy for a digital age* (pp. 1–10). London: Routledge.

Bennett, E, & Youde, A. (2010). E-tutoring. In J. Avis, R. Fisher, & R. Thompson (Eds.) *Teaching in lifelong learning: A guide to theory and practice* (pp. 154–162). Maidenhead: Open University Press.

Bernard, R. M., Abrami, P. C., Borokhovski, E., Wade, C. A., Tamim, R. M., Surkes M. A., & Bethel, E. C. (2009). A meta-analysis of three types of interaction treatments in distance education. *Review of Educational Research, 79*, 1243–1289.

Biggs, J. (2003). *Teaching for quality learning at university* (2nd ed.). Maidenhead: Open University Press.

Biggs, J. B., Kember, D., & Leung, D. Y. P. (2001). The revised two-factor study process questionnaire: R-SPQ-2F. *British Journal of Educational Psychology, 71*, 133–149.

Biggs, J., & Tang, C. (2007). *Teaching for quality learning at university* (3rd ed.). Maidenhead: Open University Press.

Blondy, L. C. (2007). Evaluation and application of andragogical assumptions to the adult online learning environment. *Journal of Interactive Online Learning, 6*(2), 116–130.

Boelens, R., De Wever, B., & Voet, M. (2017). Four key challenges to the design of blended learning: A systematic literature review. *Educational Research Review, 22*, 1–18. doi: 10.1016/j.edurev.2017.06.001.

Brindley, J., Blaschke, L. M., & Walti, C. (2009). Creating effective collaborative learning groups in an online environment. *The International Review of Research in Open and Distributed Learning, 10*(3), 1-18. doi: https://doi.org/10.19173/irrodl.v10i3.675.

Carnell, E. (2007). Conceptions of effective teaching in higher education: Extending the boundaries. *Teaching in Higher Education, 12*(1), 25–40.

Cleveland-Innes, M., & Campbell, P. (2012). Emotional presence, learning, and the online learning environment. *The International Review of Research in Open and Distributed Learning, 13*(4), 269–292.

Corneli, J., & Danoff, C. J. (2011). *Paragogy: Synergizing individual and organizational learning.* Retrieved from https://upload.wikimedia.org/wikiversity/en/6/60/Paragogy-final.pdf

Dabbagh, N., & Kitsantas, A. (2012). Personal learning environments, social media, and self-regulated learning: A natural formula for connecting formal and informal learning. *Internet and Higher Education, 15*(1), 3–8. doi: 10.1016/j.iheduc.2011.06.002.

Devlin, M., & Samarawickrema, G. (2010). The criteria of effective teaching in a higher education context. *Higher Education Research & Development, 29*(2), 111–124.

Ellington, H. (2000). How to become an excellent tertiary-level teacher: Seven golden rules for university and college lecturers. *Journal of Further and Higher Education, 24*(3), 311–321.

Fox, R. (2001). Constructivism examined. *Oxford Review of Education, 27*(1), 23–35. doi: 10.1080/03054980125310.

Garrison, D. R., & Arbaugh, J. B. (2007). Researching the community of inquiry framework: Review, issues, and future directions. *The Internet and Higher Education, 10*(3), 157–172.

114 Models and frameworks for effective e-tutoring

Garrison, D. R., Anderson, T., & Archer, W. (2000). Critical inquiry in a text-based environment: Computer conferencing in higher education model. *The Internet and Higher Education*, 2(2-3), 87–105.

Goleman, D. (2001). An EI-based theory of performance. In C. Cherniss & D. Goleman (Eds.) *The emotionally intelligent workplace: How to select for, measure, and improve emotional intelligence in individuals, groups, and organization* (pp. 27–44). San Francisco, CA: Jossy-Bass.

Hase, S., & Kenyon, C. (2013). Heutagogy fundamentals. In S. Hase & C. Kenyon (Eds.) *Self-determined learning: Heutagogy in action* (pp. 7–18). London: Bloomsbury.

Ke, F. (2010). Examining online teaching, cognitive, and social presence for adult students. *Computers & Education*, 55(2), 808–820.

Kember, D., & McNaught, C. (2007). *Enhancing university teaching*. London: Routledge.

Knowles, M. S., Holton, E. F., & Swanson, R. A. (2011). *The adult learner: The definitive classic in adult education and human resource development* (7th ed.). Woburn: Butterworth Heinemann.

Knowles, M. S., Holton, E. F., & Swanson, R. A. (2015). *The adult learner: The definitive classic in adult education and human resource development* (8th ed.). Abingdon: Routledge.

Kolb, D. A. (1984). *Experiential learning: Experience as the source of learning and development.* Englewood Cliffs, NJ: Prentice Hall.

Laurillard, D. (2002). *Rethinking university teaching: A framework for the effective use of learning technologies* (2nd ed). Abingdon, Oxfordshire: RoutledgeFalmer.

Lave, J., & Wenger, E. (1991). *Situated learning: Legitimate peripheral participation.* Cambridge, UK: Cambridge University Press.

Mason, R. (2006). Learning technologies for adult continuing education. *Studies in Continuing Education*, 23(2), 121–133.

Mayer, J. D., & Salovey, P. (1997). What is emotional intelligence? In P. Salovey & D. Sluyter (Eds.) *Emotional development and emotional intelligence: Implications for educators* (pp. 3–31). New York: Basic Books.

Mayes, T., & de Freitas, S. (2004). *JISC e-learning models desk study: Stage 2: Review of e-learning theories, frameworks and models.* Retrieved from http://www.jisc.ac.uk/uploaded_documents/Stage%202%20Learning%20Models%20(Version%201).pdf

Mayes, T., & de Freitas, S. (2007). Learning and e-learning: The role of theory. In H. Beetham & R. Sharpe (Eds.) *Rethinking pedagogy for a digital age: Designing and delivering e-learning* (pp. 13–25). Abingdon, Oxfordshire: Routledge.

Mclay, M., Mycroft, L., Noel, P., Orr, K., Thompson, R., Tummons, J., & Weatherby, J. (2019). Learning and learners. In J. Avis, R. Fisher, & R. Thompson (Eds.) *Teaching in lifelong learning: A guide to theory and practice* (3rd ed., pp. 81–107). Maidenhead: Open University Press.

Minton, M. (2005). *Teaching skills in further and adult education* (3rd ed.). London: Thompson.

Moore, M. G. (1997). Theory of transactional distance. In D. Keegan (Ed.) *Theoretical principles of distance education* (pp. 22–38). New York: Routledge.

Nicoll, K., & Harrison, R. (2003). Constructing the good teacher in higher education: The discursive work of standards. *Studies in Continuing Education*, 25(1), 23–35.

Rienties, B., & Rivers, B. A. (2014). Measuring and understanding learner emotions: Evidence and prospects. *Learning Analytics Review*, 1, 1–28.

Ruge, G., Tokede, O., & Tivendale, L. (2019). Implementing constructive alignment in higher education–cross-institutional perspectives from Australia. *Higher Education Research & Development*, 38(4), 833–848. doi: 10.1080/07294360.2019.1586842.

Salmon, G. (2003). *E-moderating: The key to teaching & learning online* (2nd ed.). London: RoutledgeFalmer.

Salmon, G. (2011). *E-moderating: The key to teaching & learning online* (3rd ed.). London: RoutledgeFalmer.

Siemens, G. (2005). *Connectivism: A learning theory for the digital age*. Retrieved from http://www.itdl.org/journal/jan_05/article01.htm

Smith, K., & Hill. J. (2019). Defining the nature of blended learning through its depiction in current research. *Higher Education Research & Development, 38*(2), 383–397. doi: 10.1080/07294360.2018.1517732.

Stenbom, S., Cleveland-Innes, M., & Hrastinski, S. (2014). Online coaching as a relationship of inquiry: Mathematics, online help, and emotional presence. In The Canadian Network for Innovation in Education Conference, May 13-16, 2014.

Wenger, E., McDermott, R. A., & Snyder, W. (2002). *Cultivating communities of practice: A guide to managing knowledge*. Boston, MA: Harvard Business Press.

Wheeler, S. (2012). *Digital learning futures*. Retrieved from http://www.steve-wheeler.co.uk/2015/03/social-mobile-and-personal-learning.html#!/2015/03/social-mobile-and-personal-learning.html

Wheeler, S. (2015). *Learning with 'e's*. Carmarthen: Crown House Publishing.

Youde, A. (2014). *A mixed methods exploration of effective tutors and tutoring in blended learning contexts* (Unpublished EdD Thesis, The University of Huddersfield, Huddersfield). Retrieved from http://eprints.hud.ac.uk/id/eprint/20351/

Youde, A. (2016). Tutor emotional competences valued by learners in a blended learning context. *European Journal of Open, Distance and E-Learning (EURODL), 19*(2), 81–97. doi: 10.1515/eurodl-2016-0008.

Youde, A. (2017). I don't need peer-support: Effective tutoring in blended learning environments for learners studying vocationally orientated degrees. In INTED 2017 Proceedings: 11th International Technology, Education and Development Conference, Valencia, Spain (pp. 1552–1561). doi: 10.21125/inted.2017.0499.

Youde, A. (2019). I don't need peer support: Effective tutoring in blended learning environments for part-time, adult learners. *Higher Education Research & Development*. doi:10.1080/07294360.2019.1704692.

Chapter 8

E-tutor competences, skills and beliefs

Introduction

This Chapter draws together a developing literature base regarding the competences and skills required for effective tutoring in online and blended contexts. Further, it considers the influence of tutor beliefs and perceptions on practice. The Chapter firstly outlines a growing body of empirical research specifically exploring the roles and competences required of tutors in online and blended learning environments. Synergies are then explored between these competences and those suggested by prominent ability and trait-based models of emotional intelligence (EI). The Chapter contributes to the academic literature by exploring online tutor competences through the lens of EI theory. Further, comparisons are made to the competences promoted by prominent theorisations within distance education discourse. The Chapter suggests aspects of theoretical triangulation (Denzin, 1970) within distance education and EI academic literature, and the growing body of empirical work around online tutor competences. Finally, the Chapter explores the influence of tutors' approaches to teaching, beliefs and perceptions, and presents empirical research suggesting that they influenced practice within blended learning modules.

Online tutor roles and supporting competences

There is debate regarding whether online tutoring requires different competences than those needed in traditional, face-to-face teaching environments. Klein, Spector, Grabowski, and de la Teja (2004) found online instructor competences were similar to those required in face-to-face contexts, however, Bawane and Spector (2009, p. 383) argued that the significance and demonstration of those competences may vary according to context. Chapter 7 presented a broad range of competences and knowledge, and argued they were necessary for effecting teaching within traditional, face-to-face environments. To develop this for online contexts, an overview of online tutor roles is provided with underpinning competences suggested for them to be effectively undertaken. This discussion makes reference to desirable personal qualities and skills that may support effective tutoring in online and blended learning contexts. This Section also makes connections with some emotional competences (ECs) already discussed within this book, particularly those outlined in Chapters 3 and 4.

Two key sources provided the basis of this literature review. Bawane and Spector (2009) analysed 14 empirical studies that explored necessary roles and supporting competences for effective online tutors. Consideration of these key online tutor roles provides a platform to explore supporting competences. McGee, Windes, and Torres (2017) conducted a Delphi study of expert online tutors that included an extensive literature review of online teaching competences on which they based their analysis. Although this Section is separated to consider pedagogic, course facilitation, social and other key competences, these were not found to be distinct groupings and they appeared to be more effective when operating synergistically.

Pedagogical competence

Of key importance for effective tutoring is a deep understanding of appropriate pedagogical practices for the particular teaching and learning context (Devlin & Samarawickrema, 2010; Stickler & Hampel, 2007). Chapter 7 noted that effective higher education (HE) tutors should possess knowledge and understanding of:

- student learning and motivation
- effective teaching and learning methods
- effective assessment methods
- effective feedback
- monitoring learner progress.

Such competences are similarly vital within online and blended learning contexts, with Chapter 7 discussing effective pedagogy in such environments.

The above competences are extended within online and blended contexts to include understanding online pedagogical design, the implementation of online pedagogical strategies, and an appreciation of the scholarship of online teaching (McGee et al., 2017, p. 336). These are enhanced by the development of appropriate learning resources and the facilitation of participation amongst students (Bawane & Spector, 2009, p. 390), with the latter now discussed in greater depth.

Facilitation competence

Whilst the competences required to effectively facilitate an online or blended programme can appear quite instrumental and functional, the underpinning skills, qualities and emotional competences are demanding for effective practices. Further, the boundaries between pedagogical and facilitation competences appear blurred when reviewing academic literature in this area. Aydin (2005) outlines two roles required for successful online tutoring. The process facilitator is expected to facilitate the range of online activities that are supportive of student learning, while the content facilitator directly focuses on facilitating the learners' growing understanding of the course content, which has clear synergies with the pedagogical roles and competences outlined above. To further reinforce these synergies, Bawane and Spector (2009, p. 390) categorise facilitating participation among students and sustaining students' motivation as part of online tutors' pedagogical roles.

Chapter 7 argued that the encouragement of learner participation and collaboration was challenging, particularly for adult learners who commonly have competing pressures from work and family commitments. McGee et al. (2017, p. 336) conception of facilitation is broader though than merely encouraging such participation and collaboration. They outline course facilitation as a key online teaching role that is strengthened by online communication skills, the facilitation of interaction between students, creating a community, and the orientation of learners through a unit of study or course. Whilst there is a growing literature discussing tutor strategies and actions to encourage learner facilitation, which includes participation and collaboration, Salmon's (2011) work remains at the forefront. However, as argued in Chapter 7, suggested approaches to communicating online can be quite mechanistic with an underlying assumption that any tutor can carry these out effectively. This underestimates the emotional competences required to understand learner emotions and feelings, and the appropriate response that each particular situation demands. McGee et al. (2017, p. 336) also include "establish and sustain a social presence" as a competence underpinning online tutor course facilitation. The establishment of such presence requires social competence, which is varied and multifaceted, with the underpinning tutor attributes, such as communication skills, similar to those needed for effective course facilitation.

Social competence

Social competence, commonly referred to as building and fostering tutor/learner and learner/learner relationships, has frequently been stated as desirable for online tutors (e.g., see Berge, 2009; Guasch, Alvarez, & Espasa, 2010; Schichtel, 2010; Varvel, 2007; Wiesenberg & Hutton, 1996). Such competence in fostering relationships would underpin and support both pedagogic competence and facilitation competence. Regarding the former, the elucidation of key concepts under study would be enhanced by constructive tutor/learner relationships. The latter would support the encouragement of learner participation and collaboration, particularly within online environments.

E-tutor competences, skills and beliefs 119

Social competences, and the facilitation competences outlined in the previous Section, support the development of a Social Presence (Garrison, Anderson, & Archer, 2000; see Chapter 7) within an online environment and can reduce the Transactional Distance (Moore, 1997; see Chapter 6) experienced by learners. Further, Moore's notion of dialogue, a key factor in narrowing tutor/learner Transactional Distance, suggests the importance of social competences.

Underpinning social competence and, therefore, pedagogic and facilitation competence, is effective communication (Schichtel, 2010). This, within online learning environments, is the ability to engage with learners online (Salmon, 2011). Zimmer and Alexander's (1996) idea of 'netiquette' is relevant here, with this relating to the attributes an online tutor needs to conduct effective and socially acceptable online conversations. The management of interpersonal relationships, particularly with adults studying at a distance, is an important factor in effective teaching in online and blended learning contexts with good communication a necessary component (Bailey & Card, 2009, p. 154; Murphy, Shelley, White, & Baumann, 2011, p. 410). Tutors need to consider body language, specialist vocabulary, language and culture (Armitage et al., 2003), however, the difficulty of this is enhanced in online environments and further emphasises the need for emotional competence when teaching in online and blended contexts. In managing these relationships, tutors will be sensitive to the needs of adults and their particular circumstances (Creanor, 2002; Holley and Oliver, 2010), therefore, being empathic to their needs. Empathy, and sensitivity to needs, have been found to be important in learner perceptions of quality in distance education (Murphy et al., 2011, p. 408).

Bawane and Spector (2009, p. 390) suggest four social roles required of an online tutor, each enhanced with the communication skills and competences outlined in the previous paragraph:

- maintaining a cordial learning environment
- promoting interactivity within the group
- resolving conflict in an amicable manner
- refraining from undesirable behaviours.

The first three of these roles would enhance course facilitation and would certainly draw on the social competences described above. The final competence has clear congruence with the Managing Emotion Branch of Mayer and Salovey's Four-Branch Model of EI (Mayer & Salovey, 1997; see Chapter 3). This branch considers a person's ability "to be open to feelings, and to modulate them in oneself and others so as to promote personal understanding and growth" (Mayer, Salovey, & Caruso, 2002, p. 7). To enable a tutor to refrain from undesirable behaviours requires emotional management, in that, they are open to certain feelings, but having the ability of emotional regulation.

120 E-tutor competences, skills and beliefs

For example, a learner may e-mail a tutor with a simple request, such as to check the submission date for an assessment. This e-mail could arrive at a time when the tutor is under severe pressure, with a range of competing demands, and an inappropriate response could be sent. This could chastise the learner for asking a question where the answer is easily available in a unit handbook held on the virtual learning environment (VLE). Appropriate management of emotions here would allow the tutor to compose a reply that politely advised the learner where such unit information could be found, thus maintaining effective tutor/learner relations.

The above example provides a link into the final element of tutor social competence in this Section, those required to support the online tutor roles of advisor and counsellor (Goodyear, Salmon, Spector, Steeples, & Tickner, 2001; McGee et al., 2017). Such a role enhances a tutor's facilitation of a unit or course by suggesting measures to learners to improve performance and provide guidance on their needs (Bawane & Spector, 2009, p. 390). However, appropriate responses to learner needs in such circumstances requires accurate perception and understanding of their emotions and feelings (Mayer & Salovey, 1997).

Other key online tutor competences

To support effective teaching and learning a number of other tutor competences are required that complement pedagogic, facilitation and social competences.

Course or unit management competence, commonly associated with organisational and administrative functions (Schichtel, 2010; Wiesenberg & Hutton, 1996), both support teaching and learning and the building and fostering of relationships in online contexts. This involves competence in managing general tasks and processes, utilising effective time management, and managing assessments, both formative and summative (McGee et al., 2017, p. 336).

In traditional educational settings workload is structured, in part, through teaching timetables. However, this characteristic may not be there when considering online elements with tutors commonly planning their own delivery and support. This requires tutors to be more organised than in face-to-face settings and manage their workload with greater autonomy (Stubbs, Martin, & Endlar, 2006). University lecturers often have formal and informal leadership positions and contribute to research and scholarship, and successful management of "these contextual factors and the associated expectations is essential for effective university teaching" (Devlin & Samarawickrema, 2010, p. 120). Further, online tutoring and support has been found to generate higher workloads than similar programmes in traditional settings (Bolliger & Wasilik, 2009, p. 113; Duncan & Barnett, 2010, p. 259). However, learners value tutors who are organised and offer timely responses to queries (Murphy et al., 2011, p. 408). The effective management of their workload, therefore, is a key e-tutor competence.

The competences of adaptability and flexibility are relevant when dealing with any form of computer mediated communications (CMCs) as, at times, technology does not work and this can adversely affect learners' study (Bailey & Card, 2009, p. 155). In face-to-face contexts, tutors can quickly switch to an alternative teaching approach, but this is not possible if there is reliance on technologies with learners at a distance. Alternative strategies have to be quickly found and communicated to learners and these can often be time consuming for tutors.

The consideration of workload resonates with a number of competences discussed within the Chapter, such as adaptability and flexibility, as it allows scope for dialogue, visibility and empathic tutoring, particularly in online environments. Enthusiasm for the subject and for teaching are generally considered important tutor qualities when teaching adults (Armitage et al., 2003; Biggs & Tang, 2007; Smith, 2004) and these are likely to be enhanced when tutors are not feeling excessive pressures from competing demands.

An element of technical competence is necessary for effective online and blended tutoring (see Chapter 9 for a more detailed discussion). Of greater importance, however, is competence in selecting appropriate tools to achieve the learning objectives (Bawane & Spector, 2009; McGee et al., 2017).

Chapter 9 argues that there are desirable tutor competences that may be difficult to develop through standard HE staff development programmes. These necessitate the recruitment and selection of appropriately skilled and qualified tutors, and their career background may provide evidence of such competences. A level of confidence in and experience of teaching in online environments have been found to be key tutor competences that would take time to acquire in post (McGee et al., 2017; Youde, 2014). Further, competence in conducting research on teaching and integrating the findings into practice can be beneficial for online tutors (Bawane & Spector, 2009, p. 390).

Congruence between key emotional intelligence theorisations and desirable online tutor competences

This Section compares and contrasts two differing academic discourses, namely that concerning EI and that which has developed in relation to online tutor roles and their supporting competences. It argues that there is congruence in the abilities promoted. Chapter 1 noted Salmon's (2011, p. 104) view that EI and the ability to influence others are important attributes, necessary when tutoring online, particularly the importance of tutor self-awareness, interpersonal sensitivity and the ability to influence others. However, little empirical work has been conducted since to add weight to this view. This Section firstly compares the above discussion of competences with Mayer and Salovey's Four-Branch Model of EI (1997) and its underpinning definition of EI. Chapter 3 noted that this Model as the prominent ability-based construction of EI. It then moves onto do this with reference to prominent trait-based methods of EI detailed in Chapter 4, including Youde's (2016) development of Goleman's (2001) Framework of Emotional Competences for tutors in blended learning environments. Whilst there was limited congruence when examining pedagogic competence, clear overlaps were found with other areas of competence, particularly facilitation and social. However, pedagogic competences are likely to be enhanced by facilitation and social competence, with this Section arguing that each can be further enhanced by tutor EI.

An ability construction of emotional intelligence

The Four Branch Model of EI (Mayer & Salovey, 1997) outlines a construction of EI that is exhibited through emotional competence in perceiving, using, understanding and managing emotions. As Chapter 2 argued, EI factors are demonstrated through emotional competences, for example, the ability to perceive emotions in others would aid the development of EC in conflict management or empathy (Wakeman, 2006, p. 72). The Model's four areas suggest intelligences that underpin a range of competences outlined earlier in this Chapter, for example, facilitation, social and advisor/counsellor. To illustrate, the four branches of the Mayer and Salovey's Model (1997) are now outlined in turn. The Perceiving Branch considers the ability to perceive emotions in oneself and others, and the ability of a tutor to appropriately express their own feelings and accurately perceive emotions in others. These abilities appear important in both face-to-face and online teaching contexts. The Using Branch considers the ability to generate, use and feel emotion as necessary to communicate feelings, such as, building trust and anticipation in students to facilitate learning. The Understanding Branch considers the ability to understand emotional information and how it can combine and progress through stages and interactions. For example, a tutor understanding a learner's feelings from receiving a poor mark and how this may affect them going forward with their studies. The tutor can then consider this as the learner embarks on the next piece of work. The Managing Branch considers the ability to be to be open to feelings, and to modulate them in oneself and others, such as, a tutor regulating emotions through a difficult conversation with a learner. The combination of these four abilities suggests an emotionally intelligent online tutor.

The range of competences required for effective online tutors is likely to be strengthened by such EI and the resultant emotional competences. Pedagogic competence in motivating learners and providing effective feedback would be enhanced by the abilities outlined above, such as understanding learners' response to positive or negative feedback. Facilitation competence requires

E-tutor competences, skills and beliefs 123

communication skills and the ability to encourage interaction, develop a community and have a social presence. Social competence requires the management of interpersonal relationships, being sensitive to adults' needs and circumstances, resolving conflict, and refraining from undesirable behaviours. All of these competences are likely to be enhanced by the abilities suggested in The Four Branch Model of EI (Mayer & Salovey, 1997), as tutors would better understand their emotions and those of their learners, thus enabling more appropriate interactions and communication.

Trait-based constructions of emotional intelligence

Chapter 4 established Goleman's (2001) Framework of Emotional Competences and the Bar-On (1997) Model of Emotional-Social Intelligence (ESI) as useful templates to evaluate tutor competences. Youde (2014, 2016) developed Goleman's Framework for tutors in blended learning environments including revised definitions of the constituent competences for this context. These trait-based constructions of EI outline competences that align with the summary of suggested online tutor competences outlined earlier in this Chapter. This Section argues that these constructions are broadly summarising this body of literature, suggesting some theoretical triangulation in this area (Denzin, 1970).

As Chapter 4 argued, there is congruence between these two major trait-based constructions of EI. Both include intrapersonal and interpersonal traits as well as consideration of self-management. Goleman's (2001) Framework was derived from research into leadership and management practices in organisations and, therefore, has a strong business focus in its constituent scales. This is particularly evident in the Relationship Management quadrant of the Framework where Leadership, Change Catalyst and Influence are cited as emotional competences. Bar-On's (1997) construction of EI is more general in orientation outlining competences that appear valuable for any social situation. This is principally represented in the General Mood scale of his Model, which includes the competences Optimism and Happiness.

The interpersonal competences outlined in both models have clear congruence with the facilitation and social competences outlined earlier in this Chapter. Bar-On's (1997) Model includes the scale Interpersonal Relationship with the establishment of mutually satisfying relationships and relating well to others as supporting competences and skills. Goleman's (2001) and Youde's (2014, 2016) frameworks include Service Orientation – a tutor's ability to identify learner's often unstated needs and concerns, and match them to HE provision, and Organisational Awareness – a tutor's ability to read currents of emotions and political realities in groups. Tutor competence in these areas is likely to enhance their ability to work with individuals and groups in online and blended contexts. However, Goleman's (2001) and Youde's (2014, 2016) Relationship Management cluster of competences has greater congruence with facilitation and social competences, in particular, the fostering tutor/learner relationships. These competences include:

- Developing Others: tutors sense learners' development needs and bolster their abilities
- Communication: tutors effectively give and take emotional information, deal with difficult issues straightforwardly, listen and foster open communication.

These align with the communication skills, developing a community and tutors having a social presence outlined in the Facilitation Competences Section earlier in this Chapter. The key pedagogic competence of motivating students would be enhanced by the above definition of Developing Others as would the key social competence stated, namely the fostering of tutor/learner relations.

Competence in refraining from undesirable behaviours and resolving conflict in an amicable manner (Bawane & Spector, 2009, p. 390) closely aligns with trait-based constructions of EI. In a similar manner to Mayer and Salovey's (1997) Emotional Management Branch, Bar-On's (1997) Model includes Impulse Control – the effective and constructive control of emotions, with Goleman's Framework including Self-Control – the absence of distress and disruptive feelings. Such competences allow tutors to effectively manage emotions, thus helping to maintain effective relations with learners. Further, when considering resolving conflict, Goleman's (2001) Framework includes the competence Conflict Management, which is defined as "tutors spot trouble as it is brewing and take steps to calm all involved" (Youde, 2016, p. 92).

Chapter 4 presented Youde's (2016) development of Goleman's Framework of Emotional Competences for effective tutors and tutoring in blended learning environments. This extended the range of Self-management competences to include the competences Coping Potential and Organised with these underpinned by a strong ability to prioritise. In this context, coping potential refers to competence in focusing on key tasks and not being influenced by less important demands of the role. This competence is likely to be supported by Organisation, the ability to plan work activities efficiently, and the ability to prioritise. These competences would support tutors in managing their workloads, which, as argued earlier in the Chapter, can require careful self-management. Further, these competences would support course or unit management, commonly considering organisational and administrative functions (Schichtel, 2010; Wiesenberg & Hutton, 1996), and in managing general tasks and processes, utilising effective time management, and managing assessments (McGee et al., 2017, p. 336). The most effective tutors in Youde's (2016) research were adept at self-management and could manage the complexities of delivering a unit of study in a blended learning context.

E-tutor competences, skills and beliefs 125

Bailey and Card's (2009) phenomenological study explored what experienced e-learning tutors perceive to be effective pedagogical practices, with the competences of adaptability and flexibility identified as significant. Youde (2016) also found adaptability important as effective tutors appeared open to a new delivery model, let go of old assumptions, and adapted their practice, therefore, demonstrating competence in this area. A key scale in Bar-On's Model (2006, p. 23) is adaptability or, as he considered, change management. Competences underpinning this scale item include flexibility – to adapt and adjust one's feelings and thinking to new situations, and problem solving – to effectively solve problems of a personal and interpersonal nature. Whilst these competences are focussed more on an individual's feelings and emotions, there is clear congruence with the more practical competences suggested by Bailey and Card's and Youde's research. Online and blended HE tutors commonly move from traditional lecturing roles and, therefore, adaptability and flexibility appear significant competences for effective practice in these contexts.

There appears to be some consensus between both online tutor competences and trait-based EI discourses around the notion of confidence and enthusiasm, although this is a broad and subjective area with varying constructions of an individual's generally positive outlook and demeanour discussed within academic literature. Within the Other Key Online Tutor Competences Section above, both confidence (McGee et al., 2017) and enthusiasm (Smith, 2004) were recognised as valuable for online and blended tutors. Chapter 3 noted Youde's (2014) research into effective tutors within a blended learning environment and found they had a tendency to respond to pictorial stimuli with positive emotions (Mayer et al., 2002, p. 15). Through qualitative analysis, this finding was tentatively linked to tutor enthusiasm for their subject and for teaching in general. Goleman's (2001) and Youde's (2016) frameworks include Self-confidence as an underpinning competence of Self-awareness. This is defined as a belief and self-assurance about a tutor's own abilities (Youde, 2016). Bar-On's (2006, p. 23) General Mood scale, or self-motivation, provides an interesting consideration regarding the impact of these competences on the other scale items outlined within his Model. This scale item includes the competences Optimism – to be positive and look at the brighter side of life, and Happiness – to feel content with oneself, others and life in general. Bar-On (2006, p. 15) suggested that this scale is an example of a facilitator to the other components, in that Optimism and Happiness can facilitate, for example, Interpersonal Relationships and Stress Tolerance. Therefore, whilst confidence, enthusiasm, optimism and happiness are differing emotional competences or general traits, there appears some congruence within the literatures and theorisations explored in this Chapter regarding their enhancement of other key emotional competences, which effective online and blended tutors should possess.

Finally, within this Section, the online tutor competence Empathy is considered, which is defined as "to be aware of and understand how others feel"

(Bar-On, 2006, p. 23). As stated earlier in this Chapter, empathy and sensitivity to needs have been found to be important in learner perceptions of quality in distance education (Murphy et al., 2011, p. 408). Chapter 6 noted the importance of personal relations between tutors and learners, with these built on trust, respect and, as discussed throughout this Chapter, empathy (Rogers & Freiberg, 1994). Prominent theorisations within distance education discourse regard empathy as an essential tutor trait when dealing with students (Holmberg, 1989, 2003). Further, it is included as an interpersonal competence in both Goleman's (2001) and Bar-On's Models of EI. This highlights the importance of tutor empathy for effective practice within online and blended learning contexts. When considering HE, particularly for adult learners, awareness, understanding and sensitivity to their needs is essential for tutors. It would appear beneficial for online and blended tutors within HE to have studied online and undertaken courses whilst in full-time employment.

The influence on practice of tutors' approaches to teaching, beliefs and perceptions

Chapter 7 established the importance of a holistic approach to module teaching, learning and assessment within online and blended environments. However, a tutor's preferred approach to teaching, epistemological beliefs, and belief system in general, can influence their decisions when designing and delivering a HE unit of study. When exploring effective practice in this context, it is therefore important to understand the choices made by tutors and to consider factors that influenced decisions. These are now discussed in relation to their potential impact on practice and student learning.

When researching relationships between conceptions of teaching, such as knowledge transmission and learning facilitation, and student approaches to study, Kember and Gow (1994, p. 69) found that university departments adopting learning-facilitation strategies (or student-centred learning strategies) established an environment that encouraged Deep approaches to study (see Chapter 5 for further discussion of learner approaches to study). Effective teaching in HE has been broadly understood as teaching that is oriented to and focussed on students and their learning (Devlin & Samarawickrema, 2010, p. 112; Kember & Ginns, 2012, p. 4). Kember (1997) found a high level of synergy between 13 independent studies into academic conceptions of teaching and synthesised the research into two broad orientations – teacher centred/content-orientated and student-centred/learning-orientated. Under these two orientations, Kember (1997, p. 264) established five conceptions considered within a continuum, which are:

- teaching as imparting information
- teaching as transmitting structured knowledge

- teaching as an interaction between the teacher and student
- teaching as facilitating understanding on the part of the student
- teaching as bringing about conceptual change and intellectual development in the student.

The first two conceptions support passive learning on behalf of learners, which could be valuable at the start of module or unit of study, as some transmission of information may be used to establish clear goals, structure and assessment requirements. Following this, other student-centred approaches to teaching can be adopted throughout remaining face-to-face and online contexts. The orientations and conceptions can be instructive for tutors as they provide criteria to evaluate their approaches when delivering modules and the resultant influence on approaches to study adopted by learners.

A tutor's broader belief system can influence their approaches and practices within online and blended learning environments. There is a broad consensus of beliefs being an effectual psychological construct in teacher education (Fives & Gill, 2015) and a key predictor of teacher behaviour (Pajares, 1992). Whilst these sources are focussed on traditional teaching contexts, links between tutor beliefs and practices have also been found in online environments (Song & Looi, 2012; Stein, Shepherd, & Harris, 2011). However, when evaluating approaches and practices, it is important to separate an online tutor's broader, general belief system and focus on their educational beliefs (Pajares, 1992, p. 316). These are broad and encompass teacher efficacy, epistemological beliefs, tutor self-concept and self-esteem, and self-efficacy.

Tutor epistemological beliefs, that is, beliefs relating to the nature of knowledge and learning, impact on the approach to teaching adopted (Jones & Carter, 2006; Kember, 2007). For example, tutors favouring a knowledge transmission orientation, and believing this to be an effective approach to teaching, are more likely to adopt didactic methods both in face-to-face and online learning environments. Whereas, tutors with predominantly constructivist epistemological beliefs are more likely to engage learners in discussion, interaction and problem-solving (Topcu, 2013, p. 233). Further, the sophistication of epistemological beliefs, whether a tutor believes knowledge is relatively simple or complex, influences whether tutor led or student-centred approaches to teaching are adopted (Kember, 1997; Marouchou, 2011). Such beliefs, and resultant teaching, could influence the approaches to study adopted by learners (Biggs & Tang, 2007). Further, Kang (2008, p. 496) highlights the slow development and changes of epistemological beliefs during initial teacher training programmes. This could be relevant for tutors who move from traditional to online and blended learning contexts as inappropriate pedagogy could be introduced. Tutors' preferred pedagogies can be hindered by, for example, reduced face-to-face contact and the limitations of available educational technologies.

128 E-tutor competences, skills and beliefs

Tutor perceptions, like beliefs, influence practices within online and blended learning contexts (Youde, 2018). Perceptions, in this context, can be defined as how tutors regard and understand their teaching practices, and these can be influenced by beliefs (Minor, Onwuegbuzie, Witcher, & James, 2002). For example, Trigwell and Prosser (2004) considered the impact of tutor perceptions on practice, and state:

> teachers who perceive that their teaching workload is appropriate, that student characteristics are sufficiently homogenous and at an appropriate academic level, that class sizes are not too large and that they have some control over what is taught, are more likely to adopt a conceptual change/student focused approach to teaching (Trigwell & Prosser, 2004, p. 419).

This comment regarding workload resonates with the earlier Section that discussed the competences required to effectively manage workloads and the challenges in doing this within online and blended learning environments (see Other Key Online Tutor Competences Section). Tutor perceptions of workload influence approaches to teaching and practice but, when it is their responsibility to manage, it becomes of greater importance that it is undertaken effectively. Further, their perceptions of the affordances of online and blended learning are likely to influence their approaches to teaching in these environments.

The exploration of tutor epistemological beliefs and perceptions of factors influencing teaching and learning, such as their workload, are valuable in understanding the approaches adopted and the resultant impact on student learning. However, there is limited empirical research and accompanying literature exploring tutor perceptions, beliefs and practices within online and blended learning. There has been consideration of university tutors' beliefs and practices regarding their uptake of VLEs (Steel, 2009) and web-based technology (Lawrence & Lentle-Keenan, 2013). Similarly, Hall (2002, p. 154) argued that tutors' views regarding the pedagogy afforded by information and communications technology (ICT) influenced their adoption and use, again, a decision potentially influenced by epistemological beliefs and perceptions.

Tutor perceptions and practices within blended learning environments

Youde's (2014, 2018) empirical study explored effective tutors and tutoring within blended learning contexts. Throughout the data analysis process themes emerged that suggested the influence of tutor perceptions and beliefs on practice when delivering modules. The research, within an Education disciplinary area, conducted a detailed study of eight tutors' teaching, learning,

E-tutor competences, skills and beliefs 129

assessment and learner support in relation to one of their modules. These tutors contributed to courses aimed at part-time learners within an HE institution, undertaking vocationally relevant degrees whilst, usually, in full-time employment. The analysis considered tutors' beliefs, which had been developed in predominantly face-to-face contexts through their previous education and teaching experiences, and examined how these beliefs influenced their blended learning practices.

All the participating tutors had previously undertaken formal study in online contexts and all had found this to be a negative experience (Youde, 2014, 2018). These perceptions of online learning appeared to influence their practice on modules and were helpful in understanding adopted approaches. They adopted alternative approaches other than online pedagogy that aligned with pedagogical beliefs, namely face-to-face delivery enhanced with learner support. A lack of tutor/learner and learner/learner interaction was found within online environments. Interestingly, although tutors were generally confident in their approach to delivery and stated their modules were successful, the lack of online learning and interaction was perceived, by some, as bad practice. This could be because the lack of interaction was potentially in conflict with their stated, preferred socially constructivist pedagogical approaches and beliefs. They outlined that these approaches were commonly adopted in face-to-face teaching.

Tutor perceptions of blended learning were more positive than those they held in relation to their earlier online learning experiences, in part, due to the face-to-face component (Youde, 2014, 2018). They considered that it created space for learning whilst enabling learners to balance study with work and family commitments. There were interesting findings when considering learner ratings of tutors. Those receiving lower ratings, on the whole, adopted a 'blame' response predominantly around time affordances, but also about limited opportunities for social constructivist pedagogy. Those receiving higher ratings indicated that there were greater opportunities afforded by the delivery model, including learner support and increased space for reflection and learning. This suggests tutors who perceive blended learning as an opportunity to enhance practice and meet adult learner needs are considered to be more effective by their students.

Further tutor perceptions considered by Youde (2014, 2018) included those relating to workload, module design, and the influence of positive perceptions. Tutors receiving higher learner ratings perceived their workload as manageable and outlined clearer approaches to module delivery. Modules that were designed specifically for blended learning contexts rated better than those adapted from face-to-face traditional delivery models. Further, this influenced tutor perceptions, particularly around time for delivery, potentially shaping learners' feedback on the module. This finding concurs with MacDonald's (2006) view that modules should be designed specifically for blended learning contexts to ensure an appropriate mix of approaches.

Generally, tutors achieving higher learner ratings were more positive about their modules, which could be potentially influencing learners' perceptions. If tutors are stating there are problems within a module, such as a lack of time for delivery, learners are likely to consider this when completing a survey about their learning experience on that unit of study.

Youde's (2014, 2018) study provided examples of the influence of tutors' beliefs, which were developed in predominantly face-to-face contexts, and how they impacted on their blended learning practices. Whilst these examples will likely be unique to that study, they do highlight the complex and nuanced nature of effective tutors and tutoring in such contexts. Consideration of the influence of perceptions and beliefs on practices will enhance the evaluation of effective teaching in online and blended learning environments.

In summary

This Chapter explored a range of skills, qualities and competences that support effective tutoring in online and blended learning environments. Devlin and Samarawickrema (2010, p. 111) note that effective teaching must continue to evolve so it reflects and responds to the context in which the teaching and learning is occurring. As it evolves, there will be changes to the skills, qualities and competences required of tutors, or as Bawane and Spector (2009, p. 383) showed, the significance and demonstration of those competences may vary according to context, and the changing context.

Tutor perceptions and beliefs have been considered in relation to their impact on practices. These are significant within Higher Education as a number of tutors have moved from traditional teaching roles into online and blended contexts. This background could influence online practices. Given the rise in the number of tutors who have solely taught in online contexts, such as those delivering on massive open online courses (MOOCs), the significance of this influence could start to decline.

The following Chapter explores training and development for tutors in online and blended learning environments. It considers some of the competences and skills discussed in this Chapter and questions whether they, and other key requirements of tutors in these contexts, can be effectively engendered within HE environments.

References

Armitage, A., Byant, R., Dunnill, R., Hayes, D., Hudson, A., Kent, J., Lawes, S., & Renwick, M. (2003). *Teaching and training in post-compulsory education* (2nd ed.). Maidenhead: Open University Press.

Aydin, C. (2005). Turkish mentors' perception of roles, competencies and resources for online teaching. *Turkish Online Journal of Distance Education*, 6(3), 58–80. Retrieved from http://tojde.anadolu.edu.tr/tojde19/articles/caydin

Bailey, C. J., & Card, K. A. (2009). Effective pedagogical practices for online teaching: Perception of experienced instructors. *Internet and Higher Education*, *12*(3-4), 152–155.

Bar-On, R. (1997). *Bar-On emotional quotient inventory: Technical manual*. Toronto: Multi-Health Systems.

Bar-On, R. (2006). The Bar-On model of emotional-social intelligence (ESI). *Psicothema*, *18*, 13–25.

Bawane, J., & Spector, J. M. (2009). Prioritization of online instructor roles: Implications for competency-based teacher education programs. *Distance Education*, *30*(3), 383–397.

Berge, Z. (2009). Changing instructor's roles in virtual worlds. *Quarterly Review of Distance Education*, *9*(4), 407–415.

Biggs, J., & Tang, C. (2007). *Teaching for quality learning at university* (3rd ed.). Maidenhead: Open University Press.

Bolliger, D. U., & Wasilik, O. (2009). Factors influencing faculty satisfaction with online teaching and learning in higher education. *Distance Education*, *30*(1), 103–116.

Creanor, L. (2002). A tale of two courses: A comparative study of tutoring online. *Open Learning: The Journal of Open, Distance and e-Learning*, *17*(1), 57–68.

Denzin, N. K. (1970). *The research act: A theoretical introduction to sociological methods*. Chicago, IL: Aldine.

Devlin, M., & Samarawickrema, G. (2010). The criteria of effective teaching in a higher education context. *Higher Education Research & Development*, *29*(2), 111–124.

Duncan, H. E., & Barnett, J. (2010). Experiencing online pedagogy: A Canadian case study. *Teaching Education*, *21*(3), 247–262.

Fives, H., & Gill, M. G. (2015). *International handbook of research on teachers' beliefs*. London: Routledge.

Garrison, D. R., Anderson, T., & Archer, W. (2000). Critical inquiry in a text-based environment: Computer conferencing in higher education model. *The Internet and Higher Education*, *2*(2-3), 87–105.

Goleman, D. (2001). An EI-based theory of performance. In C. Cherniss & D. Goleman (Eds.) *The emotionally intelligent workplace: How to select for, measure, and improve emotional intelligence in individuals, groups, and organization* (pp. 27–44). San Francisco, CA: Jossy-Bass.

Goodyear, P., Salmon, G., Spector, J. M., Steeples, C., & Tickner, S. (2001). Competences for online teaching: A special report. *Educational Technology Research and Development*, *49*(1), 65–72.

Guasch, T., Alvarez, I., & Espasa, A. (2010). University teacher competencies in a virtual teaching/learning environment: Analysis of a teacher training experience. *Teaching and Teacher Education*, *26*(2), 199–206.

Hall, R. (2002). Aligning learning, teaching and assessment using the web: An evaluation of pedagogic approaches. *British Journal of Educational Technology*, *33*(2), 149–158.

Holley, D., & Oliver, M. (2010). Student engagement and blended learning: Portraits of risk. *Computers & Education*, *54*, 693–700. doi: 10.1016/j.compedu.2009.08.035.

Holmberg, B. (1989). *Theory and practice of distance education*. London: Routledge.

Holmberg, B. (2003). A theory of distance education based on empathy. In M. G. Moore. & W. G. Anderson (Eds.) *Handbook of distance education* (pp. 79–86). Abingdon: Routledge.

Jones, M. G., & Carter, G. (2006). Science teacher attitudes and beliefs. In S. K. Abell & N. G. Lederman (Eds.) *Handbook of research on science education* (pp. 1067–1104). New Jersey: Lawrence Erlbaum Associates.

Kang, N. (2008). Learning to teach science: Personal epistemologies, teaching goals, and practices of teaching. *Teaching and Teacher Education*, *24*(2), 478–498.

132 E-tutor competences, skills and beliefs

Kember, D. (1997). A reconceptualisation of the research into university academics' conceptions of teaching. *Learning and Instruction, 7*(3), 255–275.

Kember, D. (2007). *Reconsidering open and distance learning in the developing world: Meeting students' learning needs.* Abingdon: Routledge.

Kember, D., & Ginns, P. (2012). *Evaluating teaching and learning: A practical handbook for colleges, universities and the scholarship of teaching.* Abingdon: Routledge.

Kember, D., & Gow, L. (1994). Orientations to teaching and their effect on the quality of student learning. *Journal of Higher Education, 65*(1), 58–74.

Klein, J. M., Spector, J. M., Grabowski, B., & de la Teja, I. (2004). *Instructor competencies: Standards for face-to-face, online, and blended settings.* Greenwich, CT: Information Age.

Lawrence, B., & Lentle-Keenan, S. (2013). Teaching beliefs and practice, institutional context, and the uptake of web-based technology. *Distance Education, 34*(1), 4–20. doi: 10.1080/01587919.2013.770432.

MacDonald, J. (2006). *Blended learning and online tutoring: A good practice guide.* Aldershot: Gower.

Marouchou, D. V. (2011). Faculty conceptions of teaching: Implications for teacher professional development. *McGill Journal of Education, 46*(1), 123–132.

Mayer, J. D., & Salovey, P. (1997). What is emotional intelligence? In P. Salovey & D. Sluyter (Eds.) *Emotional development and emotional intelligence: Implications for Educators* (pp. 3–31). New York: Basic Books.

Mayer, J. D., Salovey, P., & Caruso, D. (2002). *Mayer-Salovey-Caruso emotional intelligence test manual.* Toronto: Multi-Health Systems.

McGee, P., Windes, D., & Torres, M. (2017). Experienced online instructors: Beliefs and preferred supports regarding online teaching. *Journal of Computing in Higher Education, 29*(2), 331–352.

Minor, L. C., Onwuegbuzie, A. J., Witcher, A. E., & James, T. L. (2002). Preservice teachers' educational beliefs and their perceptions of characteristics of effective teachers. *The Journal of Educational Research, 96*(2), 116–127.

Moore, M. G. (1997). Theory of transactional distance. In D. Keegan (Ed.) *Theoretical principles of distance education* (pp. 22–38). New York: Routledge.

Murphy, L. M., Shelley, M. A., White, C. J., & Baumann, U. (2011). Tutor and student perceptions of what makes an effective distance language teacher. *Distance Education, 32*(3), 397–419.

Pajares, M. F. (1992). Teachers' beliefs and educational research: Clearing up a messy construct. *Review of Educational Research, 62*(3), 243–253.

Rogers, C. R., & Freiberg, H. J. (1994). *Freedom to learn* (3rd ed.). Columbus, OH: Merrill-MacMillan.

Salmon, G. (2011). *E-moderating: The key to teaching & learning online* (3rd ed.). London: RoutledgeFalmer.

Schichtel, M. (2010). Core-competence skills in e-mentoring for medical educators: A conceptual exploration. *Medical teacher, 32*(7), 248–262.

Smith, A. (2004). "Off-campus support" in distance learning – how do our students define quality? *Quality Assurance in Education, 12*(1), 28–38.

Song, Y., & Looi, C. K. (2012). Linking teacher beliefs, practices and student inquiry-based learning in a CSCL environment: A tale of two teachers. *International Journal of Computer-Supported Collaborative Learning, 7*(1), 129–159.

Steel, C. (2009). Reconciling university teacher beliefs to create learning designs for LMS environments. *Australasian Journal of Educational Technology, 25*, 399–420.

E-tutor competences, skills and beliefs 133

Stein, S. J., Shepherd, K., & Harris, I. (2011). Conceptions of e-learning and professional development for e-learning held by tertiary educators in New Zealand. *British Journal of Educational Technology*, *42*(1), 145–165.

Stickler, U., & Hampel, R. (2007). Designing online tutor training for language courses: A case study. *Open Learning: The Journal of Open, Distance and e-Learning*, *22*(1), 75–85.

Stubbs, M., Martin, I., & Endlar, L. (2006). The structuration of blended learning: Putting holistic design principles into practice. *British Journal of Educational Technology*, *37*(2), 163–175.

Topcu, M. S. (2013). Pre-service teachers' epistemological beliefs in physics, chemistry, and biology: A mixed study. *International Journal of Science and Mathematics Education*, *11*, 433–458.

Trigwell, K., & Prosser, M. (2004). Development and use of the approaches to teaching inventory. *Educational Psychology Review*, *16*(4), 409–424.

Varvel, V. E. (2007). Master online teacher competencies. *Online journal of distance learning administration*, *10*(1), 1–41. Retrieved from http://www2.westga.edu/~distance/ojdla/

Wakeman, C. (2006). Emotional intelligence: Testing, measurement and analysis. *Research in Education*, *75*, 71–93.

Wiesenberg, F., & Hutton, S. (1996). Computer mediated conferencing. *Journal of the Alberta Association for Continuing Education*, *24*, 9–16.

Youde, A. (2014). *A mixed methods exploration of effective tutors and tutoring in blended learning contexts* (Unpublished EdD Thesis, The University of Huddersfield). Retrieved from http://eprints.hud.ac.uk/id/eprint/20351/

Youde, A. (2016). Tutor emotional competences valued by learners in a blended learning context. *European Journal of Open, Distance and E-Learning (EURODL)*, *19*(2), 81–97. doi: 10.1515/eurodl-2016-0008.

Youde, A. (2018). An exploration of tutor perceptions and practice within blended learning environments. EduLearn18: 10th International Conference on Education and New Learning Technologies, Palma, Majorca. 403–412. doi: 10.21125/edulearn.2018.0176.

Zimmer, B., & Alexander, G. (1996). The Rogerian interface: For open, warm empathy in computer-mediated collaborative learning. *Innovations in Education and Training International*, *33*(1), 13–21. doi 10.1080/1355800960330103.

Chapter 9

Developing effective e-tutors

Introduction

Tutors commonly move from face-to-face, traditional, class-room teaching to work in online and blended contexts, often with limited formal training or continuous professional development (CPD) relating to online learning. They often find that effective pedagogy for the context presents both technical and professional challenges. As a consequence, inexperienced tutors often adopt traditional practices in online environments (Kreber & Kanuka, 2006), which may not be effective or appropriate.

This Chapter considers effective professional development for tutors in online and blended learning contexts. Chapter 1 outlined the current e-tutoring context and the characteristics of 'new' learners (Wheeler, 2012, 2015), with this a fast changing and developing area of education (Stickler & Hampel, 2007). This can make it difficult to prepare effective programmes for the development of online tutoring skills, particularly for university staff development departments, resulting in a reliance on tutor self-development through 'trial and error' and refection on practice (Stickler & Hampel, 2007, pp. 82–83). This Chapter firstly outlines development programmes that can be provided by HE institutions before discussing the challenges of nurturing the key competences that this book has argued are necessary for effective tutoring in this context. Finally, training for the development of tutor emotional competence is discussed, with this argued to be challenging for university staff development departments to effectively deliver.

Development programmes for online tutoring

As universities adapt delivery patterns to meet the needs of part-time (PT) students, tutors' roles are changing to meet these challenges and a transformation of their existing pedagogy is needed. CPD within face-to-face contexts is widely available and Bennett and Marsh (2002, p. 14) highlight the need for effective programmes of staff development and training to support online delivery. There are a range of sources that outline suggested training programmes for online tutors (e.g., see Stickler & Hampel, 2007; Wilson, 2007) with evidence provided to demonstrate their general success. Such sources provide guidance for tutors and HE institutions regarding the formulation of a training programme for tutors moving into this context. Pedagogical considerations (see Pedagogy not Technology Section below for further discussion) are generally included, however, often given less attention is how to provide effective support for learners and how to monitor their progress (see Chapter 10 for a discussion of supporting online learners and monitoring their progress).

Salmon (2011, 2018) provides a range of empirically based training resources for online tutors that are essential for anyone moving into teaching within this area. Further, guidance is provided to create the right environment for effective training and staff development (Salmon & Wright, 2014, p. 14), which includes:

- create a sense of urgency, if not, limited change is achieved
- understand the pressures of adapting traditional teaching ideologies and practices to the current e-tutoring context
- build a tutor's confidence and competence, as this is at the heart of any transformation in teaching practices
- establish successful outcome driven staff development.

Stein, Shephard, and Harris (2011, p. 159) add to this discussion by stating that tutors should be able to see the purpose, relevance and value of the learning in which they are engaged. Formal recognition of the successful completion of online tutor training programmes has also found to be motivating for participants (Hrastinski, Cleveland-Innes, & Stenbom, 2018; McGee, Windes, & Torres, 2017).

Although the focus of this book is on individual tutors within online and blended environments, when designing units, modules or even whole courses, a team-based approach is key (Salmon & Wright, 2014). Salmon's (2016) Carpe Diem Model is a team-based approach to learning design for online and blended environments and it provides a set of stages for participants to work through in a workshop environment. Key participants forming the team should include academic tutors, learning designers, learning technologists, and a librarian, all accompanied by an experienced facilitator (Salmon, 2016).

This Section now builds a picture of the complexity and challenge of training emotionally intelligent tutors for this context. In turn, it considers the training and development of technical skills, appropriate pedagogy for the context, the value of 'on the job' training, and the importance of reflection on practice.

Technical skills

Competence in the use of basic information and communication technologies can be taken for granted by those moving into online tutoring with a range of online tutorials available for the effective use of educational software (Stickler & Hampel, 2007, p. 83). Barker (2002) advises that online tutors should undertake CPD to keep abreast of emerging technologies and he provides a useful summary of required technical skills, including effective use of e-mail and VLEs. Effective e-mail use is significant in supporting learners at a distance and training should be provided to ensure both care and attention in construction, and to develop strategies in its use to motivate and encourage (Youde, 2014, 2016). Other educational technologies continuously emerge, such as Web 2.0 and Web 3.0 in recent years. These have included e-portfolios, blogs, wikis, social software and synchronous conferencing, and CPD is advisable for their effective use. It would be difficult to argue that technical skills are not important for tutors in online and blended environments, however, these alone will not foster learning and motivate students to achieve when studying at a distance. Of more importance to tutors is a deep understanding of appropriate pedagogical approaches for their particular context and decisions made about practices with each technology should be based on the alignment of learning, teaching and assessment (Biggs, 2003).

The VLE is a common resource for tutors and students and its effective use is important. Weller (2007, p. 5) defines a VLE as "a software system that combines a number of different tools that are used systematically to deliver content online and facilitate the learning experience around that content". VLEs are probably the most pervasive of all learning technologies in education, due partly to the number of tools they support, which include discussion boards, a repository for learning resources (text-based and multimedia), e-mail, blogs and wikis. They will also include specific areas for virtual conferences (both synchronous and asynchronous), class lists and learner homepages, assessment tools and grade books, and will allow file upload for assessed work. Increasingly, intelligent agents[1] are being integrated into VLEs with these undertaking some of the work carried out by tutors. These can be valuable when tutoring larger groups, however, a number of generally worded messages to learners may limit their impact and, at times, personal messages can be more powerful.

Used appropriately, VLEs enable tutors to improve the learning experience for students by utilising communication and collaborative tools, lowering the Transactional Distance between participants, whilst supporting course administration (Bennett & Youde, 2010). However, VLEs have been criticised for supporting a content-focussed approach to learning (Dyke, Conole, Ravenscroft, & De Fraitas, 2007, p. 89; Weller, 2007, p. 125). They lend themselves to being a repository for lecture slides and word-processed handouts, and are often concomitant with Associationist approaches (Mayes &

Developing effective e-tutors 137

de Freitas, 2004; see Chapter 7 for discussion of Associationist approaches). Nevertheless, as Weller (2007, p. 19) argues, it is also possible to design learning activities within VLEs that reflect other models of learning – for example, constructivist and problem-based learning. Training should ensure a basic level of tutor IT skills including the ability to provide an appropriately structured and scaffolded VLE, allowing PT learners to construct deeper understanding of the topics being studied (Youde, 2014).

Pedagogy not technology

As stated above and argued in Chapter 7, of crucial importance for effective tutoring is a deep understanding of appropriate pedagogical practices for the particular context (Devlin & Samarawickrema, 2010; Stickler & Hampel, 2007). The Section above argued that, while technical skills are important, in the current e-tutoring context they can be easily obtained. Chapter 7 outlined Mayes and de Freitas' (2004, p. 7) perspectives, which suggest suitable approaches to tutoring in online and blended learning contexts. These are rooted in Biggs' Constructive Alignment Model (2003), which states that all components of teaching and learning are congruent or aligned.

Youde's (2014, 2019) study made recommendations for tutor training in blended learning contexts and raised a number of relevant areas for HE institutions to consider. This study focussed on vocational courses for PT learners. Training should incorporate certain elements of the Conceptual Model of Effective Tutors and Tutoring (see Chapter 11) where it could influence tutor practice. However, with regards to teaching, learning and assessment, training could focus on areas such as outlining the fundamental principles of the Individual Constructivist Perspective (Mayes & de Freitas, 2007), which includes facilitative teaching styles and problem-based assessments (see Chapter 7 for a more detailed discussion of this research). This was found to be the most appropriate module or unit approach for these particular learners allowing some structure and facilitation, but also learner self-direction of their studies.

The influence a tutor's perceptions, values and beliefs regarding teaching and learning are significant here (see Chapter 8 for a more detailed discussion of their impact on practice). Youde's (2014) findings indicated that tutor perceptions, their previous experiences and their pedagogical beliefs were all influencing practice and, consequently, should be considered when developing training or recruiting for HE.

'On the job' training

As outlined above, there are a range of formal training programmes tutors can follow to develop their online teaching practices. Through case study analysis of an online tutor training programme, Bennett and Marsh (2002, pp. 18–19) state that prospective tutors should be placed within practical contexts to develop new teaching and learning practices quickly. It is common practice for tutors proficient in traditional settings to be moved into online contexts, although it is advised that training continues beyond the pre-experience stage and that it should be supplemented by learning technologists and technical support (Bennett & Lockyer, 2004, p. 242; Davis & Fill, 2007, p. 825). This should be developed by peer collaboration around appropriate pedagogy (Carnell, 2007, p. 33; Stickler & Hampel, 2007, p. 83). Such collaboration can help tutors develop their pedagogical understanding of emerging technologies and develop technical skills in their use. Effective tutors in blended learning environments were found to have colleagues with whom they discussed issues of pedagogy and technology (Youde, 2014). Further, Youde (2014) found that less experienced tutors had mentors with whom they could discuss practices. It was apparent that a culture of support and sharing of good practice between tutors existed, which included robust technical support. There is a growing body of evidence that tutor training and development is more effective when it is ongoing and part of a collective experience, with appropriate technological and pedagogical support on hand (McGee et al., 2017; Stein, Shephard, & Harris, 2011; Youde, 2014).

The above discussion paints a complex picture of tutor development when teaching in online environments, however, McGee et al. (2017) study of expert online tutors found a factor they valued most was prolonged experience. It is clear there can be valuable learning whilst 'on the job', however, this is enhanced by collaborative and supportive colleagues, and further strengthened by tutor self-reflection and development.

Time for reflection

A constraint for university tutors is time and this can restrict opportunities for reflection on action (Schön, 1987). When considering the development of online tutoring skills, space for reflection is important and should be included in training courses/programmes (Hrastinski et al., 2018, p. 127). This notion can be extended beyond training courses as tutors move into practice. Online elements of blended tutoring are commonly asynchronous, which can provide time for tutors to consider action or even consult with colleagues or a mentor regarding practice (Youde, 2014).

Recruiting and developing emotionally competent online tutors

Emotional competence is a learned capability based on emotional intelligence, one with massive potential to lead to effective performance in online and blended learning environments (see Chapter 2 for a justification of this definition). Empirical studies have found that emotional competences can be

Developing effective e-tutors 139

developed through training (Boyatzis, 2007; Dolev & Leshem, 2016; Neale, Spencer-Arnell, & Wilson, 2011). However, the time required to develop such competence will arguably be beyond the scope of university staff development programmes.

Dolev and Leshem (2016, 2017a, 2017b) undertook a two-year teacher targeted EI professional development training programme in one Israeli secondary school. Twenty participants undertook the training that was based on the Bar-On (1997) Model of Emotional-Social Intelligence (ESI). It was comprised of group workshops and individual coaching sessions, all led by three expert EI trainers. Qualitative findings indicated that there was a positive impact on all the participants, described by some as transformational training, however views were varied in nature (Dolev & Leshem, 2017a, p. 28). The participants also completed Bar-On's (1997) Emotional Quotient Inventory (EQ-i), both before and after the programme, with the analysis revealing the training had a modest impact (Dolev & Leshem, 2016, p. 87). This, the authors stated, was surprising given the length and intensity of the programme, and the qualitative data from participant interviews. Again, this suggests that effective EI training for tutors in online and blended learning environments is challenging.

Dolev and Leshem (2016, 2017a, 2017b) have questioned the value of an inventory to measure the EI of teachers, which is similar to Youde's (2014) finding regarding academics who completed the Mayer-Salovey-Caruso Emotional Intelligence Test (MSCEIT; Mayer, Salovey, & Caruso, 2002; see Chapter 3). In his research, an ability measure of EI was chosen to alleviate academics' tendency to deconstruct tests of intelligence, however, although advised to answer questions on instinct, tutors reported a desire to determine 'correct' answers. This suggests a need for caution in using such inventories as part of recruitment and selection processes, or as part of training and development activities. Youde (2014) also noted that one tutor's responses could have been influenced by her state of mind following two recent bereavements of close family members, making answers more negative than in normal circumstances. Further, two tutors reported the questionnaire's length as an issue and the feelings of frustration this caused affected later stages of completion. Youde (2014) also found that the eight academics who completed the MSCEIT achieved below average EI scores. Chapter 3 noted that higher MSCEIT average scores were anticipated from a group of experienced HE lecturers with established careers. The instrument's validity in identifying effective tutors was questioned.

Hrastinski et al., (2018) explored the value of digital badges[2] to encourage online tutoring skills development. The three badges under investigation related to tutors encouraging discussion and reflection, and providing emotional support to learners. This final badge was found to be the most difficult to achieve, suggesting the challenge of developing emotionally competent tutors through formal training courses.

140   Developing effective e-tutors

Emotional competences outlined by Youde (2016), such as self-confidence, adaptability, organisation and communication, are traits that take a long time to develop, often beyond the scope of university training. Therefore, selection methods will have to be used, possibly behavioural interview techniques (Lynn, 2008), to determine tutors with the mix of qualities and competences to be effective in this context. Youde's (2014) study revealed a potentially important consideration when recruiting potential tutors for online and blended learning contexts. Interview analysis identified one tutor as highly self-efficacious as he spoke confidently about practice in both face-to-face and online contexts. However, he received a low score on learner feedback questionnaires indicating some issues with regard to their perceptions of quality. VLE analysis revealed that this individual made no contributions to discussion boards where learners had uploaded assessment plans. Although the tutor responded to learner e-mails about plans, the questionnaire findings and the lack of VLE contributions highlighted the difficulties of accurately predicting practice from traditional selection interviews alone.

In summary

This book has argued that those tutoring adult learners on PT vocational courses should possess pedagogical approaches that align with the Individual Constructivist Perspective (Mayes & de Freitas, 2007). It has further argued that tutors with primarily social constructivist pedagogical beliefs may struggle to adapt their practice to online and blended contexts and may require greater training and development. Training and development programmes may be unable to influence such deeply engrained beliefs and, consequently, recruitment and selection should focus on tutors favouring individual constructivist approaches. Further, this Chapter has argued that emotional competences are challenging to train through traditional university staff development programmes and, again, recruitment practices should be adopted that selects e-tutors with such competences.

Notes

1. This is software that acts on behalf of online tutors, for example, to e-mail students who have not completed certain required activities within the VLE by a certain date.
2. A digital badge is an acknowledgement of accomplishment earned within a learning environment.

References

Barker, P. (2002). On being an online tutor. *Innovations in Education and Teaching International*, *39*(1), 3–13.
Bar-On, R. (1997). *Bar-On emotional quotient inventory: Technical manual*. Toronto: Multi-Health Systems.

Bennett, E, & Youde, A. (2010). E-tutoring. In J. Avis, R. Fisher, & R. Thompson (Eds.) *Teaching in lifelong learning: A guide to theory and practice* (pp. 154–162). Maidenhead: Open University Press.

Bennett, S., & Lockyer, L. (2004). Becoming an online teacher: Adapting to a changed environment for teaching and learning in higher education. *Educational Media International*, *41*(3), 231–248.

Bennett, S., & Marsh, D. (2002). Are we expecting online tutors to run before they can walk? *Innovations in Education and Teaching International*, *39*(1), 14–20.

Biggs, J. (2003). *Teaching for quality learning at university* (2nd ed.). Maidenhead: Open University Press.

Boyatzis, R. E. (2007). Developing emotional intelligence through coaching for leadership, professional and occupational excellence. In R. Bar-On, J. G. Maree, & M. J. Elias (Eds.) *Educating people to be emotionally intelligent* (pp. 155–168). Westport, CT: Praeger.

Carnell, E. (2007). Conceptions of effective teaching in higher education: Extending the boundaries. *Teaching in Higher Education*, *12*(1), 25–40.

Davis, H. C., & Fill, K. (2007). Embedding blended learning in a university's teaching culture: Experiences and reflections. *British Journal of Educational Technology*, *38*(5), 817–828.

Devlin, M., & Samarawickrema, G. (2010). The criteria of effective teaching in a higher education context. *Higher Education Research & Development*, *29*(2), 111–124.

Dolev, N., & Leshem, S. (2016). Teachers' emotional intelligence: The impact of training. *International Journal of Emotional Education*, *8*(1), 75–94.

Dolev, N., & Leshem, S. (2017a). Developing emotional intelligence competence among teachers. *Teacher Development*, *21*(1), 21–39.

Dolev, N., & Leshem, S. (2017b). What makes up an effective emotional intelligence training design for teachers? *International Journal of Learning, Teaching and Educational Research*, *16*(10), 72–89.

Dyke, M., Conole, G., Ravenscroft, A., & De Fraitas, S. (2007). Learning theory and its application to e-learning. In G. Conole & M. Oliver (Eds.) *Contemporary perspectives in e-learning research* (82–98). London: Routledge.

Hrastinski, S., Cleveland-Innes, M., & Stenbom, S. (2018). Tutoring online tutors: Using digital badges to encourage the development of online tutoring skills. *British Journal of Educational Technology*, *49*(1), 127–136.

Kreber, C., & Kanuka, H. (2006). The scholarship of teaching and learning and the online classroom. *Canadian Journal of University Continuing Education*, *32*(2), 109–131.

Lynn, A. B. (2008). *The EQ interview: Finding employees with high emotional intelligence.* New York: AMACOM.

Mayer, J. D., Salovey, P., & Caruso, D. (2002). *Mayer-Salovey-Caruso emotional intelligence test manual.* Toronto, Canada: Multi-Health Systems.

Mayes, T., & de Freitas, S. (2004). *JISC e-learning models desk study: Stage 2: Review of e-learning theories, frameworks and models.* Retrieved from http://www.jisc.ac.uk/uploaded_documents/Stage%202%20Learning%20Models%20(Version%201).pdf

Mayes, T., & de Freitas, S. (2007). Learning and e-learning: The role of theory. In H. Beetham & R. Sharpe (Eds.) *Rethinking pedagogy for a digital age: Designing and delivering e-learning* (pp. 13–25). Abingdon, Oxfordshire: Routledge.

McGee, P., Windes, D., & Torres, M. (2017). Experienced online instructors: Beliefs and preferred supports regarding online teaching. *Journal of Computing in Higher Education*, *29*(2), 331–352.

Neale, S., Spencer-Arnell, L., & Wilson, L. (2011). *Emotional intelligence coaching: Improving performance for leaders, coaches and the individual.* London: Kogan Page Publishers.

Salmon, G. (2011). *E-moderating: The key to teaching & learning online* (3rd ed.). London: RoutledgeFalmer.

Salmon, G. (2016). *Carpe diem learning design: Preparation & workshop.* Retrieved from https://www.gillysalmon.com/uploads/5/0/1/3/50133443/blackwhite_carpe_diem_planning_process_workbook_version18_june2016.pdf

Salmon, G. (2018) *Gilly Salmon.* Retrieved from https://www.gillysalmon.com/

Salmon, G., & Wright, P. (2014). Transforming future teaching through 'carpe diem' learning design. *Education Sciences, 4*(1), 52–63.

Schön, D. A. (1987). *Educating the reflective practitioner.* San Francisco: Jossey-Bass.

Stein, S. J., Shephard, K., & Harris, I. (2011). Conceptions of e-learning and professional development for e-learning held by tertiary educators in New Zealand. *British Journal of Educational Technology, 42*(1), 145–165.

Stickler, U., & Hampel, R. (2007). Designing online tutor training for language courses: A case study. *Open Learning: The Journal of Open, Distance and e-Learning, 22*(1), 75–85.

Weller, M. (2007). *Virtual learning environments: Using, choosing and developing your VLE.* London: Routledge.

Wheeler, S. (2012). *Digital learning futures.* Retrieved from http://www.steve-wheeler.co.uk/2015/03/social-mobile-and-personal-learning.html#!/2015/03/social-mobile-and-personal-learning.html

Wheeler, S. (2015). *Learning with 'e's.* Carmarthen: Crown House Publishing.

Wilson, G. (2007). New skills and ways of working: Faculty development for e-learning. In M. Bullen & D. Janes (Eds.) *Making the transition to e-learning: Strategies and issues* (pp. 121–138). Hershey, PA: Idea Group.

Youde, A. (2014). *A Mixed Methods Exploration of Effective Tutors and Tutoring in Blended Learning Contexts* (Unpublished EdD Thesis, The University of Huddersfield, Huddersfield). Retrieved from http://eprints.hud.ac.uk/id/eprint/20351/

Youde, A. (2016). Tutor emotional competences valued by learners in a blended learning context. *European Journal of Open, Distance and E-Learning (EURODL), 19*(2), 81–97. doi: 10.1515/eurodl-2016-0008.

Youde, A. (2019). I don't need peer support: Effective tutoring in blended learning environments for part-time, adult learners. *Higher Education Research & Development.* doi:10.1080/07294360.2019.1704692.

Chapter 10

Emotionally intelligent tutoring

Introduction

This book has argued that emotional intelligence (EI) and emotional competence (EC) are of value for those tutoring in online and blended learning environments. Strategies and actions are now presented that can make tutors appear emotionally competent in learners' eyes. Firstly, the Chapter suggests some practical measures for effective communication with learners. The 'reading' and use of emotions in text-based environments are discussed with associated strategies to guide tutors. Then, approaches to support learners studying at a distance and monitor their progress are considered. This is developed to explore the understanding of learner emotions at cohort or course level. Finally, the development of two questionnaires that elicit learner perceptions of their study within online and blended learning environments is outlined.

Communicating emotion in online environments

Emotions are a critical component of the teaching and learning process and impact on learner achievement, self-management and motivation (Rienties & Rivers, 2014). Even with the advance of synchronous communication media, when tutoring adult learners on part-time (PT) higher education (HE) courses, text-based asynchronous communication channels remain dominant. This brings challenges for the online tutor to accurately gauge learner feelings and emotions as there is a lack of visual cues, which impacts on the quality of information being transferred (Gilmore & Warren, 2007; McKenna & Bargh, 2000). However, there are some basic steps, supported by developments in educational software, to help tutors when communicating with learners in online contexts. Tutors reflecting on their expression of emotions, whilst encouraging the same in their learners, can support all in both exhibiting and developing emotionally competent traits. Chapter 2 outlined a definition of EI that included the ability to perceive, use, understand and manage emotions (Mayer & Salovey, 1997, p. 10). However, this ability

144   Emotionally intelligent tutoring

is challenging in largely text-based environments and this Chapter takes steps to support tutors in developing their EC in this context. Further, Chapter 4 presented a Framework of Emotional Competences (Youde, 2016) that were found to contribute to tutor effectiveness in blended learning environments, such as emotional self-awareness and organisation. In that Chapter, some actions were discussed regarding the operationalisation of those ECs in practice. This Chapter builds on this discussion.

This Section outlines strategies that online tutors can use to express emotions whilst helping them know and understand their learners' emotions. It firstly considers how this can be achieved at an individual level, which is supported by an analysis of two prominent psychological constructs – Transactional Analysis and Countertransference. The discussion then moves onto course level strategies to understand the emotional state of all participants within online learning environments.

Understanding emotions at an individual level

Salmon (2002) suggests practical examples of expressing emotion in text, which are helpful when communicating online. Firstly, the correct use of punctuation is essential. Table 10.1 provides an example student e-mail and considers the implications of an exclamation mark on the tutor's response. Secondly, emoticons[1] and emojis[2] provide tutors with a wide variety of options for displaying emotions themselves, and of ways that their use could be encouraged in their learners' communications. Although undertaken in relation to secondary school pupils, the study undertaken by Derks, Bos, and Von Grumbkow (2008) found that emoticons had an impact on message interpretation within online contexts. This includes more complex messages,

Table 10.1 Implications of punctuation within asynchronous, text-based online environments

---

The extract below is a learner e-mail in response to a tutor sending out a schedule for a forthcoming face-to-face class on a blended learning course.

> *Hi (Tutor),*
> *Thank you for your e-mail.*
> *Can I confirm that the start time of the next day school is 10AM as last Friday I arrived for 9AM as stated in the letter!*
> *Thank you.*

The exclamation mark at the end of the main sentence indicates learner frustration at the misinformation previously received. The e-tutor should notice this, and the repeat of "thank you", again indicating frustration, and respond accordingly to try and alleviate their feelings. However, the exclamation mark changes the whole message contained with the e-mail. Without it, the frustration is not communicated and a more rational and pragmatic response can be provided.

such as sarcasm and ambiguity, with their study noting that, to a large extent, emoticons can replace some non-verbal behaviours. A comprehensive literature review (Dunlap et al., 2016) into effective emoticon use within online educational environments suggested the following recommendations:

- they can enhance teaching presence, for example, to allow tutors to clarify their emotions or intent
- they can provide more personalised and humanised feedback
- they can soften critical feedback
- tutors should establish clear expectations for emoticon use
- tutors should use other strategies alongside emoticons to improve communication, enhance social presences, and build effective online communities.

Such strategies, as suggested in the final bullet point, are discussed throughout this book, but particularly in Chapter 7 when considering effective teaching and later in this Chapter when exploring effective learner support in online learning environments.

Further strategies for the effective communication of emotions within educational contexts involve adopting the affordances of technological developments. These could include audio or video feedback on learners' work, a common feature on current virtual learning environments (VLE), and mobile technologies. Learners themselves can submit assessments and reflections through audio or video channels, or utilise screen capture software to present evidence, such as an online resource to explain and justify its development and value.

Transactional analysis within online learning environments

The social psychological theory transactional analysis (TA; Berne, 1961, 1964) outlines a particular approach to the understanding of practices in a range of fields including counselling, management and education. It has been increasingly used within online counselling contexts, but, as yet, its value within online learning has received little attention, from both theoretical and empirical standpoints. The theory is extensive, continues to be developed (as well as critiqued), and a full discussion of its many facets is beyond the scope of this book. However, to help understand behaviour in online environments, the analysis of social transactions to determine the 'ego state' of participants can help create effective learning environments. Ego states, defined as "a pattern of thought, feeling and action that represents a developmentally and functionally significant mode of relating to self and others" (McLeod, 2013, pp. 205–206), are a central concept within TA theory. Understanding of such thoughts, feelings and actions, in the self and in others, requires EI and competence, as defined in the previous Section.

146 Emotionally intelligent tutoring

For online tutors, recognition of ego states can provide valuable self-understanding and help them relate to learners.

TA theory states that everyone alternates between one of three sides to their personality. These 'ego states' – Parent (P), Adult (A) and Child (C; Berne, 1961, 1964) – converse with each other within social interactions, known as 'transactions'. The Parent ego state represents a set of feelings, thinking and behaviours that have been copied from parents and parental figures, such as grandparents, close relatives and teachers. TA argues there are two types of Parent, the Controlling Parent (CP), who, within transactions, want the 'child' to be controlled and can be judgemental, and the Nurturing Parent (NP), who wants to encourage and comfort the child, or others. Whilst the Parent ego state is rooted the past, the Adult ego state is about a direct response to the present circumstances and approaches life rationally in order to make the best choices. The Adult is really the ideal ego state as adults are, according to the theory, seen as comfortable with themselves, and are generally considered to think rationally and talk reasonably. Finally, and again rooted in the past, the Child ego state represents a set of behaviours, thoughts and feelings which are replayed from an individual's childhood. TA argues there are two types of Child: the Free Child (FC) is curious, exploring, emotional, creative, open, vulnerable and likes playing. The Adaptive Child (AC) reacts to life around them by either changing themselves to be seen as good and compliant, or by rebelling against the forces of change and, so, being naughty.

As stated above, within TA, communications are known as transactions with Berne (1961, 1964) describing some of these as complementary and others as crossed. Complementary transactions occur when the sender receives the response they expected. When considering ego states, an Adult communication would expect an Adult response, a Parent communication would expect a Child response, and vice versa. Therefore, an online learner may ask, "when does the next unit start?" (Adult ego state) and the tutor would respond, "it starts next month, you will get an e-mail to confirm the date soon" (Adult ego state). Both communications are in the present and rational, therefore from an Adult ego state. The conversation is purposeful and comfortable for both participants. Now consider a Parent to Child communication, a tutor might say, "remember to read those chapters I suggested, they will help you get a good grade on your assignment" (NP ego state), which elicits the following response "yes, will do, I am sure they will be an interesting read" (AC ego state). Again, a comfortable and effective communication and response. While transactions remain complementary, the conversation can, hypothetically, go on indefinitely, even within online environments.

Crossed transactions occur when the response to the communication is from a different ego state than invited or anticipated. Going back to the example above, the online learner asks, "when does the next unit start?" (Adult ego state), with the following response received – "look in the course handbook! I keep telling you to look there first for course information before asking questions". This response could be from a Controlling Parent ego state, or can be from a Free Child ego state if the tutor was on the verge of a tantrum. Either way, it was not the response that the learner anticipated and the communication would break down, with this situation requiring work from the tutor to rebuild trust. An Adult ego state response would have been as stated in the above paragraph, but perhaps with a reminder that all key information was contained within the course handbook.

The e-mail in Table 10.1 highlights the challenge for tutors to judge ego states purely within online environments. As stated above, the extract was a learner e-mail in response to a tutor sending out a schedule for a forthcoming face-to-face class on a blended learning course. The response was:

> Can I confirm that the start time of the next day school is 10AM as last Friday I arrived for 9AM as stated in the letter!

The exclamation mark at the end of the main sentence indicates learner frustration at the misinformation previously provided and suggests they could be in CP ego state as the response appears forceful and fault finding. Alternatively, it could be FC as the response is complaining. Either way, a careful tutor response is required to get the transactions complementary and, ideally, Adult to Adult. However, changing the exclamation mark to a question mark changes the whole message contained with the communication:

> Can I confirm that the start time of the next day school is 10AM as last Friday I arrived for 9AM as stated in the letter?

This now appears a perfectly rational response to a mistake and is within an Adult ego state and, therefore, a complementary transaction to the original tutor message. The exclamation mark was a key piece of information for the tutor in determining the learner ego state and, therefore, providing an expected response.

A further TA consideration for online tutors when communicating with learners is the Ulterior Transaction (Berne, 1964). This refers to interaction sequences where an individual appears to be communicating from one ego state, whereas, in fact, they are sending a covert or implicit message from another ego state (McLeod, 2013, p. 208). In other words, two ego states are running in parallel, the social message (what is said) is different to the psychological message (what is meant; Berne, 1961, 1964). For example, a learner may e-mail a tutor with a request for help with understanding a particular topic (Adult ego state). The tutor responds in Adult ego state with a short explanation and some recommended further reading to help their understanding. The learner responds by saying they had read all those sources and they still do not understand the topic, which the tutor then responds to, again, try help, then another deflection communication arrives. What the learner is saying (the social message) is Adult ego state, but the psychological message is attention seeking, confused and complaining, therefore, more closely aligned to the Adapted Child ego state. Ulterior transactions can be manipulative, either consciously or unconsciously, and increase the risk of communication failure and conflict. Tutors should try to break down such transactions to a series of complementary exchanges. In the above example, the tutor could adopt NP ego state to tell the learner how well they are doing, thus providing a complementary transaction to the learner's AC. This example mirrors Berne's (1964) original stimulus for the concept of the 'games' people play – "why don't you – yes but", as, whatever the suggestion, the learner responds with an excuse for why it cannot be done.

Effective online tutoring is underpinned by an ability to communicate when at a distance. Knowledge and understanding of TA and its constituent ego states is a further tool for tutors to consider when engaging with individuals or groups of learners. Effective online communications can motivate and encourage enthusiastic learners or reassure and placate those who are less confident and/or worried. Tutors having these abilities would exhibit the emotionally competent traits outlined in Chapter 4. As stated earlier, TA is extensive, but further reading around Strokes, the Four Life Positions and the 'games people play' (Berne, 1961, 1964) would benefit those tutoring in online and blended learning environments. Further developments of Berne's theory can also be useful for tutors, for example, Karpman's (1968) Drama Triangle. This outlines a type of destructive interaction that can occur between people in conflict. It considers people who take on the roles of Persecutor, Victim and Rescuer, which can be seen within online communication environments.

Countertransference

This construct is firmly rooted within counselling discourses, nonetheless, has resonance for tutors within online and blended learning environments. Put simply, Countertransference can be considered as the emotional entanglement between a client and therapist (McLeod, 2013). Its resonance for tutors relates to their awareness of the impact of their emotions on learners and, conversely, how learner emotions can influence tutors. For example, a tutor who, as a student, was nervous of examinations, may transmit this fear to learners as an upcoming test approaches. Whilst this would have a negative impact on learners, a tutor exhibiting positivity and enthusiasm for a topic area could transmit this to learners and make them more interested in the area of study (Chapter 8 noted the importance of tutor enthusiasm and it is generally considered an important personal quality when teaching adults). It is important that tutors are aware of their emotions (Youde, 2016; see Chapter 4 for

Emotionally intelligent tutoring   149

a further discussion of the importance of tutor self-awareness) and consider how they are influencing their learners. Further, this self-awareness should extend to knowing how learner emotions are affecting themselves, such as the influence of a frustrated and demanding student who constantly criticises the tutor and their teaching.

Understanding emotions at unit or course level

With the increased availability of big data sets there are opportunities for sophisticated analytics that can indicate individual, cohort and course learner feeling (Behrens, Piety, DiCerbo, & Mislevy, 2018). The growing field of learner analytics within data analytics can provide valuable information to online and blended tutors regarding learner behaviours. Institutional VLEs can collect a wealth of learner data that can be analysed to understand their behaviours in these online spaces. Such understanding of feeling and behaviour can give some indication of learner emotions whilst they are engaged in their study. This Section explores approaches to measuring learner emotions online and this can help tutors to provide effective support to students.

Rienties and Rivers (2014, p. 1) undertook a literature review of more than 100 studies to explore emotions that influence learner attitude, behaviour and cognition. The findings of Cleveland-Innes and Campbell (2012) and Stenbom, Cleveland-Innes, and Hrastinski (2014) regarding emotional presence (described in Chapter 7) within online learning environments influenced this study. From this review, Rienties and Rivers identified seven data gathering approaches to measure, identify and understand learner emotions. The first three approaches use existing data commonly available from VLEs, and these are:

- content analysis
- natural language processing
- behavioural indicators.

Content analysis involves the interpreting and coding of written text for, in this case, the identification of learner emotions within computer mediated communications (CMCs). Whilst this technique can give great insight into learner feelings and behaviour, it can be time consuming and is therefore difficult for tutors to use consistently in their everyday practice. Automating systems are becoming increasingly sophisticated in identifying emotions in text, with the underpinning technique known as natural language processing (Rienties & Rivers, 2014, p. 7). Whilst such systems are, perhaps, beyond the scope of most HE institutions, they can be used to identify learner emotions, but also tutor emotions when interacting in online environments and providing feedback. The final approach identified by Rienties and Rivers (2014, pp. 7–8), the identification of behavioural indicators, is more readily available for tutors in online and blended learning environments. VLEs record communications between tutors, learners and other supporting systems, such as links to online library resources. Therefore, any clicks, replies, and 'likes' of others' comments can be monitored and analysed. Such information can give a tutor clues to learner behaviour, for example, a lack of interaction could indicate disengagement from a unity of study. Therefore, data can be used purposefully as strategies are developed to encourage re-engagement. An example of how this information can be used to support learners is presented in the next Section.

The above paragraph outlines methods of obtaining information regarding learner emotions when using data that is already available to course tutors. Rienties and Rivers (2014) outline four approaches to obtaining new data that helps to identify and understand learners' emotions. The first two are quantitative and qualitative methods, such as distributing questionnaires to learners or conducting interviews or focus groups. For example, tutors could distribute the Achievement Emotions Questionnaire (AEQ; Pekrun, Goetz, Frenzel, Barchfeld, & Perry, 2011), which is designed to assess various achievement emotions experienced by students within academic settings. This could be adopted for online and blended learning contexts. The 24-point scale instrument considers the emotions enjoyment, hope, pride, relief, anger, anxiety, shame, hopelessness and boredom during class, while studying, and when taking examinations. Although, courses delivered solely online would not have 'classes' and tend not to use traditional examinations as summative assessments, such a questionnaire could provide valuable information about learner feelings. Further, two questionnaires are presented later in this Chapter that can be used by online and blended tutors to obtain feedback regarding the quality of provision provided and learner approaches to study. Whilst such instruments are relatively easy to administer and analyse, interviews and focus groups would take more time, but would provide richer and deeper data. Rienties and Rivers' (2014, pp. 11–12) two remaining methods of obtaining data are using feedback to develop wellbeing word clouds and the use of intelligent tutoring systems, with the latter discussed further in Chapter 11 when the future of emotionally intelligent tutoring is explored.

Monitoring learner progress in online and blended learning environments

It can be difficult for tutors to know when a student is struggling or disengaged. Therefore, when tutoring in online and blended environments, systems need to be in place to monitor learners to help facilitate their progression through a unit of study or module. Strategies to support learners are now discussed, but they are underpinned by a range of tutor competences, including organisation and conscientiousness, which were outlined in Chapter 4. The key message within this Section is that tutors should use multiple strategies to monitor learner progress and should engage with the affordances of educational technologies to help.

When monitoring learner progress, the unit or course should be designed to encourage learner communication and interaction (Marsden & Youde, 2012). This is to ensure that learners are regularly required to complete activities that can be reviewed by tutors. This can be aided by learner analytic functions commonly provided by VLEs. For example, weekly activities could be set which involve reading and researching a particular topic, with the learner then required to contribute to a discussion or complete a quiz. Each of these activities can be reviewed to check learner engagement. Even basic VLEs have functionality to allow tutors to know where learners have 'clicked'. Such a tracking system provides data that can be valuable for tutors in giving some insight into students' study habits regarding the sections of a VLE that are being engaged with, for example, content areas or discussion forums. This data can identify a learner who is potentially becoming disengaged, but other methods are needed to support. As Chapter 9 noted, increasingly, intelligent agents are being integrated into VLEs, which can be used to support tutors in monitoring their learners' progress.

Building on the discussion above regarding designing units of study and encouraging learner engagement, Marsden and Youde (2012) argue that these activities should be complemented by the addition of:

- an e-mail folder for each student that saves every message exchanged and is kept in a shared area of the university network to allow each tutor access
- a log recording the date and a brief summary of any online, synchronous conversations, such as a video call, or even a telephone conversation, also accessible to each tutor.

Not all communications with a tutor occur within the confines of a VLE and any tutor/learner interactions should be captured and recorded in an area accessible to other course or unit tutors. Such logs should be monitored regularly and proactive contact should be made with a learner who has not engaged with course activities and who has not made contact with tutors via either e-mail or other synchronous communication media. Marsden and Youde (2012) provide an example of the importance of using such a system:

> during a recent monthly review, we noticed that a particular student had made no e-mail or phone contact, nor had that student accessed the VLE. The student's e-mail folder revealed that they were shortly moving house and would try to maintain the course of study. The tutor was then able to email the student to ask about progress on the course and how the house move was going. This type of personal communication was only

152 Emotionally intelligent tutoring

possible because of the monitoring mechanisms and the student quickly re-engaged (Marsden & Youde, 2012).

Such proactive tutoring would be motivational for learners through their knowing that their tutors were concerned about their progress. Also, by using the affordances of this system for monitoring learner progress, the tutors could appear emotionally intelligent in the learner's eyes. Knowledge of the learner's individual circumstances, such as the house move in the above example, would suggest both relationship management (trustworthiness, organisation and conscientiousness) and self-management'(developing others, influence and communication) ECs (Goleman, 2001; Youde, 2016).

Such systems to monitor learner progress are effective when tutoring larger cohorts. With smaller groups, tutors can get to know their learners individually and develop a social presence with the cohort (Garrison, Anderson, & Archer, 2000). This becomes more challenging as numbers grow and an effective system of monitoring learner progress is needed to ensure that learners feel what Shin (2002, p. 132) described as Transactional Presence – "the degree to which a distance student perceives the availability of, and connectedness with, teachers, peer students and institution". This type of system fosters learner connectedness with online and blended tutors, and broader institutional support services. Further, it allows tutors to communicate proactively with individual learners with a specific purpose in mind. Youde (2014, 2017, 2019a) found that effective tutors, as judged by their learners, were proactive in providing support and that this opened communication channels. For example, formative assessment processes were monitored closely with e-mail, phone calls or discussions at face-to-face sessions used to prompt learners and encourage dialogue.

Through analysis of theorisations of EI, distance learning and adult learning, and empirical research considering effective tutors and tutoring within this context (see Chapters 7 and 8), this book has identified synergies in relation to Humanist approaches to learning (Mclay et al., 2019, p. 94). An effective system of supporting learners and monitoring their progress is at the heart of Humanist approaches to teaching and learning in online and blended contexts.

Eliciting learner perceptions of quality within online and blended environments

When considering the practical implications of tutoring it is important to elicit learner feedback on the quality of their experience. This can be achieved qualitatively, such as through student focus groups, however, once student numbers on units of study or courses grow, quantitative feedback may be helpful in understanding broad learner perceptions. There are a range of questionnaires available through which to do this, for example, earlier in this Chapter the Achievement Emotions Questionnaire (AEQ; Pekrun et al., 2011) was outlined, which was designed to assess various achievement emotions experienced by students within academic settings. Youde (2014, 2019b) developed two questionnaires to elicit learner feedback in online and blended contexts. The study focused on adult learners in PT, vocationally relevant degree courses. Although the research was conducted within an Education disciplinary area, the questionnaires have utility in any subject area targeting adult learners on vocationally orientated courses. The questionnaires were designed to elicit:

- general learner opinion about the quality of tutoring on a unit of study within the online and blended learning environments – the Course Experience Questionnaire
- the learners' approach to their studies in both online and blended environments – the Revised Study Process Questionnaire (R-SPQ).

Each are attitude questionnaires that allow learners to express judgements, points of view and opinions about their tutors and themselves (Oppenheim, 1992). Oppenheim (1992, p. 200) argues that, as well as allowing ease of construction, "Likert scales tend to perform very well when it comes to a reliable, rough ordering of people with regard to a particular attitude".

To measure the scale reliability of these questionnaires as measurement instruments Cronbach's Alpha coefficient was used to evaluate the degree of item homogeneity. Whilst there is some discussion about an acceptable Cronbach Alpha value indicating scale reliability (e.g., see Field, 2005, p. 668), Kline (1999) argues that when measuring complex psychological constructs such as EC, values around $\alpha = .7$ can be acceptable and this was used as a guide to development of the questionnaires. Tests of reliability were run with 72 participants who completed the questionnaires. Oppenheim (1992, p. 168) recommends a correlation procedure such as factor analysis to further purify the scales of questionnaire items. However, Field (2005, p. 638) draws on a range of research to conclude that the reliability of such analyses are weak in relation to sample sizes below 100.

An overview of both questionnaires' development is now presented.

The Course Experience Questionnaire (CEQ)

To obtain general opinion about the quality of tutoring in a unit of study a modified version of the Course Experience Questionnaire (CEQ) can be used (Ramsden, 1991; a copy of the revised CEQ can be found in Appendix 2). The original CEQ (Ramsden, 1991) was designed as an indicator of teacher effectiveness on courses in HE institutions and draws on learners' perceptions of teaching, curriculum and assessment. It was designed for courses with traditional approaches to teaching and more regular tutor/learner contact than online and blended delivery models usually allow. It has been modified to make it suitable for an individual tutor [see Kreber (2003) for a similar use of the CEQ] and a blended teaching model [see Richardson & Woodley (2001) and Richardson (2009) for a similar use of the CEQ in distance education]. Kreber (2003) used a 23-item version of the CEQ in her study to explore the relationship between students' course perception and approaches to study in undergraduate science courses. In North America, where Kreber's study was based, a course was interpreted as "a semester-long seminar or lecture usually comprising thirty-six hours of class time and taught by one instructor" (Kreber, 2003, p. 62), therefore, this was similar to a unit of study in HE contexts generally. Consequently, Kreber's version of the CEQ informed the development of Youde's revised questionnaire.

The scale items adopted for Youde's revised questionnaire were largely the same as the original CEQ, but adapted in line with Kreber's (2003), Richardson's (2009), and Richardson and Woodley's (2001) studies, and were:

- good teaching communication
- good teaching feedback on, and concern for, student learning
- clear goals and standards
- appropriate workload
- appropriate assessment.

These scale items broadly concur with the characteristics of effective online and blended tutors and tutoring identified within this book. The Good Teaching scale items cover what the literature outlines as a 'good teacher' (e.g., see Brindley, Blaschke, & Walti, 2009; Laurillard, 2002), particularly as the statements cover both delivery and feedback on learners' work. Further, Lizzio, Wilson, and Simons (2002) found that the original CEQ factor Good Teaching significantly predicted student summative achievement. Kreber (2003) amended the original CEQ Good Teaching scale in relation to two factors, with these categorised as Feedback on, and Concern for, Student Learning and Classroom Teaching, both of which have relevance for online and blended contexts. Feedback on, and concern for, student learning provides data about the importance of feedback, which is a motivating aspect of tutoring in online and blended learning environments, and concern for learning, which relates to the EC of the tutor. For example, the statement "the tutor made a real effort to understand difficulties I might be having with my work" provides an indication of interpersonal relationships being developed. Kreber's Classroom Teaching scale was adapted to the Good Teaching Communication scale to include statements about clear communication, motivational comments to improve work, and tutors making the subject interesting. Clear goals and standards, together with good teaching, were also found to have an impact on academic achievement (Wilson, Lizzio, & Ramsden, 1997), and

Emotionally intelligent tutoring   155

were therefore appropriate for online and blended contexts. Appropriate student workload would appear to be a feature of good teaching particularly as a heavy student workload is associated with Surface approaches to learning (Entwistle & Ramsden, 1983; Gibbs, 1992; see Chapter 5 for a discussion of learners' approaches to study). Whilst formative assessments are more likely to be under tutor control, summative assessments in HE are developed by unit and course leaders in conjunction with course approval committees. Appropriate assessment has the same consideration as appropriate student workload. However, learner perceptions of tutors are important given the vocational nature of the courses investigated and the requirement that assessments should meet adults' needs (Knowles, Holton, & Swanson, 2015).

The reliability score for the revised CEQ was acceptable ($\alpha = .871$), as were the scores for the scales Clear Goals, Good Teaching Communication, and Good Teaching Feedback (Youde, 2014, 2019b). The CEQ scale Appropriate Assessment was problematic ($\alpha = .392$) and was removed from the final questionnaire. Appropriate Workload did not achieve an acceptable level of reliability ($\alpha = .599$), however, due to the extensive use of the CEQ in other empirical studies it was deemed to be at a sufficient level. Further testing of reliability and validity is needed.

Revised Study Process Questionnaire (R-SPQ)

Chapter 5 noted the importance of learners' approach to study and, when considering effective online and blended learning practice, some indication of their commitment can be valuable. This includes both learners' approaches and their motivation towards study. Vermetten, Lodewijks, and Vermunt (1999) found that the quality of teaching could influence learners' approaches to study and, it is assumed, this would be similar for online and blended courses. However great a tutor's impact on approaches to study, it would be incomplete to consider quality without exploring learner motivation and their approach to a unit of study.

Biggs, Kember, and Leung's (2001) R-SPQ evaluates learners' approaches and motivation towards their study (a copy of the revised R-SPQ can be found in Appendix 3). This questionnaire is appropriate for use in relation to learners studying in western universities and has exhibited acceptable validity and reliability (Leung, Ginns, & Kember, 2008; Stes, De Maeyer & Van Petegem, 2013). Zeegers (2002, p. 74) has discussed the reliability of the R-SPQ and gave reasons why he felt the original Study Process Questionnaire (SPQ; Biggs, 1987) needed revisiting. These mainly focussed on the changing nature of HE in Australia, where Zeegers was based, and these factors (a more diverse student body, increased cost to student, changes to content delivery and assessment due to funding cuts, increased use of technology) are relatively common in HE internationally. These changes, plus the R-SPQ's emphasis on effective teaching (Biggs et al., 2001), make the instrument suitable for online and blended contexts, particularly with regard to the impact of technology on delivery and assessment.

The R-SPQ was designed for full-time courses with examinations as the main method of assessment, therefore it was amended to make it more suitable for adult learners on online and blended learning courses (Youde, 2014, 2019b). Eley (1992) argues that inventories like the R-SPQ are often more sensitive when reworded for a particular subject. The changes made include; references to 'lecturers' have been amended to 'tutors', references to 'exams' have been amended to 'assessment', and 'course outlines' have been changed to 'course materials'.

Through testing with 72 participants, Youde's (2014, 2019b) amended R-SPQ achieved acceptable Cronbach Alpha scores on both the Deep and Surface scales (Deep α = .752; Surface α = .725). Given its previous scrutiny for validity (e.g., see Biggs et al., 2001; Leung, Ginns, & Kember, 2008; Stes, De Maeyer, & Van Petegem, 2013; Zeegers, 2002), it provides a robust measure of approaches to study in online and blended learning contexts.

In summary

This book has explored, in depth, the value of EI and EC for those tutoring in online and blended learning environments. Although Chapter 3 outlined research (Youde, 2014) that suggested there was no correlation between EI, as measured by the Mayer-Salovey-Caruso Emotional Intelligence Test (MSCEIT; Mayer, Salovey & Caruso, 2002), and learner perceptions of quality in a blended learning environment, Chapter 4 presented a range of tutor EC traits that appeared valuable (Youde, 2016). What has been given little attention is how these traits were exhibited and actioned in practice. This Chapter has suggested some measures that tutors could take to effectively communicate with learners and monitor their progress, thereby exhibiting EC traits, appearing emotionally intelligent, and generating positive relationships with and between learners. Finally, two questionnaires have been outlined which tutors could use to elicit learner perceptions of their practices within online and blended units of study.

The next and final Chapter presents a conceptual model of effective tutors and tutoring within a blended learning context and summarises the key arguments within this book.

Notes

1. Emoticons, short for emotion icons, are pictorial representations of facial emotions, commonly made up from punctuation symbols, letters and numbers.
2. Emojis are ideograms and smileys used in electronic communications and media. In this context, they tend to be representations of facial emotions, but can be other images, such as, a 'thumbs up' emoji for a tutor to indicate 'well done' to a learner.

References

Behrens, J. T., Piety, P., DiCerbo, K. E., & Mislevy, R. J. (2018). Inferential foundations for learner analytics in the digital ocean. In D. Niemi, R. D. Pea, B. Saxberg, & R. E. Clark (Eds.) *Learning analytics in education* (pp. 1–48). Charlotte, NC: IAP.

Berne, E. (1961). *Transactional analysis in psychotherapy*. London: Souvenir Press.

Berne, E. (1964). *Games people play*. London: Penguin.

Biggs, J. B. (1987). *Student approaches to learning and studying*. Melbourne: Australian Council for Educational Research.

Biggs, J. B., Kember, D., & Leung, D. Y. P. (2001). The revised two-factor study process questionnaire: R-SPQ-2F. *British Journal of Educational Psychology, 71*, 133–149.

Brindley, J., Blaschke, L. M., & Walti, C. (2009). Creating effective collaborative learning groups in an online environment. *The International Review of Research in Open and Distributed Learning, 10*(3), 1–18.

Cleveland-Innes, M., & Campbell, P. (2012). Emotional presence, learning, and the online learning environment. *The International Review of Research in Open and Distributed Learning, 13*(4), 269–292.

Derks, D., Bos, A. E., & Von Grumbkow, J. (2008). Emoticons and online message interpretation. *Social Science Computer Review, 26*(3), 379–388.

Dunlap, J., Bose, D., Lowenthal, P. R., York, C. S., Atkinson, M., & Murtagh, J. (2016). What sunshine is to flowers: A literature review on the use of emoticons to support online learning. In S. Y. Tettegah & M. Gartmeier (Eds.) *Emotions, technology, design, and learning* (pp. 163–182). San Diego, CA: Elsevier.

Eley, M. G. (1992). Differential adoption of study approaches within individual students. *Higher Education, 23*, 231–254.

Entwistle, N. J., & Ramsden, P. (1983). *Understanding student learning*. London: Croom Helm.

Field, A. (2005). *Discovering statistics using SPSS* (2nd ed.). London: Sage.

Garrison, D. R., Anderson, T., & Archer, W. (2000). Critical inquiry in a text-based environment: Computer conferencing in higher education model. *The Internet and Higher Education, 2*(2-3), 87–105.

Gibbs, G. (1992). *Improving the quality of student learning*. Bristol: Technical and Educational Services.

Gilmore, S., & Warren, S. (2007). Emotion online: Experiences of teaching in a virtual learning environment. *Human Relations, 60*(4), 581–608.

Goleman, D. (2001). An EI-based theory of performance. In C. Cherniss & D. Goleman (Eds.) *The emotionally intelligent workplace: How to select for, measure, and improve emotional intelligence in individuals, groups, and organization* (pp. 27–44). San Francisco: Jossy-Bass.

Karpman, S. (1968). Fairy tales and script drama analysis. *Transactional analysis bulletin, 7*(26), 39–43.

Kline, P. (1999). *The handbook of psychological testing* (2nd ed.). London: Routledge.

Knowles, M. S., Holton, E. F., & Swanson, R. A. (2015). *The adult learner: The definitive classic in adult education and human resource development* (8th ed.). Abingdon: Routledge.

Kreber, C. (2003). The relationship between students' course perception and their approaches to studying in undergraduate science courses: A Canadian experience. *Higher Education Research and Development, 22*, 57–70.

Laurillard, D. (2002). *Rethinking university teaching: A framework for the effective use of learning technologies* (2nd ed.). Abingdon, Oxfordshire: RoutledgeFalmer.

Leung, D. Y. P., Ginns, P., & Kember, D. (2008). Examining the cultural specificity of approaches to learning in universities in Hong Kong and Sydney. *Journal of Cross-Cultural Psychology, 39*, 251–266.

158 Emotionally intelligent tutoring

Lizzio, A., Wilson, K., & Simons, R. (2002). University students' perception of the learning environment and academic outcomes: implications for theory and practice. *Studies in Higher Education*, 27(1), 27–52.

Marsden, F., & Youde, A. (2012). Fostering a transactional presence: A practical guide to supporting work-based learners. In S. Oosthuizen (Ed.) *Part-time study: The new paradigm for higher education?: A Selection of Papers Presented at the 2011 Conference of the Universities Association for Lifelong Learning*. Leicester, UK: UALL.

Mayer, J. D., & Salovey, P. (1997). What is emotional intelligence? In P. Salovey & D. Sluyter (Eds.) *Emotional development and emotional intelligence: Implications for educators* (pp. 3–31). New York: Basic Books.

Mayer, J. D., Salovey, P., & Caruso, D. (2002). *Mayer-Salovey-Caruso emotional intelligence test manual*. Toronto, Canada: Multi-Health Systems.

McKenna, K. Y. A., & Bargh, J. A. (2000). Plan 9 from cyberspace: The implications of the internet for personality and social psychology. *Personality and Social Psychology Review, 4*, 57–75.

Mclay, M., Mycroft, L., Noel, P., Orr, K., Thompson, R., Tummons, J., & Weatherby, J. (2019) Learning and learners. In J. Avis, R. Fisher, & R. Thompson (Eds.) *Teaching in lifelong learning: A guide to theory and practice* (3rd ed., pp. 81–107). Maidenhead: Open University Press.

McLeod, J. (2013). *An introduction to counselling* (5th ed.). Maidenhead: Open University Press.

Oppenheim, A. N. (1992). *Questionnaire design, interviewing and attitude measurement*. London: Continuum.

Pekrun, R., Goetz, T., Frenzel, A. C., Barchfeld, P., & Perry, R. P. (2011). Measuring emotions in students' learning and performance: The achievement emotions questionnaire (AEQ). *Contemporary educational psychology, 36*(1), 36–48.

Ramsden, P. (1991). A performance indicator of teaching quality in higher education: The course experience questionnaire. *Studies in Higher Education, 16*, 129–150.

Richardson, J. T. E. (2009). The attainment and experiences of disabled students in distance education. *Distance Education, 30*(1), 87–102.

Richardson, J. T. E., & Woodley, A. (2001). Perceptions of academic quality among students with a hearing loss in distance education. *Journal of Educational Psychology, 93*(3), 563–570.

Rienties, B., & Rivers, B. A. (2014). Measuring and understanding learner emotions: Evidence and prospects. *Learning Analytics Review, 1*, 1–28.

Salmon, G. (2002). *E-tivities: The key to teaching & learning online*. London: RoutledgeFalmer.

Shin, N. (2002). Beyond interaction: The relational construct of 'transactional presence'. *Open Learning, 17*(2), 121–137.

Stenbom, S., Cleveland-Innes, M., & Hrastinski, S. (2014). Online coaching as a relationship of inquiry: Mathematics, online help, and emotional presence. In The Canadian Network for Innovation in Education Conference, May 13-16, 2014.

Stes, A., De Maeyer, S., & Van Petegem, P. (2013). Examining the cross-cultural sensitivity of the revised two-factor study process questionnaire (R-SPQ-2F) and validation of a Dutch version. *PLoS One, 8*(1), 1–7. doi: 10.1371/journal.pone.0054099.

Vermetten, Y. J., Lodewijks, H. G., & Vermunt, J. D. (1999). Consistency and variability of learning strategies in different university courses. *Higher Education, 37*, 1–21.

Wilson, K. L., Lizzio, A., & Ramsden, P. (1997). The development, validation, and application of the course experience questionnaire. *Studies in Higher Education, 22*, 33–53.

Youde, A. (2014). *A Mixed Methods Exploration of Effective Tutors and Tutoring in Blended Learning Contexts* (Unpublished EdD Thesis, The University of Huddersfield, Huddersfield). Retrieved from http://eprints.hud.ac.uk/id/eprint/20351/

Youde, A. (2016). Tutor emotional competences valued by learners in a blended learning context. *European Journal of Open, Distance and E-Learning (EURODL)*, *19*(2), 81–97. doi: 10.1515/eurodl-2016-0008

Youde, A. (2017). I don't need peer-support: Effective tutoring in blended learning environments for learners studying vocationally orientated degrees. In INTED 2017 Proceedings: 11th International Technology, Education and Development Conference, Valencia, Spain (pp. 1552–1561). doi: 10.21125/inted.2017.0499.

Youde, A. (2019b). The development of the course experience questionnaire and revised-study process questionnaire for part-time learners on blended, vocationally relevant, degree programmes. In EduLearn 2019 Proceedings: 11th International Conference on Education and New Learning Technologies (pp. 10–17). doi: 10.21125/edulearn.2019.0005.

Youde, A. (2019a). I don't need peer support: Effective tutoring in blended learning environments for part-time, adult learners. *Higher Education Research & Development*. doi:10.1080 /07294360.2019.1704692.

Zeegers, P. (2002). A revision of the Biggs' study process questionnaire (R-SPQ). *Higher Education Research and Development*, *21*(1), 73–92.

Chapter 11

Emotionally intelligent tutors and tutoring

A summary and concluding thoughts

Introduction

To conclude this book, an outline conceptual model is provided that represents an interpretation of effective practice in a blended learning context. Drawing on Youde (2014, 2019a), this model builds on the findings already presented and draws together the key arguments made. It is underpinned by a number of factors, associated with learners' views of effective practice, which can support tutors who are delivering units of study within higher education (HE) for adult learners. The Chapter then summarises two key themes emanating from this book, namely, the importance of tutor/learner relationships in online and blended learning, and the synergies identified between a number of prominent theorisations. Finally, areas for further research are discussed together with the future of emotionally intelligent tutoring.

A conceptual model of effective tutors and tutoring within a blended learning environment

This Section outlines the key findings from research that explored the practices of tutors in blended learning contexts (Youde, 2014). It investigated the skills, qualities and competences, particularly emotional competences (ECs), contributing to tutor effectiveness. The exploration included analysis of learners' perceptions of their teaching and learning experience. The study's aims identified the issues of effective practice in teaching, learning, assessment and learner support, as well as considering other factors that influenced learner perceptions of quality in the context under investigation. Stronge (2002, p. 64) stated that "teaching effectiveness draws on a multitude of skills and attributes in different combinations and in different contexts to produce the results that define effectiveness", and this was certainly apparent throughout the research conducted within the present study as the complex multi-dimensional nature of effective teaching emerged. A clear conceptualisation of effective practice is proposed and this is supported by a summary of tutor qualities and competences. This Section

Emotionally intelligent tutors and tutoring 161

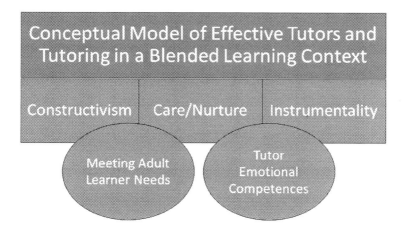

Figure 11.1 Conceptual model of effective tutors and tutoring in a blended learning context.

now develops the Conceptual Model of Effective Tutors and Tutoring in a blended learning context (see Figure 11.1).

The Model has three main dimensions, which are framed as the following higher order 'concepts': constructivism, care/nurture and instrumentality, together with 'lower level' factors which are provided to operationalise the three broad conceptual areas (Youde, 2014, 2019a). The first dimension, Constructivism, represents students' learning as achieving understanding. The second dimension, Care/Nurture, represents the support, and nature of that support, provided by tutors for learners. The third dimension, Instrumentality, represents other factors beyond constructivism and care/nurture that contribute to the effectiveness of tutors within blended learning contexts. The Model is a conceptual framework for understanding the data generated from the practices of the eight tutors investigated by Youde (2014) and their approaches to delivery of a module within a HE institution. This represents an interpretation of effective practice in a particular cultural context, but may be useful in understanding instances of online and blended learning in similar contexts. The Model suggests qualities and skills of effective tutors and provides a summary of effective tutoring, which could inform tutors, course leaders and managers in delivering successful online and blended learning programmes.

The Model is underpinned by the group of ECs (Youde, 2016) outlined in Chapter 4 and contends that, in order to be effective, tutors should possess these competences. These ECs predominantly support the Care/Nurture Dimension, such as the example of tutors being committed to learner support, but also aspects of Instrumentality, such as tutors managing competing pressures and being organised. The Model is further informed by and broadly

162 Emotionally intelligent tutors and tutoring

congruent with the proposed Andragogical Model for blended learning contexts (Youde, 2018) outlined in Chapter 5 and the factors it contained to operationalise its core principles. These factors predominantly support the Constructivism Dimension, but also elements of Care/Nurture.

The operationalisation of the conceptual model

As outlined above, the Model includes three dimensions (see Figure 11.1) detailing higher order 'concepts' and this Section now presents 'lower level' factors, which are provided to potentially guide online and blended learning practitioners, course leaders and university departments in similar contexts. These factors help operationalise the three broad conceptual areas of effective online and blended tutors and tutoring.

As detailed in Chapter 3, the modules investigated by Youde (2014) were successful with students achieving and expressing high levels of satisfaction. The Model firstly identifies factors present across all modules that were associated with learners' general success. This Section argues that these factors do not all have to be present for a successful blended learning experience, but that they appear to be associated with effective practice. Even with some factors missing, the presence of intrinsically motivated learners as found by Youde (2014, 2018; see Chapter 5) would enable modules to be delivered successfully. For example, the Model highlights robust technical support as a factor associated with general success as all tutors who participated mentioned that this was apparent when delivering modules. However, as there were no issues in relation to technical support on the modules under investigation, it is not possible to state that such support is essential for successful module outcomes. One tutor's module, heavily disrupted by external events, still had learners achieving and generally happy with their learning experience. Secondly, the Model proposes factors influencing learner perceptions of quality. These factors were highlighted by effective tutors, that is those receiving higher ratings on a learner attitude survey, and indicate practices that if not present or exhibited, would influence learner perceptions of quality.

For ease of presentation, the lower level factors are outlined in three tables that relate to:

- Constructivism (Table 11.1)
- Care/Nurture (Table 11.2)
- Instrumentality (Table 11.3).

There is a brief discussion and rationale of the dimension's content for each below. Youde (2014, 2017, 2019b) found that tutor practices showed congruence with Mayes and de Freitas's (2007) Individual Constructivist Perspective (ICP), a model of aligned practices (Biggs, 2003) within online and blended learning environments (see Chapter 7 for a more detailed description of how

Emotionally intelligent tutors and tutoring 163

Table 11.1 Constructivism Dimension's lower level factors

	Constructivism – factors associated with, and influencing, learner perceptions of quality
Factors associated with effective practice	• The Individual Constructivist Perspective (Mayes & de Freitas, 2007) was the predominant approach to module teaching, learning and assessment • A facilitative teaching style was the predominant approach • Assessments were problem-based • Tutors related theory to practice whilst demonstrating to learners the relevance of topics covered • Learner support was structured around module assessment requirements including formative assessments • Assessments were developed to encourage tutor 'availability' and 'visibility' and were the basis of tutor/ learner dialogue • Clear goals and standards were evident to learners such as detailed assessment briefs and exemplar work • Tutors appropriately structured module virtual learning environments (VLEs) with resources and access to further reading to act as a 'safety net' for learners • Tutors displayed self-efficacy in face-to-face environments and in providing learner support.
Factors influencing learner perceptions of quality	• Tutors developed strategies to manage adult learner needs, such as consideration of spread of assessment deadlines • Tutors promoted a simple module structure focussed around assessment that created more 'space' for learning • Tutors were clear of the purpose of adopted educational technologies, which align with desired learning activities and outcomes • Tutors' pedagogical beliefs aligned with the Individual Constructivist Perspective • Tutors perceived blended learning as an opportunity for learners • Tutors displayed self-efficacy in all teaching and learning environments in blended contexts.

the research findings aligned with the ICP and why this approach was appropriate for adult learners in this context).

The constructivism dimension

Table 11.1 outlines the Constructivism Dimension's lower level factors, including factors associated with effective practice and those that influenced learner perceptions of quality.

164 Emotionally intelligent tutors and tutoring

Table 11.2 Care/Nurture Dimension's lower level factors

	Care/Nurture – factors associated with, and influencing, learner perceptions of quality
Factors associated with effective practice	• Tutors were committed to learner support • Tutors motivated and encouraged learners in face-to-face environments • Tutors were empathic to adult learner needs and mindful of their competing pressures • Tutors were enthusiastic about their subject, face-to-face delivery, and learner support.
Factors influencing learner perceptions of quality	• Tutors provided proactive and not reactive learner support • Tutors provided proactive and not reactive communications, such as, communication before the first face-to-face session • Tutors taught learners at multiple points during courses when practical, thereby encouraging relationships to develop.

There are similarities between some of Constructivism's lower level factors and those of the other Dimensions. Teaching, learning and assessment factors were firmly rooted in constructivism with the support strategies helping provide a structured learning environment. This support prompted tutor/learner dialogue with further guidance provided by an appropriately structured virtual learning environment (VLE), assessment briefs and exemplar work. The VLE, which can act as a 'safety net' should learners experience

Table 11.3 Instrumentality Dimension's lower level factors

	Instrumentality – factors associated with, and influencing, learner perceptions of quality
Factors associated with effective practice	• Tutors had colleagues to collaborate with and discuss effective pedagogy in blended learning contexts • Tutors had available mentors or coaches to discuss effective use of educational technologies in blended learning contexts • Tutors' departments had a 'culture of support' • Tutors used e-mail effectively • Educational technologies were robust • There was available technical support • Tutors had a minimum basic level of IT skills.
Factors influencing learner perceptions of quality	• Tutors managed competing pressures and were organised • Tutors solved problems as they occurred and displayed initiative • Tutors had blended learning experience or developed in practice.

Emotionally intelligent tutors and tutoring 165

difficulties, could sit in the Care/Nurture Dimension, however, the structured support it can provide suggested a greater congruence with constructivism. Further, tutors' use of educational technologies, their pedagogical beliefs, and their perceptions of blended learning as an opportunity for learners, could sit within Instrumentality, but all support constructivist approaches to learning if adopted together.

The care/nurture dimension

Table 11.2 outlines the Care/Nurture Dimension's lower level factors, including factors associated with effective practice and those that influenced learner perceptions of quality.

There are similarities between some of Care/Nurture's lower level factors and those associated with the other Dimensions, particularly around notions of communication and support. In particular, providing proactive communications and support encouraged constructivist approaches to learning, however, the thought and planning required to undertake these actions suggest a greater congruence with Care/Nurture. Tutors' adopting these strategies undertook extra activities to engage with and support learners, which demonstrated a commitment beyond what could be described as effective constructivist teaching. This commitment influenced the decision to add these factors to the Care/Nurture Dimension.

All the factors in the Care/Nurture Dimension are strengthened if tutors possess the group of ECs described by Youde (2016; see Chapter 4), who proposed a framework of ECs that appeared to contribute to tutor effectiveness in a blended learning environment.

The instrumentality dimension

Table 11.3 outlines the Instrumentality Dimension's lower level factors, including factors associated with effective practice and those that influenced learner perceptions of quality.

There are similarities between some of Instrumentality's lower level factors and those identified within the other Dimensions, such as the effective use of e-mail, but there are tensions around notions of tutor collaboration and cultures of support. These factors suggest the development of practice within communities (Lave & Wenger, 1991), which are constructivist in orientation. However, as these factors were not directly related to the teaching and learning within modules, they have been located in the Instrumentality Dimension. Further, tutor collaborations around effective practice could have resulted in the adoption of behaviourist orientations throughout the modules, which would have conflicted with the predominant constructivist approaches. Again, some of these factors, such as tutors solving problems as they occur, are strengthened if tutors possess the group of ECs proposed by Youde (2016). For

166 Emotionally intelligent tutors and tutoring

example, organisation was a key self-management EC in Youde's Framework, which would be enhanced by conscientiousness and adaptability.

Implications for practice

The proposed Conceptual Model of Effective Tutors and Tutoring in a Blended Learning Context (see Figure 11.1) suggests qualities and skills that would be embodied in and exhibited by effective tutors, and provides a summary of effective tutoring in the context investigated, which could inform the practice of lecturers, course leaders and managers delivering online and blended learning programmes. The Model could:

- assist tutors' teaching, assessment and learner support by, for example, structuring support around module assessment requirements
- support the recruitment and selection of tutors for this context by highlighting the importance of, for example, pedagogical beliefs aligning with ICP (Mayes & de Freitas, 2007), specific ECs, and self-efficacy in online and blended learning contexts
- support tutors' training needs analyses by, for example, highlighting and exploring unexamined assumptions, and considering effective e-mail and VLE use
- support course leaders in the development of online and blended learning programmes to, for example, provide a course structure that encourages tutor/learner relationships to foster, and ensure there are a mix of assessment strategies appropriate for adults studying vocationally relevant degrees
- inform university managers with regard to the need to ensure that there is, for example, the provision of robust educational technologies with available technical support, and the encouragement of a culture of sharing and support amongst academic staff.

Conceptual model – Further research

This Chapter has synthesised themes from a number of sources to present a conceptual model of effective tutors and tutoring. These themes were all developed within an in-depth study of a particular blended learning context. The Model requires further research to broaden the empirical base, both within similar university contexts and across a range of subject disciplines, to enhance its construct validity. The findings, and resultant Model, may have differed if a broader mix of disciplines has been included in the study.

The importance of tutor/learner relationships

This book has highlighted the importance of tutors' previous relationships with learners (see Chapter 6), with this appearing to lower Transactional Distances if present (Moore, 1997). Previous relationships with learners

Emotionally intelligent tutors and tutoring   167

appear to have a strong influence on the availability and visibility of tutors. The three most effective tutors identified in Youde's (2014) research had course management responsibilities on learners' courses and two had taught earlier modules. It is reasonable to assume that learners knew these tutors were available and trust had emerged through positive exchanges, with a lowering of Transactional Distance occurring.

A tutor's previous relationship with the learner group has been found to influence learner perceptions and a factor underpinning this could be tutors' increased ability in understanding their students' emotions (Youde, 2014). Chapter 3 noted that the Blends task of the Mayer-Salovey-Caruso Emotional Intelligence Test (MSCEIT; Mayer, Salovey, & Caruso, 2002) is potentially providing an indication of effective online and blended tutoring in learners' eyes and this task identifies emotions that combine with other emotions. The Blends task forms part of the Understanding Branch of the Four Branch-Model of Emotional Intelligence (EI; Mayer & Salovey, 1997), and this is potentially relevant for tutors as they seek to understand how a learner's emotions are interlinked and how they change over time. For example, it appears beneficial for tutors to understand a learner's anger from receiving a poor mark and this may result in sadness in the near future. As tutors develop relationships with learners, a better understanding of their emotions may be developed. This ability, which will help a tutor to respond appropriately to learners, can help build productive relationships and potentially impact on the quality of support provided.

As argued in Chapters 5 and 6, the broad, underpinning theoretical foundation of this book could be described as Humanist. Humanist theories of learning take a person-centred approach in which true learning comes from within (Mclay et al., 2019, p. 94). This broad conception of Humanism aligns with the key finding regarding the importance of tutor/learner relationships. This book has explored a range of theories and empirical research with this notion central to its spirit and argument. These include EI, Transactional Presence (Moore, 1997), Social Presence (Garrison, Anderson, & Archer, 2000), and empathy (Holmberg, 2003). HE institutions should encourage structures that allow tutor/learner relationships to develop within online and blended courses.

Synergies of theorisations and prominent learning discourses

A key finding emanating from this book is the synergies identified between four discourses relevant to teaching adults through online and blended learning delivery models. Central to each of these discourses is the importance of personal relations, which was argued in the above Section. The Conceptual Model of Effective Tutors and Tutoring highlighted overlaps between the good practice described in prominent online learning discourses (see Chapter 8), theorisations of EI and EC [largely through analysis of Goleman's Framework (2001), but also the Four-Branch Model of EI under-pinning the MSCEIT] (Mayer et al., 2002; see Chapters 3 and 4), theorisations of adult learning (see Chapter 5), and theorisations in distance education (see Chapter 6). These discourses have been married together and provide an element of theoretical triangulation (Denzin, 1970) to form the Model, which further strengthens its validity in developing effective provision within online and blended learning contexts.

Emotionally intelligent tutoring: Required further research

This book has explored a complex multi-faceted aspect of tutors and tutoring in online and blended contexts. To develop understanding of the nuanced nature of emotionally intelligent tutoring further qualitative analysis of learner perceptions of their tutors, and their units of study or modules, could reveal other factors influencing quality. This book has considered the probability that tutor perceptions of their practice, and their general level of work satisfaction are factors that are, often unintentionally, transmitted to and understood by learners. Should tutors overtly discuss operational problems or general work issues then learner behaviour is likely to be affected and their perceptions of quality influenced. For example, a learner who perceives their tutor as busy might be reluctant to get in touch if they are experiencing difficulties or misunderstandings. Further qualitative analysis comparing tutor and learner perceptions would provide insight into this factor.

Chapter 2 noted Dolev and Leshem's (2016, p. 87) evaluation of a two-year, teacher targeted, EI professional development training programme, which found that as the participants' EI developed, they directly and indirectly improved the social and emotional learning of their pupils. Thus, EI training and development for teachers could extend to pupils and the school (ibid). This finding is potentially significant and should be researched further to understand the impact of developing tutors' EC and the resultant effects on learner achievement and emotional well-being.

What is clear from the discussion and analysis within this book, further research is required to provide a firm empirical base to Salmon's (2011, p. 104) view that EI and the ability to influence others are important attributes when tutoring online.

The future

Computers are being developed that can analyse facial expressions, interpret a person's emotions, and respond accordingly (Matheson, 2018). This process mirrors Mayer and Salovey's (1997) definition of EI that has been adopted throughout this book (see Chapter 3), particularly with regard to perceiving, using and understanding emotions. Technologies are being imbued with the ability to read, interpret, replicate and, possibly, even experience emotions themselves (Yonck, 2017, p. IX). This area of research is in the field of Affective Computing or Artificial Emotional Intelligence and related work is already exploring student interest in classrooms (Matheson, 2018). So, in the near future, the emotionally intelligent online tutor with which a learner engages could well be a computer, with all the positive potential and the negative portent that follows from such an eventuality.

References

Biggs, J. (2003). *Teaching for quality learning at university* (2nd ed.). Maidenhead: Open University Press.

Denzin, N. K. (1970). *The research act: A theoretical introduction to sociological methods.* Chicago: Aldine.

Dolev, N., & Leshem, S. (2016). Teachers' emotional intelligence: The impact of training. *International Journal of Emotional Education, 8*(1), 75–94.

Garrison, D. R., Anderson, T., & Archer, W. (2000). Critical inquiry in a text-based environment: Computer conferencing in higher education model. *The Internet and Higher Education, 2*(2-3), 87–105.

Goleman, D. (2001). An EI-based theory of performance. In C. Cherniss &D. Goleman (Eds.) *The emotionally intelligent workplace: How to select for, measure, and improve emotional intelligence in individuals, groups, and organization* (pp. 27–44). San Francisco, CA: Jossy-Bass.

Holmberg, B. (2003). A theory of distance education based on empathy. In M. G. Moore. & W. G. Anderson (Eds.) *Handbook of distance education* (pp. 79–86). Abingdon: Routledge.

Lave, J., & Wenger, E. (1991). *Situated learning: Legitimate peripheral participation.* Cambridge: Cambridge University Press.

Matheson, R. (2018). *Helping computers perceive human emotions: Personalized machine-learning models capture subtle variations in facial expressions to better gauge how we feel.* Retrieved from http://news.mit.edu/2018/helping-computers-perceive-human-emotions-0724

Mayer, J. D., & Salovey, P. (1997). What is emotional intelligence? In P. Salovey & D. Sluyter (Eds.) *Emotional development and emotional intelligence: Implications for educators* (pp. 3–31). New York: Basic Books.

Mayer, J. D., Salovey, P., & Caruso, D. (2002). *Mayer-Salovey-Caruso emotional intelligence test Manual.* Toronto, Canada: Multi-Health Systems.

Mayes. T., & de Freitas, S. (2007). Learning and e-learning: The role of theory. In H. Beetham & R. Sharpe (Eds.) *Rethinking pedagogy for a digital age: Designing and delivering e-learning* (pp. 13–25). Abingdon, Oxfordshire: Routledge.

Mclay, M., Mycroft, L., Noel, P., Orr, K., Thompson, R., Tummons, J., & Weatherby, J. (2019) Learning and learners. In J. Avis, R. Fisher, & R. Thompson (Eds.) *Teaching in lifelong learning: A guide to theory and practice* (3rd ed., pp. 81–107). Maidenhead: Open University Press.

Moore, M. G. (1997). Theory of transactional distance. In D. Keegan (Ed.) *Theoretical principles of distance education* (pp. 22–38). New York, NY: Routledge.

Salmon, G. (2011). *E-moderating: The key to teaching & learning online* (3rd ed.). London: RoutledgeFalmer.

Stronge, J. H. (2002). *Qualities of effective teachers.* Alexandria, VA: Association for Supervision and Curriculum Development.

Yonck, R. (2017). *Heart of the machine: Our future in a world of artificial emotional intelligence.* New York, NY: Skyhorse Publishing.

Youde, A. (2014). *A mixed methods exploration of effective tutors and tutoring in blended learning contexts* (Unpublished EdD Thesis, The University of Huddersfield). Retrieved from http://eprints.hud.ac.uk/id/eprint/20351/

Youde, A. (2016). Tutor emotional competences valued by learners in a blended learning context. *European Journal of Open, Distance and E-Learning (EURODL), 19*(2), 81–97. doi: 10.1515/eurodl-2016-0008.

Youde, A. (2017). I don't need peer-support: effective tutoring in blended learning environments for learners studying vocationally orientated degrees. In INTED 2017 Proceedings: 11th International Technology, Education and Development Conference, Valencia, Spain. (pp. 1552–1561). ISBN 978-84-617-8491-2.

Youde, A. (2018). Andragogy in blended learning contexts: Effective tutoring of adult learners studying part-time, vocationally relevant degrees at a distance. *International Journal of Lifelong Education, 37*(2), 255–272. doi: 10.1080/02601370.2018.1450303.

Youde, A. (2019a). A conceptual framework for effective tutors and tutoring within a blended learning context. In EduLearn 2019 Proceedings: 11th International Conference on Education and New Learning Technologies (pp. 10–17). doi: 10.21125/edulearn.2019.0118.

Youde, A. (2019b). I don't need peer support: Effective tutoring in blended learning environments for part-time, adult learners. *Higher Education Research & Development.* doi:10.1080/07294360.2019.1704692.

Appendix 1

An andragogical model for adult learners studying in blended learning contexts

The Andragogical Model presented below includes factors to operationalise the six core principles (Youde, 2014, 2018).

Need to know:

- tutors outlined key module information and key topics within face-to-face sessions with supporting documentation available, such as assessment briefs
- tutors adopted the Individual Constructivist Perspective across the whole module with student-centred learning encouraging experimentation and application of theory to practice
- tutors adopted a 'facilitative' teaching style
- face-to-face sessions included a range of student-centred activities to develop understanding of key concepts and apply theory to practice
- tutors provided a structured learning environment with modules structured around assessment requirements.

Learners' self-concept:

- tutors provided a structured learning environment with modules structured around assessment requirements
- learners had choice over focus of module assessment
- learners studied independently outside face-to-face sessions, mainly on module assessments
- tutors adopted strategies to foster student-centred learning including appropriate feedback on progress
- tutors had relevant Self-Management and Relationship Management emotional competences to effectively address this principle.

Role of learners' experiences:

- tutors adopted a variety of teaching and learning methods within face-to-face sessions, including group work, student-centred learning and application of theory to practice

172   Appendix 1

- learners had choice over focus of module assessment with application to work contexts and roles.

Readiness to learn:

- tutors adopted the Individual Constructivist Perspective across the whole module with student-centred learning encouraging experimentation and application of theory to practice
- assessments were problem-based within learners' organisations
- learners had choice over focus of module assessment with application to work contexts and roles.

Orientation to learning:

- tutors adopted the Individual Constructivist Perspective across the whole module with student-centred learning encouraging experimentation and application of theory to practice
- assessments were problem-based within learners' organisations
- learners had choice over focus of module assessment with application to work contexts and roles.

Motivation to learn:

- tutors were aware that learners generally exhibit intrinsic motivation
- tutors outlined the value of their modules in relation to learners' work context, roles and practices
- tutors provided appropriate feedback to enhance learners' belief of success and demonstrated commitment to support
- tutors showed enthusiasm for the subject area and adopted strategies within face-to-face sessions to motivate learners for the module duration
- tutors adopted strategies to motivate learners at a distance, which included interacting online and communicating proactively
- tutors required relevant emotional competences to effectively address this principle.

Appendix 2

Course Experience Questionnaire

Introduction

This appendix presents the final version of the revised Course Experience Questionnaire (CEQ), including the preceding text. Within the questionnaire, the scale items are identified. These are coded:

- GT-C – Good Teaching: communication
- GT-F – Good Teaching: feedback on, and concern for, student learning
- CG – Clear Goals and Standards
- AW – Appropriate Workload.

The italicised questions are negatively scored.

Final version of the Course Experience Questionnaire

In answering this section of the questionnaire, please think about the individual tutor and the module they have taught you. The questions relate to general aspects of the tutoring, assessment and feedback you have received whilst undertaking the module. Please circle the relevant number next to each question. The numbers alongside each question represent the following response:

1—strongly disagree
2—disagree
3—neither agree or disagree
4—agree
5—strongly agree.

I	It was easy to know the standard of work expected in this module CG	1 2 3 4 5
2	The tutor of this module motivated me to do my best work GT-C	1 2 3 4 5

3	The workload in this module was too heavy AW	1 2 3 4 5
4	I usually had a clear idea of where I was going and what was expected of me in this module CG	1 2 3 4 5
5	The tutor put a lot of time into commenting on my work GT-F	1 2 3 4 5
6	*To do well in this module all you really needed was to rework the course notes* AA	1 2 3 4 5
7	*The tutor seemed more interested in assessing learning outcomes than what I had understood* AA	1 2 3 4 5
8	*It was often hard to discover what was expected of me in this module* CG	1 2 3 4 5
9	I was generally given enough time to understand things I had to understand AW	1 2 3 4 5
10	The tutor made a real effort to understand difficulties I might be having with my work GT-F	1 2 3 4 5
11	*Feedback on my work was usually given only in the form of marks or grades* GT-F	1 2 3 4 5
12	The tutor normally gave me feedback on how I was doing GT-F	1 2 3 4 5
13	The tutor was extremely good at explaining things GT-C	1 2 3 4 5
14	*The tutor asked me questions about facts* AA	1 2 3 4 5
15	The tutor worked hard on making the subject interesting GT-C	1 2 3 4 5

16	*There was a lot of pressure on me to do well in this module* AW	1 2 3 4 5
17	*The sheer volume of work to get through in this module was too heavy* AW	1 2 3 4 5
18	The tutor made it clear right from the start what they expected from students CG	1 2 3 4 5

Appendix 3

Revised Study Process Questionnaire (R-SPQ)

Introduction

This appendix presents the final version of the Revised Study Process Questionnaire (R–SPQ), including the preceding text. Within the questionnaire, the Deep, Surface scale items are identified. These are coded:

- DA DM – Deep Approach, Deep Motive
- DA DS – Deep Approach, Deep Strategy
- SA SM – Surface Approach, Surface Motive
- SA SS – Surface Approach, Surface Strategy.

Final version of the R-SPQ

This questionnaire has a number of questions about your attitudes towards your studies and your usual way of studying. There is no right way of studying. It depends on what suits your own style and the course you are studying. It is accordingly important that you answer each question as honestly as you can. If you think your answer to a question would depend on the subject being studied, give the answer that would apply to the modules delivered by the tutor being researched. Please circle the relevant letter next to each question. The letters alongside each number represent the following response:

A—this item is never or only rarely true of me
B—this item is sometimes true of me
C—this item is true of me about half the time
D—this item is frequently true of me
E—this item is always or almost always true of me.

Please choose the one most appropriate response to each question. Choose the letter that best fits your immediate reaction. Do not spend a long time on each item: your first reaction is probably the best one. Please answer

Appendix 3   177

each item. Do not worry about projecting a good image. Your answers are
CONFIDENTIAL.

1	I find that at times studying gives me a feeling of deep personal satisfaction DA DM	A B C D E
2	I find that I have to do enough work on a topic so that I can form my own conclusions before I am satisfied DA DS	A B C D E
3	My aim is to pass the course while doing as little work as possible SA SM	A B C D E
4	I only study seriously what's given out in class or in the module notes SA SS	A B C D E
5	I feel that virtually any topic can be highly interesting once I get into it DA DM	A B C D E
6	I find most new topics interesting and often spend extra time trying to obtain more information about them DA DS	A B C D E
7	I do not find my course very interesting so I keep my work to the minimum SA SM	A B C D E
8	I include things in my assignments that I do not fully understand SA SS	A B C D E
9	I find that studying academic topics can at times be as exciting as a good novel or movie DA DM	A B C D E
10	I test myself on important topics until I understand them completely DA DS	A B C D E
11	I find I can get by in most assessments by including key topics rather than trying to understand them SA SM	A B C D E
12	I generally restrict my study to what is specifically set as I think it is unnecessary to do anything extra SA SS	A B C D E

13	I work hard at my studies because I find the a material interesting DA DM	A B C D E
14	I spend a lot of my free time finding out more about interesting topics which have been discussed in the module DA DS	A B C D E
15	I find it is not helpful to study topics in depth. It confuses and wastes time, when all you need is a passing acquaintance with topics SA SM	A B C D E
16	I believe that tutors shouldn't expect students to spend significant amounts of time studying material everyone knows won't be assessed SA SS	A B C D E
17	I usually come to my tutor with questions in mind that I want answering DA DM	A B C D E
18	I make a point of looking at most of the suggested readings that go with the course notes DA DS	A B C D E
19	I see no point in learning material which is not likely to be assessed SA SM	A B C D E
20	My approach was to do as little work as possible in order to pass the module SA SS	A B C D E

Index

Page numbers in *italics* refer to figures and those in **bold** refer to tables.

ability: build productive relationships 33; to capture information 6; construction of emotional intelligence 122–123; defined 21; emotional regulation 119; engage with learners online 119; to influence others 4, 14, 86, 121, 168; learners 6; measure 20–22, 40, 139; model 11–12, 39; to plan work activities 48, 96, 124; self-esteem and 27; to succeed 40; trait-based constructs 39, 116; to understand emotions 12, 24, 31, 33, 105, 167
abstract conceptualisation (AC) *63*, 63–64, 146, 148
accurate self-assessment 45, **52**
achievement 1, 8, 16; academic 154; adult learner 64; learner 143, 168; module 28; school 27; students 27, 44, 154; work outcomes 17
Achievement Drive **41**, 47, 53–54, 96
Achievement Emotions Questionnaire (AEQ) 150, 153
active experimentation (AE) *63*, 63–64
adaptability: CEQ scores 47; competences 54, 105, 121, 140; EQ-i scales **42**; self personal competence **41**, **52**; tutors 46, 49
Adaptive Child (AC) 146, 148
adaptive processes 102
adult learner 58–76; Andragogical Model 59–62; approaches to study 65–67; experiences as basis for learning activities 70; experiential learning 62–64; extrinsic motivators 64–65; interest in learning 71; intrinsic motivators 64–65;

motivation to learn 72–74; motive of learning 68; orientation to learning 71; part-time 59; responsibility for decisions on education 69–70; self-concept 69–70; twenty-first century 58–59; *see also* learners
adult learning 50, 59–62, 71, 152, 168; *see also* learning
Alexander, G. 119
Anari, N. N. 15
Anderson, T. 95
Andragogical Model: adult learners 59–62, 171–172; blended learning environments 67–68, 74–75; core principles 60, 171
Andragogy 59–62, 64, 103, 107, 109
Anwar, S. 16
Arbaugh, J. B. 105
Archer, W. 95
artificial intelligence (AI) 2
Ashkanasy, N. M. 11–12
Asrar-ul-Haq, M. 16
assertiveness **42**
assessment 97–100
Associative Perspective 101
Ausburn, L. J. 59, 107
Aydin, C. 118

Bailey, C. J. 125
Barker, P. 136
Bar-On, R. 11, 38–40, 96; Emotional Quotient Inventory (EQ-i) 43, 139; Model of Emotional-Social Intelligence (ESI) 41–43, **42**, 86, 123, 125–126, 139
Bawane, J. 116–119
beliefs: epistemological 126–128; e-tutor 126–130; metacognitive 27; pedagogical 129, 137, **163**, 165–166; perceptions and

180 Index

126–128; skills and 5, 105, 116–130; tutors 128; values and 137
Bennett, S. 134, 137–138
Berne, E. 146, 148
Biggs, J. 64, 66–67, 72, 96, 155; Constructive Alignment Model 82, 95, 97, 137; Study Process Questionnaire (SPQ) 155
Blaschke, L. M. 83
blended learning environments 1–2, 6–8; adult learners 58–76, 171–172; Andragogical Model 59–62, 67–68, 74–75; conceptual model of tutors and tutoring 160–166, *161*; distance education 80–92; effectiveness of tutors 53–54; effective teaching 95–112; emotional competences 53–54; emotional intelligence (EI) of tutors in 25–27; learner perceptions of quality 152–156; monitoring learner progress 150–152; motivation 58–76; personal relations within 86–92; tutor perceptions 128–130; *see also* online learning environments
blended tutoring 44–54; *see also* tutoring
blends task 26, 32
Boelens, R. 7, 88
Bos, A. E. 144
Brackett, M. A. 27
Brindley, J. 83

Cabello, R. 15
Campbell, P. 105, 149
Card, K. A. 125
care/nurture dimension 161, **164**, 165
Carnell, E. 96
Carpe Diem Model 135
Caruso, D. R. 14
Caspi, A. 84
CEQ *see* Course Experience Questionnaire (CEQ)
change management **42**, 125
changes task 26, 32
Classroom Teaching scale 154
Cleveland-Innes, M. 105, 149
Cliffe, J. 16–17
Clipa, O. 15
cognitive presence 103
communication **52**; asynchronous 3, 101, 106, 143; electronic 3; failure and conflict 148; parent to child 146; proactive 90; skills 118; social media

technologies and 111; synchronous 143; technology-mediated 2; tutors 51, 124
Community of Inquiry Framework 103–105, *104*
competences: adaptability 54, 105, 121, 140; emotional 53–54; e-tutors roles and supporting 116–121; facilitation 117–119, 122–123; pedagogic 117, 122; self personal **41**, **52**; tutors 116–121; *see also* emotional competence (EC)
computer mediated communication (CMC) 87, 97, 106, 121, 149
conceptual model: constructivism dimension 163–165, **164**; of effective tutors and tutoring 160–166, *161*; implications for practice 166; operationalisation of 162–163; research 166
concrete experience (CE) *63*, 63–64
conflict management 16, 51, 53–54, 124
connectedness 85, 152
connectivism 95, 107–108
conscientiousness 46, 48, **52**, 53–54, 105
Constructive Alignment Model 82, 95, 97, 137
constructivism 110, 161–165, **163**
content analysis 39, 74, 149
continuous professional development (CPD) 96, 100, 134, 136
Controlling Parent (CP) 146–147
Conversational Framework 95, 102, *103*
coping potential **52**, 54, 105
Corcoran, R. P. 4, 15, 21–22, 27
countertransference 144, 148–149
Course Experience Questionnaire (CEQ) 28, 67–68, 70, 73–74, 153, 173–175; Appropriate Assessment 155; Clear Goals 155; competent mean score 31; Good Teaching Communication 51, 155; Good Teaching Feedback 155; reliability score 154; total mean score 30; tutors **29**, 32, 44, 48, 50
Cronbach Alpha scores 156
Curci, A. 27

Daus, C. S. 11–12
Dawda, D. 43
Deep and Surface scales 156
de Freitas, S. 95, 97–98, 100–101
de la Teja, I. 116
Delphi study 117
Derks, D. 144
developing others 16, 51, **52**, 124

Devlin, M. 96
De Wever, B. 7, 88
Dewey, J. 59, 62, 80
digital immigrants 58
digital literacies 8
discursive processes 102
distance education 80–92; based on
empathy 81–82; emotional competence
85–86; Holmberg's theory of 81–82;
humanist theories of learning 80–81;
Moore's transactional distance theory
83–85; personal relations within
blended learning environment 86–92;
Shin's transactional presence theory 85;
theorisations of 81–86, 90–92
Dolev, N. 15, 22, 139, 168
Drama Triangle 148

education *see* distance education;
higher education (HE)
educational research 15–17
effective teaching 95–112; e-learning
frameworks and models 100–106; in
higher education 95–96; learning and
assessment 97–100, 110–112; learning
theories for twenty-first century adults
106–110; overview 95; *see also* learning
ego state 145–148
e-learning frameworks and models 100–106
Eley, M. G. 156
Ellington, H. 96
emotional competence (EC) 4, 12–13, 70,
140; blended learning environments
53–54; defined 13; distance education
85–86; emotional intelligence (EI)
44–54; Goleman's framework of 40–41,
41; relationship management 83, 91; *see
also* competences
Emotional Competence Inventory
(ECI) 40
emotional intelligence (EI) 1–2, 4, 11–17,
38–55; ability-based construction
122–123; ability measure 20–22; ability
model 11–12; background 11–13;
blended tutoring 44–54; of clerical
workers 14; competencies and skills **42**;
defined 12; educational research and
15–17; emotional competences 44–54;
e-tutor and 121–126; Four-Branch
Model of 22–25; literature 13–14;
overview 38; score **25**; training and
development for teachers 168; trait-based

models 38–43, 96, 116, 123–126; of
tutors in online and blended learning
environments 25–27
*Emotional Intelligence: Why it can matter
more than IQ* (Goleman) 12
emotionally intelligent blended learning
tutors 23
emotionally intelligent tutoring 143–156;
communicating emotion in online
environments 143–150; conceptual
model of effective tutors and tutoring
160–166, *161*; future 168–169; learner
perceptions of quality 152–156;
monitoring learner progress 150–152;
research 168
emotional management 24, **42**
Emotional Quotient Inventory (EQ-i)
43, 139
emotional regulation **42**, 119
emotional self-awareness 16, **42**, 45–46, **52**
Emotional-Social Intelligence (ESI) 38,
41–43, **42**
emotions 13; ability to understand 33;
to facilitate thought 23; learners 144;
learning process 105; managing 24–25,
27; perceiving 22, **25**; understanding
23–24, **25**; understanding at individual
level 144–145; understanding at unit or
course level 149–150; using **25**, 27
empathy **42**, 49, **52**, 81–82
enthusiasm 32, 34, 46, 73, 121, 125, 148, 172
empirical research 27–29
epistemological beliefs 126–128
EQ-i SCALES **42**
e-tivities approach *see* Five-Stage Model
e-training models 100–101
e-tutor(s) 116–130; beliefs 126–130;
emotional intelligence theorisations
and 121–126; on the job training
137–138; overview 116; pedagogy 137;
perceptions 126–130; recruiting and
developing emotionally competent
138–140; reflection 138; roles and supporting competences 116–121; teaching
126–130; technical skills 136–137
e-tutoring: blended learning environments 6–8; current context
5–6; development programmes for
134–138; digital literacies 8; online
learning environments 6–8; overview
1–5; peer-to-peer interaction 6–8;
see also tutoring

182   Index

Experiential Emotional Intelligence (EEI) **25**, 26
experiential learning 62–64, *63*, 102
extrinsic motivations 72–74
extrinsic motivators 64–65, 74

Facebook 7
facilitation competences 117–119, 122–123; *see also* competences
facilitation task 26, 31
Falloon, G. 84
feelings 13
Fernández-Berrocal, P. 15
Field, A. 153
Fineman, S. 16
Five-Dimensional Model 11, 40, 43
Five-Stage Model 95, 101–102
flexibility **42**
formative assessment 87
Four-Branch Model 20, 39, 91; of emotional intelligence 22–25, 119, 122–123, 167
Fox, R. 100
Framework of Emotional Competence 40–41, **41**, 44–45, 86, 96, 122–124, 126
Free Child (FC) 146–147

Galindo-Villardón, M. P. 15
Gall, M. 14
Garrison, D. R. 85, 95; Community of Inquiry Framework 103–105, *104*
Ghanizadeh, A. 15
Gibbs, G. 66
Goel, L. 84
Goleman, D. 11–13, 38–40, 42, 45, 51, 53; Achievement Drive 96; Framework of Emotional Competence 40–41, **41**, 44–45, 86, 96, 122–124, 126; service orientation 123
Good Teaching Communication 51, 154–155
Good Teaching Feedback 155
good teaching practices 2
Gorsky, P. 84
Gow, L. 126
Grabowski, B. 116
Grewal, D. 14

Hall, R. 128
happiness **42**, 125
Harris, I. 135
Harrison, R. 96

Hart, S. D. 43
Hase, S. 108
Hassan, M. 16
heutagogy 95, 108–109
higher education (HE) 2–3, 6, 49, 58, 69, 82, 98; effective teaching in 95–96; emotional intelligence (EI) and 11–17; institution 129; part-time (PT) courses 143; staff development programmes 121; summative assessments 155; tutors in 11–17, 117
Hill, J. 6
Holmberg, B. 50, 80; consideration of personal relations 82; theory of distance education 81–82; *see also* distance education
Holton, E. F. 60, 84
Hrastinski, S. 105, 139, 149
humanist theories of learning 80–81

Ignat, A. A. 15
impulse control **42**, 124
independence **42**
Individual Constructivist Perspective (ICP) 99, 110–112, 137
influence 51–52, **52**
information and communications technology (ICT) 128
initiative 47, **52**, 54, 105
instruction systems design perspective (ISD) 101
instrumentality dimension 161, **164**, 165–166
intelligence 21, 40
Intelligence Quotient (IQ) 12
interactive processes 102
interpersonal relationships **42**, 125
interpersonal traits **42**
intrapersonal traits **42**
intrinsic motivation 72
intrinsic motivators 64–65

Jelfs, A. 1
job performance 16

Kadis, J. 14
Kang, N. 127
Karpman, S. 148; Drama Triangle 148
Kember, D. 66, 96, 126, 155
Kenyon, C. 108
Kingston, E. 15
Klein, J. M. 116

Knowles, M. S. 59–61, 68–70, 75, 84, 107
Kolb, D. 62–63; Experiential Learning Cycle *63*, 102
Kreber, C. 154

Lanciano, T. 27
Laurillard, D. 83, 85; Conversational Framework 95, 102, *103*
leadership 51–52
learners: ability 6; achievement 143, 168; approaches to study 65–67; dialogue 88–90; emotions 144; experiences 60–61, 80, 171–172; intrinsic motivation 72; monitoring progress 150–152; part-time 105; perceptions of quality 72–74, 152–156; relationships 166–167; self-concept 60–61, 80, 91, 110, 171; tutors' support of 87–88; *see also* adult learner
learning: assessment and 97–100; digital age 107; humanist theories of 80–81; social constructive approaches to 105–106; theoretical perspectives on 98; theories for twenty-first century adults 106–110
Leshem, S. 15, 22, 139, 168
Leung, D. Y. P. 66, 155
Lizzio, A. 154
Lodewijks, H. G. 67, 155
Lopes, P. N. 4, 14

MacDonald, J. 129
managing branch, MSCEIT 33, 122
managing emotions 24–25, 27
Marsden, F. 151
Marsh, D. 134, 137–138
Marton, K. 65
Maslow, Abraham 80
Massive Open Online Courses (MOOCs) 3, 5, 59, 62, 66
Matthews, G. 21
Maul, A. 12
Mayer, J. D. 11–12, 14, 22, 39, 168
Mayer-Salovey-Caruso Emotional Intelligence Test (MSCEIT) 11–12, 20–35, 139; ability measure of EI 20–22, 40; branch- and task-level analysis of 30–34; EI of tutors in online and blended learning environments 25–27; empirical research 27–29; Four-Branch Model of EI 22–25, 119, 122–123, 167; identifying effective tutors 29–34;

positive-negative bias scores 33–34; structure of **25**; tutors score **29**; utility of **30**
Mayes. T. 95, 97–98, 100–101
McDonald, P. L. 59
McGee, P. 117–118, 138
Mclay, M. 62–63, 100
McLeod, J. 13
McNaught, C. 66, 96
Minton, M. 96
Moafian, F. 15
mobile devices 6
Model of Emotional-Social Intelligence (ESI) 41–43, **42**, 86, 123, 125–126, 139
mood **42**
Moore, M. G. 80, 91; Theory of Transactional Distance 83–85, 90
Mortiboys, A. 4
motivation 64; blended learning environments 58–76; extrinsic 72–74; intrinsic 72; to learn 60, 72–74, 172
MSCEIT *see* Mayer-Salovey-Caruso Emotional Intelligence Test (MSCEIT)

need to know 60–61
netiquette 119
Nicoll, K. 96
Nurturing Parent (NP) 146

online learning environments 1–2, 6–8; adult learner 58–76; andragogical model 59–62; distance education 80–92; effective teaching 95–112; emotional intelligence (EI) of tutors in 25–27; learner perceptions of quality 152–156; monitoring learner progress 150–152; motivation 58–76; transactional analysis within 145–148; *see also* blended learning environments
online tutor *see* e-tutor
Online Tutoring Questionnaire (OTQ) 28, 31–32
on the job training 137–138
Oppenheim, A. N. 153
Opre, A. 12–13
optimism **42**, 46, 125
organisation **52**, 54, 96, 105, 124
organisational awareness 50, 123
orientation to learning 60–61, 71, 172
Orton-Johnson, K. 81

184 Index

paragogy 95, 109–110
Parrish, D. R. 16
part-time (PT) 2, 44, 58–59, 105, 129,
    134, 143
passive learning 127; *see also* learning
Patino-Alonso, M. C. 15
pedagogical beliefs 129, 137, **163**,
    165–166; *see also* beliefs
pedagogy, e-tutors 137
peer-to-peer interaction 6–8
perceiving branch, MSCEIT 30–31
perceiving emotions 22, **25**
perceptions: e-tutor 126–130; of quality
    72–74; tutors 128–130
Personal Learning Network (PLN) 7–8,
    95, 110–111
personal relations within blended learning
    environment 86–92
positive-negative bias 27; scores of
    MSCEIT 33–34, 45
Prensky, M. 58
Price, L. 1
problem-solving **42**
Prosser, M. 128

qualitative research 16

Ramsden, P. 44, 67
readiness to learn 60–61, 71, 80, 172
reflection, time for 138
reality-testing **42**
reflective observation (RO) *63*, 63–64
reflective processes 102
relationship management **41**, 44, 51–53,
    52, 83, 91, 123
reliability score 154
reporting bias 21
Revised Study Process Questionnaire
    (R-SPQ) 67, 153, 155–156, 176–178
Richardson, J. T. E. 1, 154
Rienties, B. 105, 149–150
Rivers, B. A. 105, 149–150
Rogers, Carl 80

Säljö, R. 65
Salmon, G. 4, 14, 86, 118, 121, 135, 144,
    168; Carpe Diem Model 135; Five-Stage
    Model 95, 101–102
Salovey, P. 4, 11–12, 14, 22, 39, 168
Samarawickrema, G. 96
scaled open courses *see* Massive Open
    Online Courses (MOOCs)

self-actualization **42**
self-assessment 45, **52**
self-awareness 16, **41–42**, 44–46, **52**,
    53–54, 125
self-concept: adult learner 69–70; learners
    60–61, 69–70, 80, 91, 110, 171
self-confidence 16, 45–46, **52**, 53, 125
self-control 46
self-esteem 27
self-expression **42**
self-management 16, **41**, 46–49, **52**, 54,
    105
self-motivation **42**
self personal competence **41**, **52**
self-regard **42**
self-reporting tests 21
sensations task 26, 31–32
service orientation 50, **52**
Shah, N. A. 15–16
Shephard, K. 135
Sherratt, C. 85
Shin, N. 84; Transactional Presence
    theory 85, 90–91, 152
Siemens, G. 8, 111
Simons, R. 154
situative learning 100
Situative Perspective 99
skills: beliefs and 5, 105, 116–130;
    communication 118; competencies **42**;
    technical 136–137
Smith, K. 6
social awareness 16, **41**, 44, 49–51, **52**, 91
social competence **41**, **52**, 118–120, 123
social constructive approaches to teaching
    and learning 105–106
Social Constructivist Perspective
    (SCP) 99
social media 6
social presence 103
social responsibility **42**
Soleti, E. 27
Spector, J. M. 116–118
staff development 135
Stein, S. J. 135
Stenbom, S. 105, 149
Strategic Emotional Intelligence (SEI) **25**,
    26–27
Straus, R. 4
stress management **42**
stress tolerance **42**, 125
Study Process Questionnaire (SPQ) 155
Swanson, R. A. 60, 84

Tang, C. 64, 66, 72, 96
teaching: e-tutor 126–130; presence 103; social constructive approaches to 105–106
technical skills, e-tutors 136–137
technology 137
Templeton, M. 84
text-based online environments **144**
theorisations: distance education 90–92; of distance learning 81–86, 90–92; emotional intelligence 121–126; prominent learning discourses 167–168
Theory of Transactional Distance 83–85, 90
Tormey, R. 4, 15, 21–22, 27
Torres, M. 117
Tough, A. 72
transactional analysis 145–148
Transactional Presence theory 85, 90–91, 152
Trigwell, K. 128
trustworthiness 46–47, **52**, 53–54, 105
tutoring: conceptual model of effective tutors and 160–166, *161*; emotionally intelligent 143–156; *see also* e-tutoring
tutors: actions to develop tutor/learner relations 90; adaptability 46, 49; availability 85, 87–90; beliefs 128; CEQ results **29**; communication 51; competences 116–121; Course Experience Questionnaire (CEQ) **29**; effectiveness of 53–54; emotionally intelligent blended learning 23; epistemological beliefs 126–128; extent and quality of 88–90; in higher education (HE) 11–17, 117; learner relationships 166–167; MSCEIT scores **29**; perceptions 128–130; preferred pedagogies 127; support of learners 87–88; visibility 88–91; *see also* e-tutor(s)
Twitter 7

understanding branch, MSCEIT 32–33
understanding emotions 23–24, **25**
using branch, MSCEIT 31–32

Vaida, S. 12–13
values: beliefs and 137
Vega-Hernández, M. C. 15
Vermetten, Y. J. 67, 155
Vermunt, J. D. 67, 155
virtual learning environment (VLE) 7–8, 28, 44, 49–50, 74, 86, 89, 101, 111, 120, 128, 136–140, 145, 149–151, 164; content and communications 67; e-mail and 166; synchronous conference 43
Voet, M. 7, 88
Von Grumbkow, J. 144

Walti, C. 83
weaving 106
Weller, M. 136
Wheeler, S. 2, 6–7, 108–109, 111
Wilson, K. 154
Windes, D. 117
Woodley, A. 154
work activities 48, 96, 124

Youde, A. 16, 61, 64, 69, 124–125, 137–140, 151–152, 153, 161; Accurate Self-assessment 45; Achievement Drive 47; alternative approach for social media 110; distance education theorisations 90–92; effectiveness of tutors 53; effective tutors and tutoring 128; emotionally competent 21; Emotional Self-awareness 46; learner attitude survey 28; learner self-direction 70; learners' intrinsic motivation 72; peer support and collaboration 112; perceptions of learners 44; predominant approaches to teaching and assessment 67, 75; research on tutors 49, 86, 96; service orientation 123; student support mechanisms 73

Zeegers, P. 155
Zhang, P. 84
Zimmer, B. 119

Printed in the United States
by Baker & Taylor Publisher Services